Endorsements

C.W.E. Johnson's new book *It's About You! Know Your Self* presents a brilliant and provocative interpretation of the psychological concepts in the channeled literature. I highly recommend this book.
Dr. Brian L. Weiss—Author of *Many Lives, Many Masters.*

In *It's About You! Know Your Self,* Chris Johnson peels away the layers that make up our personal identity to reveal a composite that is much more complex and majestic than we commonly believe. This book is a blueprint for discovering what really matters in life, a template for joy and fulfillment.
Larry Dossey, MD—Author of *One Mind: How Our Individual Mind is Part of a Greater Consciousness and Why It Matters.*

In this critical time for humanity, where our physical world is in deep trouble, each of us needs to know who we really are from a nonphysical perspective to understand how we are all co-creating our future. Chris Johnson is a true scholar of our consciousness in all its aspects of knowing, being and action. The wealth of information he brings together from a remarkable number of sources and perspectives, along with its superb organization, makes this volume an unsurpassed resource for understanding yourself and others as we play out this and many more lives as co-creators in a conscious cosmos.
Elisabet Sahtouris, PhD—Evolution biologist and futurist, author of *EarthDance: Living Systems in Evolution.*

At a time when psychology is becoming ever more reductionist and brain-based, Chris Johnson offers a new cartography of human consciousness that opens up the widest vista of understanding and thus provides a much more comprehensive

picture not only of the deeper structure of the self but also of our potential for expansion and evolution through discovery of our deeper intent. The book is very clearly written and invites the reader on an exhilarating journey of self-discovery, integrating physical and nonphysical understandings in a highly accessible fashion and providing some practical principles for more conscious living.
David Lorimer, MA, PGCE, FRSA—Programme Director of the Scientific and Medical Network. Editor of *Science, Consciousness and Ultimate Reality*.

Our long dominant worldview of materialism is giving way in a shift in our individual and collective psyches awakening to a more spiritual knowing. Therefore, now more than ever before, we humans need teachers and guides grounded in an emerging truth we can trust. Johnson provides us here with an outstanding 21st-century metaphysical textbook to empower us to use more consciously our intention to change and enrich our lives and the reality we are manifesting. *It's About You! Know Your Self* is an excellent, clearly-written and well-organized body of much-needed teaching for our challenging times.
Professor Jon Klimo—Author of *Channeling: Investigations on Receiving Information from Paranormal Sources*.

It's About You!

Know Your Self: A New Edition

It's About You!

Know Your Self: A New Edition

C.W.E. Johnson

BOOKS
Winchester, UK
Washington, USA

JOHN HUNT PUBLISHING

First published by O-Books, 2019
O-Books is an imprint of John Hunt Publishing Ltd., 3 East St., Alresford,
Hampshire SO24 9EE, UK
office@jhpbooks.com
www.johnhuntpublishing.com
www.o-books.com

For distributor details and how to order please visit the 'Ordering' section on our website.

ISBN: 978 1 78904 292 4
978 1 78904 293 1 (ebook)
Library of Congress Control Number: 2018965987

A CIP catalogue record for this book is available from the British Library.

Design: Stuart Davies

UK: Printed and bound by CPI Group (UK) Ltd, Croydon, CR0 4YY
US: Printed and bound by Thomson-Shore, 7300 West Joy Road, Dexter, MI 48130

Contents

Previous Books

First edition of *It's About You! Know Your Self* (2013)
ISBN: 978-1-78099-111-5

Dedicated to the lifetime of
Harold Edward Johnson (1923–2012), aka Hari Jansingh.
One "focus personality" of an Essence committed to the evolution of human consciousness. Harry was the editor-in chief of the first edition of *It's About You! Know Your Self.*

In the forecourt to the 6th Century BCE temple of Apollo at Delphi an inscription reads:

> **Know Thyself**

It became the guiding principle of Socrates and many scholars over the centuries.

> **Knowe thy selfe: that is to saye, learne to knowe what thou arte able, fitte and apt vnto, and folowe that.**
> (1545. R. Ascham, *Toxophilus* ii. 36)

Preface

During the breakdown of my marriage in 1988, my father suggested I read a book that may help me come to terms with this most common of life crises. The book was *Seth Speaks* by Jane Roberts. I knew that my father had had his own marital problems, as was apparent when he divorced my mother, but he was now happily married to the love of his life and lived in a manner approaching the bliss I envied.

I concluded that I would take his advice and began reading *Seth Speaks* in earnest anticipation of finding the answers to my woes. I stopped reading it after the first paragraph of the introduction:

> This book was written by a personality called Seth, who speaks of himself as an "energy personality essence" no longer focused in physical form. He has been speaking through me for over seven years now, in twice weekly trance sessions.[1]

I rang the old man. I told him that although I could respect any pearls of wisdom that came from him or from learned philosophers who had demonstrated a very *definite* physical form, I wasn't too happy about a dead guy lecturing me through a dodgy psychic medium type he liked to hang around with. (My father was always frequenting weird spiritualist churches and their like.)

"Read it," he said, "and keep reading it, despite any statements that trigger beliefs and attitudes you hold that will attempt to get you to stop reading it. Simply recognize that you have a *belief* that doesn't agree with what you're reading. Acknowledge that to be the case, turn a page or two, and continue reading."

It proved to be sound advice.

I completed the book while staying with a friend, and over the next eighteen months I worked my way through several tomes of enlightenment produced by Seth, Jane Roberts, and her husband Rob Butts. The knowledge I absorbed certainly lifted my mood and helped steer me through a time fraught with emotion.

In 1989 I attended my first Seth conference, venturing all the way into the Rocky Mountains next to Denver, Colorado—to my untraveled self, America's "Wild West"—with my new partner in life and my old man and his. By 1992, I had read a great deal of what became known as *The Seth Material* and was probably one of the most enlightened people in the entire world.

Alas, by the end of 1992 my "enlightenment" had morphed into depression.

The cause was elusive. I went to see several eminent psychologists and psychiatrists who were very sympathetic to my plight and a regular consumption of antidepressant drugs ensued. In the May of 1993, after lengthy periods off work, my employers dismissed me—which, like the drugs, did little to alleviate my depression.

Then it dawned on me! Seth's guidance throughout the time of my marital morass had provided me with not only a better understanding of myself, but had also helped me, through some simple exercises, to lighten my mood. I returned to my Seth studies and found that on the second or perhaps third reading, it was clear that I was not quite as enlightened as I had previously imagined. Further study, along with renewed practice of various exercises, finally did the trick in getting rid of my depressive interludes, which freed me to consider my next course of action in life.

Discussions with my father ensued. We bounced our understandings of the Seth material off each other and then decided upon a way forward for me that took into consideration aspects of the material that held me in fascination.

Seth's portrayal of the psyche in *The Nature of the Psyche* was an aspect that enthralled me; I wanted to study the psyche and know more about the nature of our minds. Seth tells us that before a physical reality manifests it begins creation in the mind. I wanted to understand the mechanics of *how* that might be true. I concluded that the first step on my path of fascination would be to learn more about how academia approaches the subject of the psyche.

Supported by my partner, in 1994 I returned to full-time education and became an undergraduate in Psychology at the University of London. I subsequently began to study the psyche from two disparate perspectives, one backed by objective empirical research over the past century, the other supported by subjective personal experience and the information contained within metaphysical literature.

Perhaps mesmerized by the empirical approach and the success it brought the classical sciences during the 20th Century, psychology appeared to me to have taken its eye off the ball. Psychology looked to the brain, our physical senses, abnormal behaviors and animal experimentations to reveal the workings of the psyche and its nonphysical associates—not least, the ever-elusive phenomenon of consciousness.

Disappointed by the narrow academic approach, I looked to broaden my knowledge of the mind and psyche through metaphysical offerings. With the Seth's material as my gold standard, I expanded my examination of channeled information to include other sources.

Lazaris (Jach Pursel), Abraham (Esther Hicks), Elias (Mary Ennis), and Bashar through Darryl Anka, were some of a burgeoning group of metaphysical scribes whose messages I began to compare and contrast for consistency and similarity during the late 1990s. I also took a Master's Degree in Occupational and Organizational Psychology after graduating. I'm not quite sure why. In retrospect, it was probably a subconscious drive to enhance my credibility as a scholar. A degree in an "ology" sounds good, but a Master of Science qualification would provide me with an educational background better suited to the purposeful life I was about to live.

By the new millennium, metaphysical tuition had led me to investigate the links between the mind and the body—how physical or psychological symptoms, or "dis-ease" (as channeled sources would have it), point to nonphysical elements within our minds (thoughts, beliefs, feelings, and emotions) as the instigators of such dis-ease. I am indebted to the works of Gary Craig, Louise Hay, Debbie Shapiro, and Donna Eden and David Feinstein—to name but a few—who have contributed pioneering work in establishing a clearer, more holistic depiction of the structure of a human being. Much of their work confirmed the assertions made by our channeled friends on the complex, multifaceted, and multidimensional nature of the Self.

The emerging discipline of *Energy Psychology (EP)* became the next focus of my studies. As its title suggests, EP addresses both the mind and our energy systems. Our energy systems are those subtle forces associated with the physical body that Eastern medicinal practices promote as Qi (chi) energy centers and flow pathways. Only relatively recently in the West have we begun to observe and map these energies through instrumentation.

After two years of training and research in EP, then marrying its healing approaches with recommendations on healing from channeled sources, I began a complementary health practice in 2000. I found that the various treatment methods of EP were indeed as powerful as its promotional literature suggested. I soon began to regard myself as "the complete physician," a term used by Seth to describe the doctor of the future—a healer with a genuinely holistic approach.

My health practice trundled along for the next six years with an excruciatingly small client base that tended to get smaller as the clients got better.

Things then took a dramatic change on the day before my fifty-third birthday.

Following a week of feeling very weak, I took to my bed.

Awakening the next morning, I was amazed to see the floral patterning of the bedroom curtains revealing erotic images—Rubenesque female forms were writhing amongst the roses. An ambulance was called—alas, the hallucinations were due to lack of oxygen to the brain—and I was rushed to the intensive care unit of the nearby hospital.

For the next six days I lay in a drug-induced coma as the medical staff took charge of fighting a virulent form of the streptococcus bacterium that was freely expressing itself in my body creating pneumonia, septicemia and pleurisy.

When I regained consciousness, my family informed me that the medical staff had not really expected me to do so. I had had my very own near-death experience. Back home, the bedroom curtains no longer excited me.

While convalescing and ruminating over this experience I had created for myself, my thoughts turned to some clients that had showed a limited response to treatment. Although repeated sessions were reassuring to my income, their loyalty to their condition was perplexing. Until I realized that perhaps their loyalty was more to do with a persistent residual energy "held" within them by an elusive subconscious element. I began to surmise that the causal event anchoring this held energy might be unrelated to the experiences of their current lifetime—perhaps a far deeper layer within their Self required attention.

In 2007, thanks to financial backing from my father and my now long-suffering partner, I travelled to the Omega Institute in New York State to train under Dr. Brian Weiss in Past Life Regression Therapy (PLRT). On graduation, I hastened home to include the technique in my practice. I thought I was surely now the most complete of any complete physician!

Apparently not.

Despite continued success with EP clients and further success with PLRT cases, my client base remained precariously low. If it had been up to me to be the breadwinner I would have had to abandon things for a more conventional means of income. I began to get ever so slightly depressed again. Aha!

Depression meant it was time to get more creative, so I returned to the metaphysical teachings for some more inspiration. I quickly found what the underlying problem was.

Seth had touched upon it when speaking of the "Families of Consciousness," however, it was what Elias had to say about it, and the ways in which it's expressed, that astounded me. My problem was to do with my ignorance of the concept of *intent*. Intent is the force that drives all action, a force that governs the direction behind any reality we create for ourselves—the spiritual element within us that steers our path through life. Discovery of the nuances of intent as expressed through our Selves reveals what we should be *doing* with our lives—thus reminding us of our "forgotten" sense of purpose.

In 2008 I discovered my own intent and purpose in a session with another channeled guide—Rose, through Joanne Helfrich. Rose revealed my purpose to me. I was not to focus solely on *healing* others on a one-to-one basis, but to concentrate on artfully *teaching* others.

"O–k–a–y," my brain clunked slowly in reply. "Thanks for that." End of session.

Teach? Teach what? A moment's contemplation helped me realize and appreciate an edict put forward by virtually all channeled sources: *all experiences have meaning*. Experiences perceived by us to be "negative" in nature (as I perceived my lack of success as a healer to be and my near-death experience) are in fact our souls' way of communicating to our conscious minds that we have strayed from our intentional path. To get back on this road to fulfillment, we need to examine what we are *doing*.

Is what I am doing in alignment with my current life's purpose and intent?

Disappointment, depression and negativity tell us it isn't.

Rose was encouraging me to look at a different path forward, one of teaching. Nevertheless, *what would I teach?* Well, you can only teach what you know. What I now knew about the nature of being human, how life works, and what's happening when it doesn't, had taken me more than twenty years to build. I admit, while its architectural plans were submitted by characters of questionable credibility, it is nonetheless an extensive library of knowledge about who we are and why we are here. It is, as most readers will find, a library containing a fascinating collection of ideas that allow us to understand our Selves from a far broader perspective than the narrow conventional modern worldview.

My studies have taught me that we each have the ability and the knowhow to create the reality we desire. We achieve our desires by understanding our personal intent and adhering as much as possible to the purposeful actions that our intent prescribes. By *doing* this, we can feel the bliss of fulfillment and live a life well lived. It is my desire that this book will begin to teach you this.

Since learning of and fully engaging with my own purpose, I have attained, both in my personal and work life, new heights in clarity of communication and empathic understanding. *Applying* the knowledge I have accrued has freed me from the grip of my ego's superficial needs and fearful reactions. Life has become delightfully content. Challenges still arise of course, but I am now far more adept at clearing them with relative ease, and indeed, *appreciating* them for the messages they contain. I get to be grateful and appreciative of my life, and compassionate towards those around me. Moreover, I enjoy communing with my *inner self* on a far more regular basis. You can't beat your inner self for a best friend.

This trilogy of books will take you through much of the process I went through—hopefully minus the depressing interludes and the near-death experience!

Sure, you must put in some work to get the most out of these books. The work involved revolves around practicing various exercises and living with a certain set of principles in mind. The exercises are highly efficient at producing an awareness of the breadth of your Self beyond just your ego's estimation—to genuinely and comprehensively *Know Your Self* (Book I). They intend to clear one's emotional and psychological baggage—so that you can *Free Your Self* (Book II). In addition, they instill a routine that hones your mental and emotional faculties for a clearer overall picture of who you are and what you are here to do—*Live Your Purpose* (Book III).

A lighthearted approach to this self-discovery stuff runs through the books as much as possible. Don't get bogged down with any particular point that may be tricky to understand. Do as my father suggested to me when reading the Seth material and move onto the next section making a note to read the skipped section later. This is particularly relevant to when you find a topic that makes you angry or cranky—this just means that this part of the material challenges your current beliefs. So, make a note if you want to, but move on. Such uncomfortable or challenging moments, I can assure you, will be minimal compared to the many moments of delight and reassurance you will experience for your Self.

Above all, enjoy your Self.
C.W.E.J.

Acknowledgements

I am grateful to many people who have contributed to this first book of a trilogy. Quite a few of them were contributing by simply being part of my life over the past 25 years or so and unwittingly reflecting behavioral evidence back to me that validates the knowledge contained within.

Since setting off on an educational journey that has brought me a profound sense of Self and a broad base of knowledge that best describes the nature of our existence, there are four people who deserve my deepest gratitude—without whom the journey would never have started or have come to a premature end.

They are: my extraordinarily patient partner over this period, Judy Johnson, who has afforded me the time and space to work things through without me needing to concern myself with "earning a living" in some conventional sense. My father, Harry Johnson, whose Self I know has always been collaborating with my Self on more than just the physical plane, to bring this project to paper or whatever newfangled electronic medium of expression is on offer. And my dear friends Joanne and Paul Helfrich, for keeping me on my path of intent, as well as help edit my thoughts into a legible form.

I'm grateful to my friends and family members for bearing with me over the last eighteen months as I learnt how to write proper English, without chiding me too often with, "When are you going to get a proper job?" I'm also grateful to my granddaughter Georgia for allowing me the time to write when I really should have been creating paintings with her to stick on the fridge.

Others that deserve my heartfelt thanks for a variety of reasons connected or otherwise to this project are Darryl Anka, Alan Aspinall, Bronwen Astor, Anne Baring, Andreas Bauer, Dana Beardshear, Teresa De Bertodano, Mark Bukator, Laurel

Butts, Tilda Cameron, Andrew Cohen, Jim Colvard, Lynda Dahl, Mary Dillman, Andy Dooley, Larry Dossey, Tim Dungan-Levant, Wayne Dyer, Paul Ekman, Mary Ennis, Lloyd Fell, Tina Fiorda, Jim and Carol Funk, Sarah Gerrard, Jim and Loretta Gilbert, Paul Gilbert, Neil Gilson, George Goodenow, Amit Goswami, Serge Grandbois, Claire Harmsworth, Arthur Hastings, Esther and Jerry Hicks and the Abraham-Hicks team, John Hunt, Anodea Judith, Jon Klimo, Joyce Kovelman, Bruce Lipton, David Lorimer, Alison Marks, Joanna Martin, Julia McCutchen, Dawn and Morgan McKay, Richard Merrick, Florence Meyer, Wendy Millgate, Anita and Danny Moorjani, Tony Neate, John L. Payne, Christine Poulter, Leanne Rhodes, Elisabet Sahtouris, Jennie Smith, Rick Stack, Helen Stewart, Vianna Stibal, David Tate, Robert Waggoner, Nancy and Helen Walker, Brian, Carole, and Amy Weiss.

A special thanks goes to Joseph Webb for his reediting work on this new edition.

Introduction

This new edition of *It's About You! Know Your Self* came about through the reviewing and rewriting of the chapters from the first edition when producing an online course based on the book. First published in June 2013, I realized a lot had happened in the five years leading up to formulating the course, both personally, not least in the expansion of my metaphysical knowledge, and collectively, as we all accelerate into what metaphysical guides term our "shift in consciousness."

When the second running of the course ended, I planned to knuckle down to completing Book II, *Free Your Self,* of the *It's About You* trilogy. As circumstance would have it, 2019 would be an appropriate time to do this as both my hips needed replacement (so much for all that healthy sporting exercise in my youth) and I would therefore need to be sitting down in recovery rather a lot. Preparing Book II highlighted the need for a reworking of *Know Your Self,* to represent and better clarify the metaphysical wisdom—particularly considering a growing awareness of the global crises we face.

In 2013, few people were talking about the spiritually driven "purpose" of one's lifetime. Fewer still were ready to accept that "consciousness" is primary—not a by-product of the physical realm (the brain), but *the* patterning force underpinning all that is, all configurations of energy whether perceived as physical or nonphysical phenomena. And there was little realization that the realities we create for ourselves, personally and en masse, are manifestations emanating from the human psyche. Realizing this means that, as with the individual experiencing a life crisis, any attempt to "solve" or "cure" our world in crisis must begin with the originating distortions within our psychological makeup.

I entitled the trilogy *It's About You* because "it" is the reality we experience. *You* choose that reality from an infinite number of probable realities available to you in the "spacious present" of the psyche. So "it" is always pertaining to you and, because of this, knowing who you are becomes essential to managing your choice of reality.

Know Your Self will open your awareness to the magnificence of who you are. When you know where you're coming from and have begun resolving any distortions (challenges) within your own psychological makeup, you will be in a better position to express your own intent and purpose in the serving of humanity as it gets to know itself over this evolutionary period.

Book II (*Free Your Self*) offers help on maintaining the natural state of well-being. It's a book that takes the reader deeper into the process of freeing the ego-self from its fears and subsequent challenges that impede full expression of one's personality. It also continues to expand one's knowledge of the many layered Self.

Book III (*Live Your Purpose*) looks to guide the reader on how to live a mostly healthy, mostly joyous (life would not be the learning experience it is if it were all completely plain sailing) lifetime, with an invigorated sense of purpose.

It's About You is a fusion of thoughts, beliefs, ideas, and theories about the structure of our Selves and how the reality we call the physical realm comes into being. Over more than twenty-five years of study, I have taken a dual track approach to learning and examining such knowledge. The main line of enquiry focuses upon metaphysical literature—specifically the information relayed by characters from the nonphysical or spiritual realm through a process known as "channeling." The other line has been the study of learned contributions on this vast subject matter from scientists, philosophers, psychologists, and spiritual leaders who we all acknowledge to be solidly situated in the physical dimension—either now or at some time in the past.

The nature of the subject matter is of course extraordinarily complex, with some ideas and notions almost impossible to describe within the vocabulary of the English language. Because of this, I provide a Glossary of Terms at the back of this book which contains much of the new language and alternative definitions thrown up by my studies. Readers of the first edition have found it useful to familiarize themselves with the glossary before embarking on the main content.

This trilogy builds upon the bedrock of wisdom provided by the *Seth Material*—a body of work channeled by Jane Roberts and authored by Jane and her husband Rob Butts now archived at Yale University's Sterling Memorial Library in New Haven, Connecticut. Consisting of thirty books produced from recorded sessions between 1963 and 1984, there is considerable recognition and praise (albeit whispered in academia) within the scientific community for its clarity of insight. Many transpersonal scholars regard it as *the* leading metaphysical information source.

Despite the Seth Material remaining mostly ignored by those holding modern and postmodern worldviews, I am convinced that the current shift in human consciousness will see a revitalized examination of Sethian philosophy and the metaphysical literature in general as a new post-postmodern worldview begins to emerge.

There is some personal work to do

Seth advocates a proactive approach to self-development, exploration, and healing. His works therefore include many exercises designed to promote learning through experience and encourage the development of our latent *extrasensory* abilities. His foundational exercises furnish us with the opportunity to commune with our *inner self* (or soul) and to begin utilizing those extra senses we rarely engage consciously. Rudolf Steiner referred to these as our "organs of supersensory perception"—whereas Seth simply calls them our *inner senses*.

My trilogy follows this proactive pattern by presenting a

variety of exercises reformulated from suggestions by several channeled guides as well as proven practices taken from more conventional schools of learning.

The exercises are important in initiating an educational process that encourages the reader to apply and experience the perennial wisdom voiced by many inspirational characters—wherever their voices come from! Their design is to help you take the next step forward from just an intellectual *understanding* of what you and the world are all about, to a confidence boosting *assimilation* of that knowledge. They are chosen for their ability to gently introduce you (your ego-self) to your inner self and your inner senses and to bring you in contact with the greater part of your Self that holds all knowledge of who you are, why you chose to participate in this world at this time, and most importantly, what may be blocking you from participating more joyfully.

The practices will clarify any psychological or emotional blocks that create challenges in your life and provide the means to remove them. Collectively, their intention is to nurture *total* Self-development, encourage ego-self-healing, and promote a love of your Self that includes the much-maligned ego-self.

Your intent to get to know your Self

The primary aim of this book, and my work in general, is to awaken the reader to their personal intent and, by so doing, clarify the purpose of their current lifetime.

As Abraham (channeled by Esther Hicks) reminds us, "You came forth into this physical environment with enormous, excited intention. You are pure positive energy expressed from Source Energy."[2]

The idea that *intent*—the directing force behind all actions and all creations—is an absolute property of our existence is something the modern, scientific worldview cannot accept because it implies that everything in our reality—whether in the objective physical realm or the subjective nonphysical mind—has both meaning and purpose. You may be pleased to hear that much of the channeled literature categorically informs us that intent impregnates *all* our realities. It follows, then, that if we are to believe the channeled literature, by identifying our own intent, we have a good chance of identifying the purpose of our current lifetime.

Our intent and purpose are the steering forces behind a life of joy and fulfillment. As you will discover, your intent drives personal psychological change, like sorting out those problematic beliefs as you come to know your Self.

The intent of *our shared human consciousness* drives changes in our collective psyche, a case in point being our shift in consciousness—meant to instigate a radical review of our collective problematic belief systems. And the intent of *Consciousness itself* is ultimately supporting the drive of all such changes as it gets to know itself through the experiences of all its individuations, not least those created by our species.

In deference to the biblical notion that a little piece of God resides in each of us, you can equate your own personal intent with that very portion of God. So, your purest personal intent is an outworking of God's intent. *Chapter 5* explores the nuances of intent as they relate to human consciousness.

The human articulation of intent loosely conforms to nine distinguishable types of expression—first referred to metaphorically by Seth and then by other channeled guides as the *"families of consciousness."* For now, know that essentially, they are differing developmental paths of activity peculiar to humankind, involved with the growth, learning, and evolution of each individual and humanity itself.

Contrary to the modern, scientific worldview, you have a higher reason for being and a personal meaning to your existence.

You exist to expand and evolve Consciousness, which begins with the consciousness of your current personality. The learning and expansion of your current personality in the physical realm simultaneously involves the evolution of the entirety of your Self in the nonphysical realm. *Your* evolution adds to the evolution of the collective consciousness of our species, which in turn expands and evolves Consciousness itself.[3]

Riding the shift

Our metaphysical friend Seth mentions that we will see the completion of a fundamental "change" in human consciousness by around 2075. It matters not how old we are at present though, what matters is that we make the effort to understand as fully as possible the way we think and the beliefs we currently hold and, where appropriate, shift our patterns of thinking so that we, our children, and future generations benefit from the work we do now for our Self. A change in our personal beliefs, which triggers our thoughts and behaviors, *reverberates through the entirety of our Self* and *our collective consciousness*—inherited by future generations.

For most of us, some preliminary work is likely necessary before we can strap our Selves in for the ride through the shift. All of us will need to work at remaining strapped in. This book and those that follow serve as a seatbelt, a guide, and a driver's manual.

Know Your Self will provide you with an awareness of how we create the realities we do—as individuals and en masse. With this reawakened awareness, we can begin to fathom the underlying "hidden" messages of our firsthand experiences. We may also gain a better grasp of the underlying communications from our collective psyche that explain our co-created experiences. In other words, we can begin to exercise our psychic abilities—which essentially entails self-channeling valuable information from the subjective (spiritual) realm to our objective, conscious-mind.

Our collective psyche informs us of the meaning of shared events, just as our inner selves inform us of the meaning of personal events. Mass events reflect the workings of our collective psyche—they are physical manifestations that echo the effects the shift is having upon the thoughts and beliefs of our prevailing worldviews.

Our shift in consciousness is the catalyst in producing the various events (crises) we consider part of a fundamental cultural upheaval. The word "fundamental" means "relating to primary principles or rules." The latter part of the word—mental—suggests where the upheaval is really taking place.

The foundations of our thinking are shifting. Religious fundamentalism, a feature of mass events since the beginning of the millennium, "naturally" arises from the shift's effects upon our spiritual beliefs. Other mass events (such as global warming and rising sea levels) highlight other changes needing to occur in the way we think and what we believe to be true. The foundations—a word etymologically linked to "fundamental"—of our financial systems are trembling for example, as too are the underpinnings of antiquated systems of government such as dictatorships and even the democratic system. Certainly, our actions relating to our quest for energy resources require new ways of thinking.

The shift is set to continue over the next few decades and for those of us not willing to review our personal set of beliefs it is likely to be an anxious, if not traumatic time. It's possible, however, for us to ride the change relatively unscathed if we are prepared to put in some work on identifying how much our personal worldview aligns with the developing new or post-postmodern one.

In short, if you're feeling anxious about the shift, look to your current thoughts and beliefs and become aware of those that may require adjustment. This book will help you in this.

Changing our beliefs and our habits of thought isn't as

straightforward as simply trashing the inappropriate and replacing them with affirmations of the newly preferred. Subtle energies are involved that need consideration for a permanent change to occur. We need to open a clear path of communication between our *ego-self* and our *inner self*—the part of our Self that knows which of our beliefs are problematic and what energies supporting them need dissolving.

The trickiest element in addressing our beliefs is to become *consciously* aware of them in the first place! We are prone to cunningly conceal our core beliefs within a subconscious security vault as they surreptitiously go about governing many of our undesired behaviors.

This book supplies you with a variety of keys and combinations for accessing your personal vault and methods for dissipating the energy held by belief systems that inhibit you. I'm sorry to have to inform you that for many of us there is indeed some work involved, but it is important work that leads to personal transformation.

It's equally important to maintain a lighthearted attitude as we do the work, so that new habits of thought are *in-formed,* rather than resisted, by a suspicious ego-self. My books adhere to the metaphysical rule of keeping things fun throughout the learning process.

I advise you to get a work journal to keep track of your progress through the exercises. It is important to do the exercises, usually more than once, and write down what comes up for you. You should include in your work journal any revelations noticed during or after an exercise, or at any other time—recalled dreams are an example.

Physics and metaphysics

Quantum physicists have recently begun to realize the capacity for explaining the reality of the nonphysical realms of probabilities and potentials—what religious doctrine describes as the spiritual realm and the channeled literature regards as the myriad expressions of Consciousness. Wolfgang Pauli, a pioneer of quantum physics, urged us to seek ways of marrying Eastern mysticism with Western science, a spiritual/scientific divide that Consciousness also seeks to resolve through the intentional forces of the shift. Indeed, part of the shift's design is to draw us closer to Rudolf Steiner's desire for the conception of a *spiritual science*.

It's About You! Know Your Self will lead you through the maze of knowledge found in both metaphysical literature and classical fields of study and identify similarities in their core messages. My intent is to clarify exactly what the shift entails, how this relates to you, and what you can do for your Self, and thereby others, to ease your passage through this era of collective transition.

The truth of metaphysics

My desire to translate Sethian philosophy into more easily digestible bytes led me to look for parallels in other philosophical works—from scientific theory to religious doctrine and to other metaphysical sources. Hence the inclusion in the content of this book of some snippets from a variety of scientific, philosophical and metaphysical sources that help confirm and match what Seth describes as the *perennial philosophy* in spirituality, and what the contemporary philosopher Ken Wilber refers to as our quest for what is "forever true" about the nature of our universe. Wilber states:

> The aim of metaphysics—which means, basically, all of Western philosophy—was to provide an account of reality that would be logically proved to be the Last Word on the subject—a presentation of what was "really true" for all time. Something like: "This is the real structure of reality; this is what is true, and this is what is good, and this is what is beautiful; and this account is the one and only real account of

> the true nature of the world." The whole point of philosophy was to figure it all out, once and for all—the Last Word. No philosopher wrote anything thinking that it would be true for only a year or two and then vanish forever. **Metaphysics means finding what is always true, always the Last Word on the subject.**[4] *(My emphasis.)*

The Seth material set the gold standard for metaphysical philosophy. However, Seth himself advises that we should not take his word as the Last Word on the subject, but to utilize what he proposes and see how much of it rings *true for you*. He informs us that beneath the relative truths we grow from our beliefs are some fundamental absolutes ("laws of the inner universe") on the nature of our physical reality. From these fundamental (foundation-to-the-mind) truths are a discernable set of principles by which the mind can generate the physical reality of our choosing. I outline these *natural* principles in *Chapter 4* and Appendix I.

The intricacies of creating your own reality

From the start of this book it is important for you to learn of the metaphysical *natural principles*. Familiarity with these mental behavioral influencers gives you a head start when you come to consciously utilize your inner senses. Once understood as a foundational mental outlook, it is then a matter of assimilating them into your everyday thoughts and actions to create the reality you desire. Easy-peasy. Well, it would be, if we didn't have an ego-self with some myriad beliefs, of which some may be keeping us from fully expressing our creative abilities.

Of course, there are some people, and Seth tells of this, that lead a relatively trouble-free life, experiencing few difficult challenges, while remaining oblivious to the hardships experienced by the majority. When we understand that we usually have numerous lifetimes on this physical plane, many of which are to do with fathoming the man-made issue of "suffering," and that our Essence self (Higher Self or Soul if you like) creates these lifetimes for many reasons to do with learning and the expansion of its *individuated* consciousness, then a lifetime absent of challenges can be seen as part of a theme of learning played out over several lifetimes. The intent and purpose of such a life might be to take a break, as it were, from the theme of suffering (a theme we are not obliged to take up incidentally), or to see if we can become *consciously* aware of the basic principles for living a joyful, fulfilling life and set an example to others.

Be encouraged when you come across a Mr. or Ms. Riley. They are a mirror, reflecting what is entirely possible for you to attain—and reminding you that you can create such a relatively challenge-free lifetime at any moment within this one!

For most of us, though, creating our preferred reality involves understanding how our ego-self works and consciously managing the creation tools at its disposal. Before we can do this, and eventually get around to showing our ego-self some compassion for its endeavors, it's important to gain a broader understanding of where the ego-self fits into the overall Self and the Self's overall reasons for being.

Part I of this book is concerned with establishing the *why* of our existence and *how* the Oneness of Consciousness creates us as a part of All-That-Is. Our reason for being is precisely the same as that of Consciousness itself—to evolve and expand through experience. Consciousness does this by creating realities in an infinite number of planes and dimensions of existence, whereas we confine ourselves to the physical dimension and a few planes of Consciousness strongly associated with it. Driving the expansion of Consciousness is the principle of intent—our human translation of which, the *Families of Intent*, offers tangible clues as to what our Essence self had in mind for its expansion when committing to the experience of having a physical life.

Chapters 1 and 2 offer a new creation myth that requires a radical reassessment of our "spiritual" beliefs, whether they be obscured by religious doctrine, or entrenched within a modern scientific worldview that sees no value in exploring nonphysical dimensions of reality.

I felt I needed to present the most intellectually thought-provoking material early on as it offers an immediate challenge to the ego-self. The challenge is to keep your mind open to the innovative ideas long enough for them to make sense—or rather, to invigorate an inner sense, a *knowing* of its foundation-to-the-mind truths. Be aware that the ego-self abhors change. It will resolutely defend its currently held beliefs and "truths" about *its* self, *its* identity (essentially its collection of beliefs), and *its* understanding of spiritual matters.

It's rare that the written word will convince a defensive ego-self to change things. Real learning comes through experience (because that's what Consciousness is all about), so the book exercises offer you the chance to *experience* some of the material presented. Practicing the exercises will eventually, if not immediately, create an experience that will give your ego-self something to think about! The importance of practice and repetition cannot be overstated—it will eventually bring you revelatory experiences that will encourage a new set of life-enhancing habits of thought and action. Trust that your inner self will know the timing of such revelations and don't be put off by your ego-self's excuses or fears. The EFT exercises will quell the fears and dissipate the doubt. EFT has become for me a lifetime's tool for self-administering relief from held emotional energy and for investigating my errant beliefs.

To create a habit of practice, you need to engage the experience at least five times. Be gentle and patient with all of this though, allow your inner self to dictate the speed at which your ego-self can cope with what is likely to be a radical (but liberating) shift in your consciousness.

Included in our *collective* shift in consciousness is a new paradigm for the understanding of our spiritual self. This is the nonphysical aspect of our existence ignored by science as it rose to prominence in our collective worldview over the last 150 years—the side to our Self that religious factions have disturbingly manipulated in interpretation for hundreds of years.

Science, through quantum theory, is beginning to acquiesce to the idea of other dimensions of reality and in so doing is broadening its thoughts and beliefs about reality in general. Here, Werner Heisenberg, the father of quantum theory, comments:

> Some scientists [have been] inclined to think that the psychological phenomena could ultimately be explained on the basis of physics and chemistry of the brain. From the quantum-theoretical point of view there is no reason for such an assumption.[5]

Paul Davies a leading figure in modern physics has this to add:

> It is often said that physicists invented the mechanistic-reductionist philosophy, taught it to the biologists, and then abandoned it themselves. It cannot be denied that modern physics has a strongly holistic, even teleological flavour, and that this is due in large part to the influence of quantum theory.[6]

Accepting the belief (remember it is always about what you *believe* to be true that sets your approach to life) that you are an individuation of the One energy patterning force of Consciousness (described in religious terms as God) can be difficult (for your ego-self), but with this thought literally seeded "in mind," you have a liberating opportunity to grow your thinking about your Self and your capabilities.

According to Elias (channeled by Mary Ennis), we are

coming to the end of the religious era. The repercussions of this collective mass event are reflected in major religious doctrines being examined and challenged by their followers. Religious institutions are losing *control* (the basis of some for their existence) over the public. Fundamentalism is a symptom of religious unrest. We are changing the *foundations to our mind* and the foundation of religious doctrine is beginning to crumble as the earthquake of our shift in consciousness plays out. A new foundation to the mind is the *trust of inner guidance* on what to believe, instead of the outer guidance (more often dictates) of institutions. Elias:

> You hold wonderings. You look to your present now and you hold questionings of validity of purpose, of missions, (grinning) of action. Within this present now, you are experiencing what I have termed to be a shift in consciousness. You are moving out of your religious era and moving into a new reality which you are creating.[7]

Know thy Self to free thy Self

Being freely able to fully express the uniqueness of yourself while in the physical domain requires a new set of beliefs about your Self, beliefs unrestricted by the ego-self's solipsism. *Chapters 6 and 7* present a comprehensive metaphysical guide to the primary expressions of the Self—your *spiritual self* and your *physical self*—on the understanding that, as Seth reminds us, there is no actual separation between these two expressions within your consciousness, or indeed between what is Self and what we currently believe to be "not Self." ***There are no separations within Consciousness.***

Contemporary philosophical debate now abounds with the notion that reality is an illusion created by the mind. Metaphysical philosophy, on first reading, would appear to agree with this idea. However, metaphysical guides are quick to point out that although we each create our own personal reality through the psychological elements of our mind, this seemingly individual reality is not illusory or unreal to its creator. We still think that there is only one *real* reality—that which is manifest "out there." Consciousness has room for everyone's personal reality, all consensus realities, and all probable realities. We are yet to assimilate into our belief systems the understanding that there is no *one* reality in existence but an infinitesimal number of personal and agreed upon co-created realities.

Chapter 9, It's All in Your Mind, presents the broadest structure of your Self and where the Mind (I use a capital "M" at times to indicate when I'm talking about the collective of minds within the Mind!) comes into play. Knowing how your Mind works may appear daunting, but familiarization with the major characters influencing your Mind—ego-self, personality, conscious-mind, inner self and body-consciousness—will make things easier for you when taking some time-out to "go within."

The subconscious area of the Mind, accessed through the metaphorical subconscious library, is the key area within the Self where we store or hold important psychological elements (thoughts and beliefs) and energies (feelings and emotions) for possible investigation. Investigation at present is difficult as the ego-self is nearly always reluctant to cooperate, fearing a change to its identity if we decide to change a belief or two. Therefore, methods to relax the ego-self before investigation are highly recommended—I highlight meditation in this book, but any form of relaxation of the ego-self can be just as effective.

We are basically talking about giving ourselves a little quality time every day (as little as 20 minutes), to calm the ego-self's chatter of information whirling in our Mind and allowing our inner self to come through with some information of its own. Take a walk in nature, do some vigorous exercise, get artistically creative in some way, have a whole-body massage, practice mindfulness, or indulge in an energy balancing session such as Reiki, Yoga, Qi gong, Shiatsu, T'ai Chi or Reflexology once or twice a week to gently and compassionately subdue your ego-self's reluctance to take on the responsibility of conscious creation.

Know thy inner senses

At present, we usually create our personal reality as a *reactive response* to the present situation—after it has been measured and assessed by only the physical senses. Our shift in consciousness is awakening us to the inner senses, the spiritual senses that work within the greater expanse of the Self unencumbered by the vagaries of the linear-time oriented physical world. It's all about exercising our intuition—tuition that comes from within. This from Bashar (channeled by Darryl Anka):

> You have to give up the dependence on logic and reason. Start practicing a higher level of logic with a greater perspective. Relinquish the ***how*** of creation. The impulse or intuitive drive is the encapsulation of the higher logic of the inner self—a communication, so follow it however illogical it seems to the ego-self.[8]

The metaphysical literature often states that becoming familiar with the inner senses will offer far more information about the reality we've just created and what choices are now available to us. The inner senses are our link to our inner self and the broader picture it has of what is important for us to know before deciding on how to act. In short, they expand and enhance our awareness.

Chapter 11 brings the inner senses into your awareness and begins a measured and gentle introduction of their use. Like with anything we haven't used too often, there is a need for caution and patience when getting them up and running properly.

Stimulation of your inner senses through the various exercises will eventually bring a heightened sense of awareness into your everyday experiences. This will enhance your interactions with others and offer greater clarity on what and why you are creating a certain reality for yourself. You experience the inner senses as *feelings*, always sent by your body-consciousness in consultation with your inner self.

Most of us confuse feelings with emotions or lump them together as being the same phenomena. The aim of *Chapter 12* is to clarify the differences between the two energy forces so that you are better able to recognize the inner senses when they talk to you through your feelings. It's important to understand that an *emotional-signal* feeling is the precursor to an emotion—which provides inner information on your current state of being, as well as a bucket full of energy for you to propel your mental and physical actions. As you become attuned to your inner senses, you'll be better able to channel that emotional energy into considered, conscious actions, rather than reactionary ones.

Furthermore, you'll find it easier to follow up on the communication contained within an emotion and act upon it. Which invariably means uncovering a belief or two that is preventing you from fully expressing yourself in some way.

You create your reality *through* your beliefs

Beliefs are at the center of the reality creation process. They form a vibrational energy filter that sifts out the probable realities deemed impossible for us to create. If, for example, we believe we are not worthy of living in abundance, then that belief will screen out the probable realities we could have manifested where the abundance of something prevails.

It is, of course, a little more complicated, so *Chapters 14,15, 16, and 17* explore the nature of beliefs, how they interact with thoughts and activate feelings, how they mobilize our imagination, play with our emotions, and set up a final filter of expectation. Expectation is often the obstacle to manifesting our desires. Our beliefs affect an expectation's likelihood of coming to fruition. Elias advises that expectation can only lead to disappointment (because beliefs will distort the outcome), and Bashar tells us of the golden rule for manifesting your desires—concentrate on what you desire for not too long, then *follow your excitement with absolutely no expectation* as to the outcome.

Our core *systems of beliefs* (*Chapter 15*), outlined by Elias, describe the basic themes of human thought we like to concern ourselves with. In one such system, *Relationships*, a seed of thought can grow into a belief we have about our relationship with someone, and that someone can be yourself. For example, the relationship between our ego-self and our inner self is often tense because of any self-belittling beliefs the ego-self is holding on to. If our ego-self fervently believes we are not worthy of a happy, fulfilling life then it is always going to shy away from having an intimate relationship with an inner self that promises such a life is possible. As the belief strengthens, it begins to dictate how we behave in the relationship (the ego-self ignores the inner self, or worse, cuts it off completely, as in schizophrenia), thereby creating a reality of constant struggle and suffering.

Unworthiness can also become a deep-rooted belief within our subconscious mind. Beliefs about self-worth abound in the recesses of our collective psyche. Many of us propagate a lack of self-worth because we have taken on beliefs from our parents, or an institution has sown the thought in our Mind—usually both. Because of the prevalence of self-worth belief issues, I felt it important to introduce the *Tapping for Self-Worth* exercise (*Chapter 4*) early on. You will find, as I did, that this exercise will prove invaluable long after completing this book.

Ready to jump in?

While writing this new edition of *It's About You! Know Your Self*, I've been continuing my lifelong learning by following an online course facilitated by the contemporary philosopher, teacher, and integralist Terry Patten. The course derives from his latest book *A New Republic of the Heart* and this passage from the book does an excellent job in rounding off this introduction:

> If we face the questions of our time, if we recognize that they really cannot be avoided; and if we acknowledge how important, real, and existential they are, we will have accepted our mission. If we don't numb and distract ourselves, these deep questions will inevitably affect us. Facing them will deepen, awaken, and transform our consciousness, our whole way of being, and our behavior.
>
> Once this challenge is accepted, the real work takes place both inside and outside of us. It requires quantum leaps in consciousness, as well as in technological and social innovation. It requires new creativity at the levels of the individual, the local community, the virtual community, institutions, corporations, cities, and nations. It requires us to develop and express creative potential that has been virtually untapped—or, all too often, sabotaged—until now. It involves, in countless ways, the need to translate abstract ideas into concrete terms, and to discover what mandates such knowledge creates. And—starting at the level of every individual—it involves taking stock of where we are, and *who* we ultimately are.[9]

Jump in to find out who *you* ultimately are and what you have to offer. Enjoy.

Part I

The Essence of Your Intent

Chapter 1

Before Your Beginning

Most of us at some point in our lives ask ourselves, "Why do I exist? What's the purpose of my life? Is there something I should do that will provide me with contentment and fulfillment? Will I continue to exist when I die? Will I reincarnate?" And of course, you have likely asked, "If there is such a thing as reincarnation, can I come back as someone who is fabulously good-looking with no health, financial, or relationship problems to speak of… please?"

The briefest of answers to these questions are:

- Because you are important to the learning and expansion of Consciousness,
- To follow your lifetime's intent,
- Yes, follow your lifetime's intent,
- Yes,
- Yes, but not as your current personality,
- And… if that's what your Essence desires as part of its learning.

During this book I will elaborate on these answers. For you to grasp the detail of my elaborations, and how *you* came to be in this world, we need to begin with a brief outline of the two classical creation stories familiar to us in the West on how *everything* came to be here.

These opposing stories form part of the worldviews of traditional Judeo-Christian ideology and that of modern scientific theory. A *new* worldview, a new story of how we came to be here and what it's like to be human, is emerging from a reconfiguration, an evolutionary leap, in our collective psychology—a shift in the way we think, what we believe, and what we value. As we are at the initial stages of this psychological reconstruction, now is an appropriate time to offer up an alternative creation story. Such a story, I believe, can help bridge the mythos of religious ideology with the logos[10] of scientific theory.

I've deduced my alternative creation story from a variety of metaphysical offerings, particularly from the philosophy contained within the Seth material. As you become familiar with this alternative creation "myth-logos," you will hopefully realize that *your* existence is not only an integral part of *all* creation, unseparated from the ongoing action of creation, but also intimately involved in the moment-by-moment, nanosecond-by-nanosecond pulsing of the universe into being! But first...

From traditional mythos to a modern logos

Described in the Book of Genesis, the Judeo-Christian religious story of creation (creationism) tells the account of God taking seven days to bring everything into existence. When he came to creating humans, God created a man first (Adam), in his own image (which is why God looks like a man and not a woman of course), and then made Adam a companion from one of Adam's ribs. Adam then called this creation a wo-man because she had come from his flesh and bone. Because of this, Adam had power over the woman (Eve). God gave these first humans, along with their progeny, power over the animals and the natural world and thereby seeded the belief that humans have the right to control and manipulate nature.

You can see why this view of creation leaves the female of our species somewhat at a disadvantage and therefore a tad peeved—hence the advent of the women's emancipation movement; as well as why the natural world is in such crisis—because of man's neglect of his custodial duties—hence the advent of the Green movement.

The scientific story of creation (integral to scientism) tells of a big bang happening around 13.8 billion years ago, which brought every "thing" (matter) into existence. There was no intelligent force behind this occurrence, as it happened according to chance. Before this momentous event, there was nothing. No "thing" was in existence—not even the dimension of time. These "facts" give rise to the modern scientific worldview:

- The physical dimension exists through happenstance.
- There is no *other* (i.e., spiritual) dimension to our existence.
- There is ultimately no reason or meaning behind the physical dimension's existence, or anything that exists within it.
- The natural world is a resource for man to exploit in order to survive. (A belief ironically derived from religious doctrine.)

In comparison to the religious story, you can see why this view of creation leaves both women *and* men somewhat depressed, fearful, and quite literally, "dis-spirited"—hence the need for *personal* psychological counseling; as well as uncaring of the natural world as we continue to plunder its resources—hence the need for ***collective*** psychological counseling.

An alternative myth-logos

When asked by an interviewer in the 1980s what the world needed most, the American mythologist Joseph Campbell (1904–1987) replied, "A new myth." He suggested it would need to encapsulate a more holistic view of the planet and its peoples, a suggestion that gave birth to a postmodern myth within the postmodern worldview. Paul Helfrich states:

> We now face the dawn of a new worldview struggling to be born. Old ways no longer provide all of the answers. We need new ways to help us solve our problems and get along on an unprecedented global scale. Change is in the air, and the

> birth pangs involve a shift in consciousness never seen before in human history.[11]

The Seth material provides the fertile ground and seeds of inspiration for Campbell's new myth, Helfrich's new worldview, and our myth-logos. The creation myth is one of the core topics within the Seth material. Seth presents his own version of creation in the first of two volumes entitled *Dreams, "Evolution," and Value Fulfillment*. Notice that "evolution" is in quotes, to signify that our current theory of evolution is constrained by a lack of understanding that it is not just a linear (time-dependent) process. Our modern scientific worldview doesn't allow for nonlinear (time-free) dimensions of existence beyond the physical. Nonlinear dimensions, Seth informs us, are where a great deal more happens in our personal evolutionary process and in the creation process in general. In such dimensions a "spacious present" exists where a process can occur all at once, or in "simultaneous time!"

Science has shown us that the created universe, the physical dimension, is essentially all about energy (E) prefigured into matter (m), within the electromagnetic spectrum that includes light (c). Einstein's famous equation $E = mc^2$ tells us how much energy is involved in the prefiguring of any particular piece of matter.

He also, in his general theory of relativity (1916), proved that time is *relative* (dependent upon other conditions) and not an *absolute* (free from influence, intrinsically pure). All of which tells us that linear time, although intimately involved with the physical dimension, is a *nonphysical* construct (formed within our collective psyche) so that we may perceive the matter of physical reality.

Consciousness: the element missing from the equation

Because the modern scientific worldview clings to "chance" being the explanation for any creation and is routinely opposed to any traditional religious worldview it does itself a disservice. Even with the advent of quantum physics a hundred years ago, until recently (within the last 30 years), science has failed to even contemplate using its own methodology to investigate the notion of a spiritual intelligence influencing the reality we perceive through our five senses and the instruments that enhance them. Seth describes the problem:

> Science has unfortunately bound up the minds of its own even most original thinkers, for they dare not stray from certain scientific principles. All energy contains consciousness. That one sentence is basically scientific heresy, and in many circles, it is religious heresy as well. A recognition of that simple statement would indeed change the world.[12]

Some scientists are coming around to this view. Quantum physicists are beginning to discover an all-pervading intelligence involved in the patterning of energy—that energy has an ability *to be aware of its surroundings and of itself* (its patterning). Scientific enquiry is getting us closer to recognizing the truth of the matter (!)—that as all energy is aware[13] it thus has consciousness, as Seth described. In other words, consciousness is *integral to everything* we perceive (All That Is)—or better still, consciousness ***is*** All That Is. Consciousness is the absolute cause of everything in existence. It is, as traditional worldviews recognize, the intelligence behind the story of creation.

Theoretical nuclear physicist Amit Goswami, echoing the mystics of his native India, asserts that consciousness, not matter, is "the ground of all being." He holds that the universe is self-aware, and that consciousness creates the physical world. Calling this theory "monistic idealism," he claims it is not only "the basis of all religions worldwide" but also *the correct philosophy for [post] modern science.* He continues:

> Everything starts with consciousness. That is, consciousness is the ground of all being. In this view, consciousness imposes "downward causation." In other words, our free will is real. When we act in the world, we really are acting with causal power. This view does not deny that matter also has causal potency—it does not deny that there is causal power from elementary particles upward, so there is upward causation—but in addition it insists that there is also downward causation. It shows up in our creativity and acts of free will, or when we make moral decisions. In those occasions, we are actually witnessing downward causation by consciousness.[14]

In view of such reasoning, I propose that our myth-logos story of creation begins with an acknowledgement that an intelligence beyond our own drives all creation. As everything is ultimately composed of energy, all energy contains consciousness—the intelligence underpinning all creation.

You have your consciousness and I have mine

Because included within the modern scientific worldview is the belief that *matter* is the ground of all being, it assumes that what we understand to be consciousness *must* be created from the matter of our brains. Your awareness, *your* consciousness, is a by-product of brain function—plain and simple. Moreover, that's the be-all and end-all of consciousness. There is no other form of consciousness, no other spiritual awareness or intelligence independent of a brain. Some other life forms might have consciousness if they have a brain, but there cannot be consciousness without some physical material producing it. This belief drives neuropsychology's preoccupation with brain mapping techniques such as fMRI (functional magnetic resonance imaging) in the hope they may provide clues about where and how consciousness emerges from the material of the brain.

What science needs to accept into its post-postmodern

worldview is that there is indeed an intelligence involved in the creation of anything physical.

It really doesn't matter what you call this energy-patterning force. Seth refers to it as All That Is, other metaphysical characters as Source. Calling it God is fine, although I advocate we call it Consciousness with a capital C. For one thing, it should appease those scientists who can't abide by the connotations of the word "God," and for another, the capitalization helps to distinguish this ubiquitous force from all the gradations, sophistications, and degrees of awareness that capital-C Consciousness has created for itself—your consciousness being one example.

To prevent possible confusion, from this point on, I use a capital C for Consciousness in written documentation when referring to the *primal cause of all creation*—aka All That Is, Source, or God. When you come across the word "consciousness" with a small *c*, it refers to *an expression* of capital-C Consciousness—an individuated portion of Consciousness. This can take the form of a collective entity, such as human consciousness or Gaia (Earth's consciousness), or an entity further along the individuation process, such as *your* consciousness or that of a tree.

Metaphysical sources categorically state that Consciousness is primary. Importantly, it is not a thing, which is why science will not be able to find the "God particle"[15] or map, plot, and tie it to physicality. It exists *before* anything material, such as a brain. Furthermore, consciousness is *the* causal factor in any phenomenon created either in the nonphysical (spiritual) realm—including our own psychological structures (e.g., a conscious mind, an ego)—or in the physical dimension.

Consciousness shapes energy into simple patterns and extraordinarily complex patterns, such as living organisms and, of course, our Selves. It is independent of our Selves, as well as being implicit to our psychological and physical being. It is integral to our brains' functioning but is not a phenomenon born *of* its functioning.

The emerging myth-logos of the story of creation

The proposed alternative story of creation recognizes the traditional worldview that there is an intelligent dynamism at the causal heart of all phenomena we perceive. The postmodern worldview of science is on the verge of accepting this proposal.

Any descriptions of how and when the universe came into existence can (and should) cater to the level of understanding of someone with average intelligence. The original traditional stories, like those of the great religions and philosophies, were told in ways that the majority of people could understand. Such stories gave someone a rudimentary knowledge of the bigger picture of where they and their community came from, along with their role in society—their life's purpose—and how to conduct themselves while performing their role. The "facts" of the matter were of no consequence because:

- No one really knew there were any.
- Any mystic or shaman who might know something could only present his or her knowledge in a way that could be understood (usually through metaphor).
- We had not yet invented using logic and reason and having a definitive methodology for finding the facts about matter.

The modern scientific description of how and when the universe came into existence is still a story. Moreover, it's not a particularly good one, as few but the highly intelligent can understand it. Once again, there is something missing, this time from the scientific storytelling equation. That something is a broader perspective on what we regard as *real* other than physical phenomena, a better understanding of the transient nature of beliefs and their tendency to become "truths" or "facts," and, as Einstein intimated, to remember to go beyond the level of thinking we were at when the story was last told.

The myth-logos version of creation begins then before the beginning—with Consciousness.

The basic "levels" of Consciousness

These are the basic levels of Consciousness we need to grasp before we get into how and why Consciousness created our physical world and all its wonders, such as *you*:

- **Consciousness (with a capital *C*)** is the only absolute.[16] It is not physical, yet it permeates all that is physical. It is an intelligent force that underpins the patterning of energy into nonphysical and physical forms in many dimensions and on many levels of existence.
- ***Your* consciousness** (small *c*) is a nonphysical, individuated expression of Consciousness. It is part of your psychological structuring, part of your psyche, which utilizes a mind for entertaining thoughts and ideas and exercising your imagination. There is *only a correlation* between your consciousness and brain activity. Your level of Consciousness allows you to ***self-reflect***, a sophistication of being ***self-aware*** and having the freedom of ***self-expression***.
- Put as succinctly as possible, ***your consciousness is a pure stream of energy, imbued with intent, which emanates from Consciousness***.
- **A third level of Consciousness** belongs to nonhuman living organisms. Living organisms have a sense of ***self-awareness*** and the freedom of ***self-expression***.
- **A fourth level of Consciousness** is that of inorganic, physical matter or individuated, solidified, patterns of energy that fall within the electromagnetic spectrum of light. No matter how small the particle of matter, it is still "aware-ized" of its individuality—the most rudimentary form of ***self-awareness***.

Chapter 2

Consciousness Gets Busy

Chapter 1 essentially declares that before your beginning, even before the physical universe began—whether you view that through a traditional mythical story of creation or a scientific theoretical one—there was (and is) an intelligence that does not rely upon the physical dimension for its existence. Consciousness is that intelligence, and it is the absolute cause of everything in existence. It permeates *All That Is,* including physical things like you and me, a rock and a tree, and nonphysical things, like a dream, a thought, an idea, and an emotion.

A broader understanding of the meaning of the term "consciousness," to include more than just our ability to be aware of our surroundings, has been with us for some time.

An interpretation of capital-C Consciousness dates back centuries in some Eastern philosophies and religions, but this elevated, more encompassing meaning has also crept stealthily into the minds of leading philosophers, scientists and psychologists in the West—particularly since the end of the 19th Century and more so with the emergence of quantum physics.

William James, the American philosopher and psychologist, suggested that *our* consciousness (awareness of our surroundings): "—is but one special type of consciousness, while all about it, parted from it by the filmiest of screens, there lie potential forms of consciousness entirely different."[17]

More recently, the quantum physicist and philosopher Amit Goswami stated:

> In our efforts, we miss the simple thing—the simple truth that it is all God, which is the mystic's way of saying that it is all consciousness. Physics explains phenomena, but

> consciousness is not a phenomenon; instead, all else are phenomena in consciousness. I had vainly been seeking a description of consciousness within science; instead, what I and others have to look for is a description of science within consciousness.[18]

When we come to acknowledge that Consciousness is essentially a force that patterns energy into coherent mental (nonphysical) or physical forms, we might then accept that everything, however limited in physical complexity (such as protons, electrons, atoms and molecules), is *conscious* in the sense that it is an *expression of Consciousness*.

Consciousness getting busy

The "job" of Consciousness is to utilize *energy* (its very lifeblood) in the creation of realities—that is, definable phenomena, or arrangements of energy, whether in the physical dimension or otherwise, that have a quality to their existence, a "tone or vibrational signature,"[19] that is perceivable as real.

This reality-creating process emerges from the inner vitality of Consciousness, a dynamism referred to by Seth as "value fulfillment," or "Divine Love."[20] (We'll explore the power of Divine Love in *Chapter 3*.)

Remember that Divine Love refers to the inner vitality of Consciousness; it provides the impetus towards all creative action[21] in physical and nonphysical terms.

Now you might ask, "*Why* does Consciousness create realities?"

The short answer is that *this is how it gets to know Itself.*

The predominant name given by our metaphysical friends to the primary force stirring Consciousness to get to know itself is—*intent*.

The force of intent, stimulated by the vital impetus of Divine Love, drives Consciousness to act—to perform acts of creation—that produce realities. The creation of a reality—or think of this as the creation of an *experience*—provides a means for learning and growth. Consciousness is constantly learning about its own Self, in order to grow!

The next question is, why does Consciousness *want* to know itself?

To answer this question, we'll need to tap into the wisdom of Consciousness for a moment. *It* knows that the more one *knows* about one's Self, the more one comes to *understand* one's Self; and it also knows that when we fully understand something, fear ceases to exist.

Being in fear is the opposite of being in Divine Love. In other words, fear disconnects us from Divine Love. Therefore, Consciousness remains permanently within the state of Divine Love because it is constantly striving to know and understand itself. It recognizes that being in Divine Love invigorates creative *action* (more experiences), while disconnecting one's Self from this state of being (through becoming fearful) leads to *inaction*. (Inaction meaning a severe weakening of one's creative abilities.)

Consciousness recognizes that by being in the state of Divine Love, your Self is free to express itself! Creativity thrives in this ultimate state of Self-expression.

Remember that as your consciousness is an individuated expression of Consciousness, you too have a deep-seated intent to know your Self.

Consciousness getting to know itself

Consciousness chose to explore the possibilities of its expansion and growth by creating dimensions of existence—playgrounds of experience. Our beloved physical reality is one playground of experience. Apparently, there are others, some more physical and some less.

The process of *individuation* facilitates Consciousness knowing itself. That is, Consciousness separates out (as our ego-selves understand it) distinct portions of itself to focus upon particular aspects of learning and growth within the medium of physicality. Consciousness makes all these portions aware-ized and independent; they also have an identity that can utilize the power of intent for exploring the physical dimension. These individuated portions are *all* forms of matter—subatomic particles, atoms, chemical elements, compounds of them, life forms, plants, animals—*you*.

An *inorganic* portion of Consciousness has an awareness of Self but is extremely limited in the expression of its individuated self on the physical stage. Compounds of the elements (coming together under the natural principle of *cooperation*, discussed in *Chapter 4*) expand the repertoire of expression for matter, but life forms add a profoundly new level of expression for individuated portions of Consciousness.

Life forms bring freedom of expression to such individuated portions.[22]

The new level of expression allows for greater complexity of cooperation and a greater sense of Self-awareness and thus a greater way for Consciousness to develop its exploratory process. Consider for a moment how nature has run with this freedom of expression under its intentional belt!

At this point, we need to bear in mind that all expressions of Consciousness in the physical domain are subject to *natural principles*—primarily the natural power of Divine Love mentioned earlier. This means that no one organism or species, given the freedom of life, can ever dominate the physical environment to the detriment of other expressions of Consciousness. To prevent this from happening, Consciousness can end participation in the physical realm for such individuated portions—death, or even extinction, eventually ensues.

Our own individuated expression of Consciousness

Our awareness of Self—integrated within our *personality*[23]—has been married with another psychological structure as part of Consciousness's evolutionary drive for experiential knowledge—an ego! This dual ego/personality psychological combo ratchets up the individuation experiment by giving us *conscious awareness* of the totality of the Self operating in realities other than just the physical dimension. In other words, our consciousness can utilize *levels of awareness on other planes of our existence* (the spiritual planes as it were), but for most of us our ego-selves have yet to realize such potentials in the construction of our realities.

With *conscious* awareness of Self comes the ability to Self-reflect.

However, for many centuries the ego-self has insisted that *it* represents the entirety of the Self and that the only reality is the physical one. Such narcissism has thus narrowed our ability to reflect on the totality of our Self. The ego-self's myopic form of self-reflection, with a focus upon its own physicality-based perceptions, has meant we are yet to truly explore the gift of Self-reflection. The shift in consciousness[24] humanity is currently experiencing aims to correct the psychological bias on Self-reflection created by the ego-self.

Albeit, Seth is quick to point out that we should not abandon the ego-self or seek to remove this part of our Self from our psychological structuring. It is, after all, extremely adept at reasoning, logic, and planning—essential psychological attributes for operating within the physical realm. The ego-self simply needs to be brought back into harmony and cooperation with the other aspects of our Selves. Better to be kind to your ego-self as you go about your own personal psychological readjustments in association with our shift in consciousness.

Our troublesome times suggest Consciousness has it in mind to see humanity's consciousness regain the full scope of conscious awareness. Our shift in consciousness moves us from the limited ego-self's evaluation of who we are to the big Self's potentials that will expand who we are.

Chapter 3

How To Be In Divine Love

After reading the introduction and the first two chapters, I hope you understand that your *Self* is an individuated portion of the absolute Oneness of Consciousness—and that this is basically a good thing!

Because of this truth, in imitation of Consciousness itself, you have an instinctive urge to know your Self. This primal urge is the power of *intent*. Consciousness recognizes that the more you learn about your Self, the more you come to understand yourself. For us individuated humans, this crucially means the more you understand about the structure of the entirety of your Self, the more you come to understand your *ego-self—and how it operates*. Moreover, the wonderful thing about understanding something is that any fear around it dissolves. In the case of your Self, because your ego-self generates fear, understanding how it operates and what causes the fear will give you a better chance of living a life free from it.[25]

Learning about ourselves through reality creation

Consciousness has created a life form—humans—with a remarkable psychological advantage over most other life forms—***conscious*** *self-awareness*. Perhaps alarmingly to some, we are a fabulous learning experiment for Consciousness. It wants to see what it can learn from allowing a portion of itself (us) to take up the brushes and vibrational palette of the physical medium and do the creation thing for itself. Consciousness has given us the means to get on with the reality creation process all by ourselves! Conscious self-awareness gives us the psychological means to reflect on what we've created, so that we might adjust our thoughts and beliefs—the elements that control our creative expression—and create anew. Particularly if what we've already created is, well, total crap.

As Seth and other channeled sources constantly remind us, we can't get away from this truth—we create our own reality—whether we *believe it*, or not. Most people at present *don't* believe this, and certainly, it is exceedingly difficult for us to understand the psychological processes involved. Therefore, many of us create our realities in the blind, unaware that we must look to our beliefs if we want to change what we have made real. However, we will find that our collective shift in consciousness, mentioned earlier, will lead to a better understanding of personal and collective reality creation.

The how of reality creation

You create realities (experiences) for yourself to learn not only about your Self but also about *how* the reality-creation process itself works. My years of study of metaphysical material reveal that Consciousness provides us with a *best way* of going about this entire reality-creation process. There is a guiding set of principles for getting the best out of our creative abilities. Furthermore, as they are not particularly difficult to understand and apply, they save many of us the need to stretch our intellectual capacity to a place of confusion. I refer to these perennial guiding principles as the *Natural Principles*, which I elaborate upon in *Chapter 4*.

In a moment I'll elaborate on *Divine Love*, first mentioned in *Chapter 2*. Here, know that if you want to create the realities you desire, you first need to bring your personality's current vibrational frequency into better alignment with that of your primal tone or vibrational signature.[26] In other words, you need to get your ego-self into psychological balance with your natural state of being—nested within Divine Love.

Exercise 1: Touching Your Tone
Go to Appendix IV for directions on this 15-minute exercise. Its design is to get you acquainted with your vibrational signature, the tone of your spiritual identity—your Essence self.

Divine Love teasing your ego-self

Because we have the gift of ***free will*** (discussed below), we can choose to ignore the best way of going about the creation process. Collectively, this is what our ego-self has chosen to do by doing things in a way that relies solely on the abilities of the intellect. Divine Love doesn't abandon our ego-self because of this apparent rejection in favor of reason and logic. It can't, as there is no separation from Consciousness and therefore Divine Love! It remains in the spiritual wings and from there continuously reminds us of the better, more principled way to create.

The way Divine Love reminds our ego-self that something we have created is not in accordance with natural principles is to tease it with *emotional-signals*.[27] At present, it invariably focuses upon the signal and engaging the emotional energy attached to it, rather than recognizing that the signal is in fact carrying a message. That message is primarily to do with acknowledging that the creation is flawed and that the ego-self needs to use the attached energy for self-reflection and some belief processing—as opposed to habitual reactionary venting.

A flawed creation, or "negative" experience, is primarily a teaching instrument. Consciousness, through the power of Divine Love, teaches us to get back to the best way to create, to return to our natural state of being. However, as our ego-self generally has yet to learn the deeper message of a negative experience and always has the last word on what we create in the physical world, our individual and collective creations often remain alarmingly defective.[28]

Our universe is still a safe place to be

Difficult as it may be for our ego-self to recognize, Seth tells us that we live in a *safe* universe. Despite the ego's naiveté and the wayward course it has taken humanity, we remain connected to Consciousness—and therefore Divine Love.

The mass media provides us with our on-the-surface view of reality. This superficial view reflects the beliefs we currently hold to be true *of* reality. The news media's reports tend to focus on events that stimulate our fears—which are generated by our collective core beliefs. As you may have gathered from the media, the prevailing worldview suggests we live in an *unsafe* universe—echoing a primal fear within our collective psyche, that we are separated from Source. The beliefs of both science and religion predominantly support this view.

Seth often reminds us that All That Is (Consciousness) is of *good intent*—which means that ***everything*** *created has a positive aspect to it*. Divine Love allows for the creation of ***all*** manifestations in the learning-about-your-Self process—even negative manifestations. When we understand that negative manifestations are integral to our learning, we will be better able to control what we create. So, while the manifest universe can appear to be unsafe, in actuality the underpinning forces of manifestation are always looking out for us. To *feel* safe in the physical world we must understand *how* we manifest our realities.

Eventually, we'll find that our collective shift in consciousness incorporates the understanding that we create our own reality. Seth informs us that Divine Love is "*always* a protection"—protecting, quite literally, the integrity of all the systems of your Self: the biological, chemical, electromagnetic, and psychological.

The divineness of Divine Love

We often talk of love as being an emotion. *Divine Love* ***is not*** *an emotion.* This misconception comes about because for our consciousness to fathom its nature, we employ emotional energy in our interpretations.

Besides being an action (described in *Chapter 2*), Divine Love is a *way of being*—the way of being of Consciousness. It is a *quality* of all actions (including emotions), and the primary principle that *applies* to all actions, in whatever field of existence they occur.

Divine Love is about the total, nonjudgmental acceptance of what is. This is because any and every creation, whether perceived as good or bad, is at its very core an expression of Consciousness born of its quest to know itself through experience. Consciousness, human consciousness, *your* consciousness, can't know itself, can't decide on what is preferable, can't make choices, can't change things, without the contrast provided by *undesirable* creations.

Divine Love powers the process of the individuation of Consciousness. As it is a primary principle of action, it demands that actions adhere to certain qualities of expression: acceptance, allowance, appreciation, and compassion. In reality, in *Truth*, all actions, all expressions, whether made physical or otherwise, are individuations of Consciousness. This is how Elias (Mary Ennis) explains Divine Love:

> Love is a quality of consciousness. It is the action of becoming. Love is a truth, and the translation within your physical dimension of love is not attraction. It is that of knowing and appreciation, genuine appreciation, which appreciation is expressed in acceptance. In this, the knowing is also significant, actual knowing of yourself and knowing of another individual and expressing an acceptance which generates an appreciation. This is the genuine expression of love.[29]

Elias reminds us that when it comes to understanding the *truths*[30] of our reality, we show little interest in them, other than Divine Love, which our current definitions show to be misinterpretations of its truth. We misinterpret and poorly define Divine Love because of our preoccupation with defining everything—which by default must occur through the language of our belief systems, an extremely limited and biased medium for expressing what we want to know or think we already know.

As Anita Moorjani comments in her book *Dying to Be Me,* when coming to terms with her near-death experience (NDE) she realized it was a state of pure awareness (couched in Divine Love), which suspends "all previously held doctrine and dogma." She continues:

> I've found that subsequent to my NDE, I'm at my strongest when I'm able to let go, when I suspend my beliefs as well as disbeliefs, and leave myself open to *all* possibilities.[31]

Moorjani's NDE is a testament to the fact that Divine Love is an action, a quality underpinning all experiences, a state of being and becoming—not a *thing* that we can describe, even if we had the language to do so.

It is impossible to express such truths as Divine Love through language associated with belief systems. As we come to recognize and uncover the truths to our existence, we get to realize the nature of our beliefs and the belief systems we construct to describe our existence. We get to know that beliefs are merely a tool for physical existence, a medium by which we paint our physical dimension.

Your will to love

Omni[32] states that Divine Love is at the core of your being and becomes a magnet within your personality. *You have a will to love* because it is within the nature of Consciousness and all its expressions. Your will to love is your direct link to Consciousness and its *modus operandi*—Divine Love. Our gift of free will is a natural by-product of having conscious self-awareness. Omni explains:

> You are beings of absolute and total free will. Free will is the natural result of [Divine] love, for love is the total and complete acceptance of what is. As love is the very nature of the All That Is [Consciousness], it is also your deepest desire, for it acts like a magnet upon your personality. All that is not love is not natural to whom you are, and all things seek to operate according to the natural laws [Principles] of the Universe. Your physical reality was created so that you may experience that which you are not. In experiencing that which you are not, you began to experience that which is not love, that which is not acceptance, that which does not allow.[33]

So there is a profound irony involved in our new story of evolution and creation. When Consciousness took the evolutionary step to bestow a life form (us humans at least) with conscious self-awareness, it gave us the ability not only to be aware of positive and negative creations but also to *choose* what we create as a reality. Because we have the free will to choose, we are even free to ignore the one influencing factor that exists to protect and sustain our free will—our will to love, provided by Divine Love.

Getting back to being in Divine Love

Way back in time when our ego-selves first used the ability to self-reflect, we began to imagine that the totality of who we were could be described by our physical appearance, our personality, and what we did to occupy our time. Such parameters would provide us with our identity, and this then separated us from other expressions of Consciousness.

This egotistical leap into loneliness led us to believe that death must be the end to our existence. We observed how other animals defended themselves against death and took this as indication of a need to protect ourselves against it. Eventually, we developed a deep-rooted belief system that sees all "others" as potential threats, and thus we cannot *allow* another the benefit of our love.

Our shift in consciousness incorporates a conscious remembering that Divine Love is the fundamental principle of creation and that we need to make a conscious effort to bring our creational skills back within its guidelines.

Our free will has taken us along a path of experiences that demonstrate how ignoring Divine Love's guidance affects our creations. We've spent centuries discovering how the absence of acceptance, appreciation, allowance, and compassion creates realities that none of us prefer. Suffering has been our immensely sad and disturbingly perverse way of teaching our Selves the fact that we have free will and can choose how to live. The shift required of our consciousness is to accept that there also exists a how-best-to-go-about-it creation scheme, the way of Divine Love.

Our will to love has never gone away as it cannot do so; we have been pretending it's not there to see where our free will would take us.

Our shift in consciousness is a step that takes us *within* an acceptance of the power of Divine Love. The only other alternative step, *outside* of this acceptance, is to allow our collective ego-self to play out its own inevitable next step, one taken by many individual ego-selves that cannot accept how things divinely work and are unable to adjust their beliefs—suicide.

Seth suggests that the personality of any individual who commits suicide soon realizes in the *transitional area within consciousness*[34] that their actions are inconsequential to the grander scheme of their Essence self, and the even grander scheme of Consciousness. This is because, as Omni reminds us, we cannot extinguish the spark of Divine Love within us. No matter how far into the darkness we go, this spark of Love, this will to love, brings us back to Consciousness—back from "lovelessness" to unconditional love.

All of which points us back to the truth that we live in a safe universe.

There is really no need for humanity to commit suicide—it's a *futile action*. In the grander scheme of probable realities floating in the timeless sea of the *"spacious present,"*[35] Consciousness is aware of this futility. It remains a probability, but the alternative probability of expanding our consciousness further offers more enticing experiential possibilities. *All* actions (even the probable one of our suicide) are a product of Consciousness getting to know itself through experiences, and *contrasting* experiences are the best way of doing this when exploring the physical domain.

What we don't realize as individuals is that suicide, like any death, returns our personality to Essence and our Essence will deliberate on whether to create a lifetime with similar challenges to complete its learning cut short by the act of suicide. Our individuation reflects the workings of Consciousness. What humanity doesn't realize is that the probable reality of our annihilation through egocentric eccentricity already exists. We are at a point in time where we must choose for ourselves what probable reality we desire for ourselves.

Consciousness couldn't care less what we choose, as *within itself* all our choices on what probable reality to take are contained, and thereby it continues to learn and expand, even if we don't!

Humanity has spent a great deal of time misinterpreting what contrasting experiences bring to the creation process. We have repeatedly demonstrated to ourselves what happens when we ignore the natural principles of the universe encapsulated within the power of Divine Love. The last evolutionary step in our consciousness—conscious self-awareness and self-reflection—gave us the free will to explore this ultimate contrast of experience. This next evolutionary step or shift in our consciousness is inevitable because we have taken this exploration as far as it can go—to the gates of self-annihilation.

Now I for one am keen to see what we can create for ourselves when the majority of us are living and practicing the natural principles of Divine Love. What fun too will be had when we appreciate the fact that we are not separate from Consciousness and that we are all equally important to the evolution of humanity and understanding how *conscious Self-awareness* works. Is it not time for us to explore contrast without judging either element and to choose a personal preference without the need to justify our choice or denigrate that which we don't choose to experience?

Chapter 4

Conquering Fear Through the Natural Principles

I take it that like myself, you are keen to explore the possibilities of what a life of being in the state of Divine Love can bring. For someone like Anita Moorjani, a person who has dallied with death and reconnected with the state of Divine Love and can recall the experience, a *knowing* prevails:

> Even with this inner excitement, however, with this feeling that I was on the precipice of some great adventure, I still didn't feel that I had to *do* or *pursue* anything for it to happen. *I just had to be myself fearlessly!* In that way, I'd be allowing myself to be an instrument of love. I understood that this was the best thing that any of us could possibly do or be, for both the planet and ourselves.[36]

Moorjani's precarious route from simple understanding to this spiritual knowledge on how to lead her life—*just to be herself without fear*—took her past the veil of death to the transitional area within consciousness and back again to the physical realm. The circumstances of her miraculous story—a body riddled with cancer going through spontaneous remission at the point of death—is not something we need to experience to acknowledge this primary spiritual message. However, two questions are worth considering: What or who is my Self that I need to be, and how do I get rid of fear? You'll find an answer to the first question during the course of this book; in the meantime, let's get on with answering the second question by first remembering that if you can fully *understand* fear and how it's generated, you will be mentally predisposed to dissolve it before it can interfere with the creation of your experience.

Our greatest fear

Because physical reality is an experiment in experience for Consciousness, all physical dimensions[37] exist for Consciousness to explore itself. Humanity's consciousness is helping in this regard, although at present we are hampered by an ego-self that believes it is separated from Consciousness and has no understanding of its role in the grander scheme of things.

Our greatest fear, according to our channeled teachers, is perhaps the greatest paradox. At the very core of our collective psyche sits a deeply felt fear of the physical dimension itself.

To explore what or who our "Self" is involves going where no one has gone before (my apologies to *Star Trek* aficionados)—seeking out the unknown, facing new and unfamiliar experiences, and *engaging with that which is not understood*—all of which inevitably generates fear.

Emotions are the primary energy resource for our creational use in the physical realm. They are autonomous energy configurations originating from outside the physical dimension that find expression in it through sentient forms of life.[38] Emotions serve as the stimuli to action. They are neutral in their expression—it is we who label them as positive or negative. They just love to be part of the creation process, regardless of the label.

When connected to the power of Divine Love, we translate emotions positively—as joy, happiness, contentment, excitement, for example. When we are losing our connection to Divine Love, fear takes the opportunity to infiltrate our mental outlook, and our ego-self, depending on the fragility of its belief systems, will often find itself attempting to clear it through venting emotional energy. During such times, we label the energy in negative terms—as anger, sadness, anxiety, frustration—all products of the *feeling* of fear.

Fear is on one end of a continuum of emotions with the state of Divine Love at the other. You can think of this continuum as a measuring stick of how close you are to Divine Love. Your overall state of being moves back and forth along this pole at a pace dictated by your personality's beliefs. You cannot get away from the fact that fear becomes a primary element entangled within the creation process as you live out your physical life.

Importantly, however, as fear (other than a primal fear to survive) is a by-product of belief systems and beliefs tied to the physical expression of Self, you can rest assured that fear does not exist outside the physical realm. Fear only exists within the psychological elements formed for you to operate within the physical realm—that is, within the structuring of your ego-self's mind.

As with any *thing*, there is, though, *good* reason for fear's existence. Fear *can be* motivating, when received as the impulse to act immediately, for instance. It is also beneficial in the sense that the nature of its emotional expression advises your *conscious-mind*[39] of the psychological reasons for its being—problematic beliefs. Nevertheless, because it originates as a *feeling*,[40] as opposed to an emotion, it will distort the flow of energy through you, drain your energy, and thereby psychologically immobilize you.

However, you can reverse these debilitating effects when you understand you are dealing with energy. Understanding fear and the problematic belief patterns behind it allows you to manipulate its energy and the energies it attracts (emotions) to your benefit. Such manipulation is fundamental to all energy-balancing intervention techniques such as EFT (Emotional Freedom Techniques).

Fear of loving

Kris, channeled through Serge Grandbois, teaches us about the fear of loving.

In coming to terms with our greatest fear of what the physical realm has in store for us, we have learnt to suppress our feelings and emotions, including those related to Divine Love. Kris suggests that this act of suppression comes about through a subconscious awareness that we cannot possibly understand the driving force behind all creation—and thus fear it, even though this force is our salvation.

One of the main reasons for fearing Love, or *acting in a loving way*, is that we believe doing so will put us in a vulnerable position. Our collective limiting beliefs about *vulnerability* (primarily that we leave ourselves open to attack) stem from our misinterpretation of the *survival instinct*[41] of Consciousness. To act in a loving manner is therefore dangerous.

We have learned that human love often leads to heartache and pain. It therefore *makes sense* to the ego-self to suppress our will to love, our sexuality in expression of love, and our desires, which come out of our natural affinity for love.

We have come to a stage where we fear loving and consequently dislike or even loathe our Selves for having the will to love.

As we cannot appear to be seen acting in a loving manner, we assume it to be far safer to hate. Hating war is what we need to do to end it, rather than loving peace. We justify hate by fearing love, which leads us to hate everything rather than love everything.

A very limiting fear

A limiting fear we all have relates to Self-examination; we are afraid of what horrendous traits and behaviors we might find within our Selves and what horrific experiences we might create. So frightful are the contents of this Freudian black hole that we rarely *consciously* go anywhere near it.

This is a shame, because all there is in anyone's deepest black hole is a collection of dubious beliefs—admittedly, some more dubious than others. We have acquired them over our formative years, together with perhaps a few reinforcing beliefs gleaned from issues pertaining to other lifetimes. Our black hole contains only the beliefs most skillful at getting us to disparage ourselves in some way. They are the ones we have invested a great deal of energy in, beliefs that suggest that we are not worthy, not powerful, not able, and not as accomplished or good as someone else.

Unhappiness with life stems from this fear of Self-examination. Without any form of regular belief-checkup, the beliefs in our black hole remain unchallenged and continue to generate feelings of unhappiness more frequently.

Just to make it perfectly clear: your *beliefs* generate fear and, thereby, feelings of unhappiness. To dissolve fear or unhappiness, you need to examine your beliefs, and before this, you simply need to be aware that *all* beliefs, however entrenched, are malleable.

In becoming aware that your beliefs are at the heart of your personality's emotional climate, and that even though a few may establish themselves as truths for you—*yet are still open to adjustment*—you liberate your thinking.

Our beliefs form a membrane[42] around the ego-self, which influences the vibrational tone we send out to the universe. This membrane also acts as a filter, allowing in information our ego-self is prepared to receive, while filtering out the energies of impending "probable experiences" that do not align with those of our vibrational tone.

As we broaden our awareness and begin to accept the nature of beliefs, also be aware of the ego-self's arrogance! Although your ego-self would like to think so, the widening of your awareness is not creating a "better" you. This is an assumption made by the ego-self's adherence to the belief system of *duplicity*[43] (refer to *Chapter 15*), which has to do with a constant need to justify the choices it makes.

In fact, by widening our awareness we are creating a platform of *acceptance* (a facet of Divine Love closely related to *compassion*) of the entirety of the Self and our beliefs. The ego-self might think this makes for a better you, but it is more of a remembering, a reconnecting, to the breadth of who we truly are. Mastering self-compassion begins with accepting rather than denigrating the dubious beliefs we may hold in our black hole.

Of course, acceptance of *unacceptable* beliefs can be tricky! The trick is to recognize these types of beliefs as elements within us that supply the contrast required to define what our preferences are and thus steer us on our path of intent and purpose. Elias elaborates:

> Therefore, the key to acceptance is to be accepting of ***all*** of your reality, be it in your belief systems, good or bad, ***all*** of which is your creation, which is ***You***; and as you are not accepting of certain elements of your creations, your systems—***You***—you reinforce your element of fearfulness.[44]

So, a wider awareness and acceptance of your beliefs, without judging them, will lessen the hold of your belief systems as well as your fears about what your Self has to offer the world.

Eliminating fear

You cannot eliminate *beliefs* from your psychological structuring; they are the medium through which you create your reality. You can, however, manipulate their energies and the energies of emotions to quiet, if not eliminate, your fears.

All "negative" experiences are associated with a fear of some kind. Such experiences bring fears to our attention for examination and remedy, which is why they fascinate us more than positive experiences—news media reporting highlights this leaning toward the negative. At present, our collective awareness is not broad enough to realize the function of the experiences; instead, we play with them like a cat with a mouse, until the mouse bores us and we catch another interesting plaything. Albeit, negative experiences are the most objective and succinct guide to Self-knowledge.

Your inner self is aware of the function of negative experiences. Your Essence self[45] does not operate under the confines of beliefs. Duplicity (judging your choices), the most pervasive of belief systems, does not exist outside physical experience. There is no positive or negative, right or wrong, good or bad where your Essence is concerned. You exist, and that's it; judgments don't mean anything. You experience duality and judgment, as they are part of a system of beliefs, and they generate emotions, negative or positive, *for the experience* of them!

Abraham (Esther Hicks) reminds us that fear springs from a resistance within us that affects the natural flow of energy relating to our desires. A contradicting belief generates the resistance. In other words, all that fear means is that we have a belief that does not marry with our desire. So once again, dealing with the belief, by adjusting the thoughts it stirs up, will nullify the fear.

Your ego-self cannot reach a place that does not contain the contrast of negativity. Therefore, fear, the source of negativity, is always with you, just as Divine Love, the source of positivity, is always with you. More accurately, fear comes in when your ego-self is resisting, detaching itself from, suppressing, or belligerently ignoring Divine Love. Fear can only leave you when your ego-self leaves the physical dimension. Rose (Joanne Helfrich) adds this on eliminating your fears:

> And that is most of what suffering is: fear. When you lose your fears, you find less suffering and may end it. For when you fear, you only perfect your ways of suffering, and there's no reason for this. In spite of what your religions have spoken about suffering, suffering is not a sacred thing. Indeed, there is no need for suffering in any way except to end it. So do so.[46]

To eliminate fear, we must trust and accept our Self—dodgy beliefs and all. *Assimilating* this knowledge is a requirement for each of us to evolve our thinking—understanding is not enough. We will still have beliefs capable of generating fear, but we will know how to deal with them. We cannot ignore fear. We must determine to deal with it when it arises. If we try to ignore it, it *will* come back to haunt us.

As we practice dealing with fear, it will become a rare experience—perhaps, ideally, confined to an *impulse* concerned only with self-preservation.

Principles for conscious living

We know that Divine Love is expansive. It encourages us to be all we can be, empowers us, and removes limitation. Divine Love is not jealous, angry, or afraid; it does not judge or question. It is simply accepting of All That Is. Now that we have a good understanding of the nature of fear and how we generate it, let's look deeper into the specifics of Divine Love and how we might go about maintaining this natural state of being.

In the coming months and years, we will want to achieve a personal shift in consciousness, which essentially requires us to change our habits of thought. This in turn means dissipating the energy behind any beliefs that have us thinking negatively or fearfully about something we wish to encourage within us. For example, if we want to instill *forgiveness*, we need to dissipate any negative emotional energy associated with this act that causes fear. We need to manage *consciously* the energies that flow through our Selves, utilizing them in the promotion of new thoughts and beliefs that support our natural state of being—nestled within Divine Love.

The ten natural principles

Appendix I presents a concise description of a set of *natural principles*.[47] These principles are primarily a derivation of Seth's "laws of the inner universe" and Omni's (John L. Payne) *Four Principles of Creation*. They arise from the vital spiritual strengths that exemplify Divine Love and are translated into understandable human concepts.

The natural principles are not a set of laws or commandments from on high; they are a purified set of behavioral guidelines—chiefly *mental*—unadulterated by institutional dogma. Familiarity with them will initiate certain mental states, which in turn will open the gates for intuitive information to flow from your Essence self to your conscious-mind.

As you practice the natural principles, adhering to them as much as you can, you will become less fearful, more self-assured, and more trusting of your innate capabilities—thereby attracting to you the experiences you desire. Practice is the key for new behaviors or traits to become automatic. It's a good idea to take a minute at the start of your day to remind yourself of them.

When you can respond automatically to any situation in accordance with the natural principles *you will be in Divine Love*. In this state (okay, perhaps not achievable all the time), your elevated *vibrational signature* will have an exponential affect upon the collective vibrational tone of humanity.

Remember that a principle "tells of the nature of things… more of a state of being" (Omni), which infers that these principles do not *govern* you. They describe the *nature* of the universe and how things work. These principles are another human translation of how you can gain the most from knowing how your Self works and how the universe works—according to the metaphysical literature. If you can observe most of them much of the time, then you're primed for a life enriched by joy, abundance, and fulfillment.

It's common to find difficulty in practicing one or more of the natural principles. This is because many of us hold debilitating beliefs regarding our self-worth. Lack of self-worth can affect us in a variety of ways, not least by preventing us from assimilating the natural principles.

Don't worry, this gives me the opportunity to introduce an exercise involving an energy psychology technique known as EFT (Emotional Freedom Techniques). Appendix II presents a basic shortcut version of EFT that you will need to familiarize yourself with before practicing Exercise 2 below. Its design is to dissipate energy held by beliefs regarding lack of self-worth, thereby nullifying their effect. It is an exercise that will prove to be invaluable as you come to know your Self through this book.

Exercise 2: Tapping for Self-Worth

Go to Appendix V for directions on this 20- to 30-minute exercise. If you're not familiar with EFT, then go to Appendix II before practicing this important exercise.

Chapter 5

Intent—Your Personal Expression

From *Chapter 2* we know there is an all-pervading *reason* for the creation of anything in existence, whether that existence is in the physical dimension we know and love, or the nonphysical dimensions of the spiritual realm from which love originates. That reason is inexorably concerned with the exploration, learning, and growth of the Self through experience—the *intent* of Consciousness. Because Consciousness is the architect of intent, its individuations such as you and me are, consequently, on the very same mission.

Scrutiny of Appendix I, the ten natural principles, should make you reasonably conversant with the "rules" under which Divine Love powers the creation process. Moreover, now that you are *consciously* aware of these principles for getting the best out of the game of life, you are in an advantageous position to address any psychological obstacles—self-limiting beliefs—that prevent you from openly engaging any one principle.

With this information, you may be inclined to rush back into the game of life. But you would be prudent to first have at least a rudimentary idea of which areas of human expression you are best suited to. Your existence alone shows you are important to the game and have something to contribute—you would not be part of the humanity squad if this were not the case! Consciousness created you to play a role in a game that has no end, only a fascinating raison d'être—the evolution of human consciousness. However, how *you* best explore, learn, and grow within life is decided upon through a specific mix of expressions of human intent. These expressions include areas of human endeavor such as teaching, the arts, healing, communication, physical athleticism, and more—so what is it that you feel drawn to do? What is it that you love to do? What are you passionate about?

Many of us have little or no idea of our innate, intentionally set, skills and abilities. Often, even when we are aware of our talent for something, we harbor a self-limiting belief or two that has us spending most of our lives suppressing that talent—sitting on the bench in fear, rather than getting immersed in the game. This book is ultimately about helping you reveal to your conscious-mind your inherent talents so that when you get back into the game of life you can effortlessly display those talents and enjoy yourself!

Revealing your intentional leanings

According to several channeled sources, your personality conforms to a discrete and distinguishable blend of intentional drives for the purposes of self-expression in the physical world. Before you were born, your Essence self chose which nuance of human intent it would like you (its individuation) to explore. Its choice affects what aspects of life you feel drawn to. It steers you toward certain actions and psychological behaviors that your Essence self knows are important in the grander scheme of acquiring total Self-knowledge.

The nine families of human consciousness

Seth made an important contribution to our understanding of the different expressions of human intent. We understand "family" to mean a distinguishable primary bloodline produced by unique individual variations. By calling the different intentional leanings the "*families* of consciousness,"[48] Seth attempts to convey a sense of the idiosyncratic psychological variations within the family of humanity.

Seth only briefly described nine such families of intent in his legacy,[49] with an emphasis upon his own so-called Sumari family's intentional leanings, as he, Jane Roberts, and her husband, Robert Butts, all belonged to this particular psychic grouping.

In the main, other channeled sources agree on the psychical groupings.[50] The metaphysical literature suggests that as with the differing attributes of the human physical form (skin coloration in accordance with exposure to the sun, or the Inuit people's physical adaptation to the cold, for example), we have differing *psychical* attributes—psychological frameworks that display their own distinct characteristics. (This is not meant to suggest that certain psychical groupings favor specific physical peoples.) The families are similar to the classification of personality *types* used in psychology, although they are far more complex because of their interdependency.

For ease of understanding, you should be aware that there are nine loosely delineated ways in which human consciousness pursues intent. Essentially, they are differing developmental paths of activity peculiar to humankind, involved with the growth, learning, and evolution of each individual and humanity itself. Although your personality encapsulates *all* the intentional drives, it chooses to experience the physical dimension with certain drives to the fore.

Here are the nine families of consciousness first mentioned by Seth during sessions 734–737. The brief intentional function of each family is attributable to Robert Butts:

Gramada: To found social systems
Sumafi: To transmit "originality" through teaching
Tumold: To heal, regardless of individual occupations
Vold: To reform the status quo
Milumet: To mystically nourish mankind's psyche
Zuli: To serve as physical, athletic models
Borledim: To provide an earth stock for the species through parenthood
Ilda: To spread and exchange ideas
Sumari: To provide the cultural, spiritual, and artistic heritage for the species.[51]

At around the time of the above-mentioned sessions, Jane Roberts, after consideration, wrote this cautionary caveat:

> But the names and designations aren't meant to be taken *too* literally; these aren't to be interpreted as esoteric clubs or brotherhoods, but as natural psychic "conglomerations" to which we all belong.[52]

Belonging to and aligning with

Seth's omission of an in-depth exploration of the psychical groupings left the metaphysical door ajar for other channeled sources to offer their own understandings. Confirming elaborations are found in the Elias transcripts, the *Kris Chronicles* (Serge Grandbois), and the teachings of Rose (Joanne Helfrich).

One complexity, initially explored by Elias, is the notion of a family of *belonging* and a family of *alignment*. Elias states that our Essence self *belongs to* a particular family of intent (in relative perpetuity), while our lifetime's personality *aligns* itself with a family, either the same as our Essence or otherwise. Our Essence self chooses the alignment family to support our overall Self's growth and development.

With Seth's rudimentary guide to the families of consciousness and the subsequent broader elaborations, we are able to discern dominant interests, roles, and physical pursuits for each group. Further, with the help of several channeled teachings on this subject, it's possible to produce simplified and succinct generic names for the nine types of human intent, as many new to Seth are put off the subject by Seth's nomenclature.

Your current personality's family of *alignment* may become apparent if you compare the descriptions with your primary concerns and interests. In addition, gauge which of the actions described by a family resonates with what brings you the greatest pleasure.

Alternatively, which described actions would you like to do

most given the right circumstances, the time, and the resources? Does any passion of yours leap to mind, especially more than once, as you ruminate on the characteristics of the families?

Don't worry if more than one family seems to resonate. You can have more than one family in alignment; they are constantly merging with one another, and your personality will express each of them at some time depending on the situation. We automatically engage our healer intent when confronted with a loved one who is suffering in some way, for example. For the moment, just have some fun as you read through the descriptions.

Below is a minimal guide to the characteristics of each family of intent. You can find a fuller description of how these intentional activities transfer to personality traits in Appendix III:

Innovators/Formers—(Gramada)—The intentional energies here are vital, inventive, innovative, and creatively aggressive. It is an intent that inspires people toward forming social systems and organizations. Those aligned with this psychical grouping tend not to take the spotlight but allow others to take on and develop their originating ideas.

Teachers/Seers—(Sumafi)—This family has an intent to keep and convey knowledge in its purest form. The focus is upon accuracy and detail. An aim is to encourage originality through teaching and promote learning through experience.

Healers/Readers—(Tumold)—People who resonate with this family have an ability to read the distortions or "dis-ease" of energy flow within physical and nonphysical structures. A primary focus is upon the healing of physical, spiritual, and psychological structures within cultures and individuals.

Reformers/Hearers––(Vold)––Those with this intent are restless and passionate about reformation, with a focus upon examining, challenging, and changing the status quo. They are revolutionary and activate reforms in the collective belief systems reflected in world institutions.

Spiritualists/Rememberers––(Milumet)––Individuals aligned with this group are apt to explore the spiritual and mystical. They have a great connection with nature, keeping us aware of the natural rhythms of life. An intent that is involved with true spiritual connection, directing our energies inwardly.

Imagers––(Zuli)––In this group is a focus upon the aesthetics of design and appearance of physical forms. The intent is to bring the fullest expression of physical forms, particularly the human body, into manifestation. Included here are inspired design capabilities.

Nurturers/Bearers––(Borledim)––Those related to this group possess the qualities of patience, affection, and understanding. The intent includes a focus upon the nurturing of individuals, particularly children, in relation to a balanced, healthy upbringing.

Exchangers/Tellers––(Ilda)––Here, the intent is to spread ideas and information amongst all cultures. Those aligned enjoy traveling to trade religious, social and political concepts. They have an ability to see and form connections, "join the dots," as Rose might say.

Artists/Speakers––(Sumari)––Nonconformist *doers* are the ones who feel an affinity with this intent. They have attention to detail, are artistically inclined, and are apt to speak out for change and the expression of creativity through the arts. They have a playful sense of humor, are prone to be impatient and enjoy the spotlight.

Like Jane Roberts' caveat quoted earlier, the channeled guides supporting these descriptions of the nuances of human intent are quick to point out that the separation is solely to do with ease of understanding. Rose[53] elaborates on Jane Roberts' caution, "Do not make the mistake of thinking of these types as groups or tribes that exclude others. This will not be a healthy expression of your Divine Source." In other words, don't imagine that any one family of characteristics, *your* alignment family, is superior to or more desirable than another.

The crucial point to understand here is that your personality *usually* prefers to adhere to the characteristics displayed by one of the families, when environmental circumstances are in harmony and you have complete freedom to choose. Your family of alignment is your personality's *primary* expression of intent. *It is a fundamental statement of character that your Essence self has chosen for your personality to explore.*

With this understood, you can then factor in the complexity of your *Essence self's* intentional leanings. Remember that your Essence self *belongs* to its own family of intent. Because your Essence self continuously influences your personality, its family of belonging plays a crucial part in describing more precisely your overall intentional predispositions. As it does so, it *brings subtlety and definition* to your alignment family's characteristics.

Discovering your own combination of both intentional directors can have you realize the general purpose of your current life.

One of the functions of your inner self (the emissary to your Essence self) is to ensure that your ego-self does not stray too far off its purposeful intentional path. Here is an example of how this complexity of intent translates to the real world:

If your personality's family of *alignment* is Artists/Speakers (Sumari—artistically inclined), then you may gravitate toward doing something artistic as a main occupation—the *overtly expressed* intent. Let's say you become a painter. Now, if your Essence's family of *belonging* is Teachers/Seers (Sumafi—teaching, accuracy of information transfer), then this subtly expressed underlying intent may draw you to teach art, with a probable penchant for fine art (attention to detail).

This is but one extrapolation drawn from numerous possible activities that remain in accordance with these families of alignment and belonging. This combination can just as easily produce a fulfilling path for someone involved with educational reform—promoting change (Artists' intent) in teaching methods (Teachers' intent). So, your intentional leanings do not necessarily restrict the fields of activity you can successfully take part in.

You can mine life fulfillment from virtually any field of endeavor provided you focus upon those activities within that field that allow you to express your intentional leanings.

Your purpose in life has nothing to do with fate

Imagining that fate governs your actions is a misinterpretation of your subconscious knowledge regarding your life's intentional leanings. In the future, should life-changing events appear to have no explanation, say to yourself, "My purpose took hold," rather than, "It must have been fate." Here is a succinct definition of what is meant by your life's purpose:

Your purpose is your own unique goal that you plan to attain in this lifetime while utilizing the directional impetus supplied by your personal families of intent.

The *goal* is a Self-developmental one set by your Essence self in deference to *its* overall evolution in Consciousness. Your inner self[54] constantly seeks to remind you of this spiritual directive, particularly when you are way off track.

I reiterate that, for most of us, it is extremely unlikely that there is but one occupation that we *must* follow to fulfil our purpose in life. However, armed with a *conscious* knowledge of our own intentional drives, we become far more able to find fulfilment in whatever occupation we choose to become involved with. Moreover, with these psychological footings, we become more confident in approaching the developmental elements within our purpose—namely, the challenges we aim to explore and resolve.

You can think of the families of consciousness as a palette of nine main colors that you use to paint your reality. As with Picasso and his blue period,[55] you restrict your use of color to the hues and tones of one of the families, apply definition with the hues and tones of another, and occasionally make use of the remainder. Like Picasso, you explore and experiment with your chosen primary color for a time—in the case of *primary* intent (family of alignment), for a lifetime.

Choosing your own expressions of intent

Seth and Elias make the key point that when it comes to choosing your intentional leanings, your *individuality* comes first.

What they mean is that as Consciousness begins to coalesce into your Essence self with its unique vibrational signature, the *psychic* structures that contribute to your physical expression are also in configuration, which includes your intentional drives. Your *primary* intent becomes your innate intent, which fuels the balancing and learning activities of your Essence self working within its family of belonging. Remember that your Essence self incorporates and manages many physical expressions—individuated portions of *itself* that your ego-self regards as other lifetimes.

Elias states that your Essence is not born into a particular family of intent, nor does it so much choose it—it "magnates" [sic] to one, "the family being the magnet. You within your individual intents are the metals being drawn to the families."[56] Or as Seth puts it, "Your individuality places you in a particular family or species of consciousness."[57]

The complexities behind this process include balancing processes of the collective psyche and intent of human consciousness—a subject beyond the scope of my introductory aim here.

When it comes to your current personality's family of alignment, again, extraordinarily complex issues are involved, but, yes, you—or more accurately, your Essence self—get to choose this one. Well... sort of! The decision about your current personality's psychic structure and nuances of intent are inexorably linked to the balancing of your overall Self's identity and individuality. Your Essence *usually* chooses one family for alignment, but it may have you align with more than one—again, a complexity that we shall leave for another time. Your Essence carries out this alignment process before you are physically born. Elias states:

> Each individual manifest [current personality] incorporates an intent, a reason that they have manifest into this physical reality, an intent that they had focused upon before they chose to manifest within this physical reality.[58]

So the choosing of families of intent is subtle in its action. If intent is all about growth and evolution through creation and experience, then choices need to be made on how this is achieved. As we are imbued with intent, we consequently always have choice, even when it comes to choosing our families of intent. During our lives, it is possible to change our allegiances to the families, although according to Elias such changes are extremely rare.

When asked about the importance of knowing our families of affiliation, Elias stated that its value is in the *understanding of our Selves, our personal intent, and the subsequent realities we create for ourselves*. A stern warning added to this statement was that we should not overplay the importance of this knowledge. We collectively entertain belief systems at present that stimulate a need in some of us to exaggerate important concepts for self-centered (egotistical) reasons, or to foolishly imagine that an ultimate blueprint exists to explain all of creation. Elias states: "The importance should not be exaggerated to be all-consuming; for this creates more belief systems, and you shall create your cults around your belief systems of your families!"[59]

Colorful characters

Elias informs us that each family can, tentatively, be assigned a color because each has a certain tone and resonance that we can associate with the different wavelengths of light perceived as colors. (You may perceive a color or colors when you practice Exercise 1, *Touching Your Tone*. If so, this could be an echo of your unique intentional tone.)

We can extend this analogy between color and intent somewhat further. We know that within the seven distinct hues in the color spectrum are millions of different shades. Similarly, within the nine distinguishing hues of the families of intent there are myriad tones, or subdivisions of the originating family.

Even though certain colors associate with the families of intent, thus hinting at possible familial subdivisions, we should not get carried away with a Victorian love for categorization. Whereas partitioning structures of matter can aid our understanding of physicality, it is not a reliable method for fathoming the features of our consciousness. In the subjective world of shifting vibrational boundaries, we need to dissolve our desire for division.

The defining lines between the different hues of our personalities are very thin. Think of the subtlety in difference between identical twins within a conventional family. Surface, physical features may well be virtually the same, and preferences within lifestyle choices may be remarkably similar too, but distinctions certainly remain within their personalities.

According to the channeled literature, our primordial psychic groupings are not absolute truths,[60] as they either do not exist or have different characteristics in other dimensions. They are, however, the guiding forces behind all choices and decisions we make in creating our individual and collective realities.

Our choices, then, do have some limitations, although from our simplified physical perspective there would appear to be none. Limitations are confined only by the way intent is explored through the collective psyche of humanity. Human consciousness is entering a phase of dramatic expansion and further sophistication. Another level of complexity within self-awareness awaits us. *Total* Self-awareness affords us the opportunity to take our individuation to new heights in terms of choosing our experiences.

A contemporary coincidence

Many channeled sources refer to coincidence or synchronicity. Contrary to the scientific worldview's assessment of the phenomenon as inconsequential—a happening due to nothing more than chance—metaphysical teachers insist greater meaning is behind such an occurrence.

While searching a plethora of personality-profiling systems

to find a contemporary approach to somewhat validate the metaphysical families of characteristics and intentional roles, I came across the *Enneagram* system. I took a closer look because of the *coincidence* of its *nine* basic types. Further study confirmed parallels in thinking that indicate an intuitive, deeper understanding of the concept of human intent. One example is the use of differing colors in the explanatory text, reflecting the analogy of the hues and tones of color referenced earlier.

The mists of time cloud the origins of Enneagram theory. It's believed to have been part of a program of spiritual enlightenment passed down through several religious doctrines, primarily Sufi mysticism from Islam. George Ivanovitch Gurdjieff (1866–1949), a spiritual teacher around the time of Carl G. Jung (1875–1961), devised a self-development system originally called the *Fourth Way* and later *The Work*, which revived interest in Enneagram theory. Present-day proponents of the enneagram system have taken up Jung's ideas on the Self and the psyche to explain the idiosyncrasies of its personality-profiling system.

Like a family of intent, an *enneatype* doesn't so much define *who* you are (your personality) as it does *what you are drawn to do*. Like your family of *alignment*, your enneatype is a lifelong psychological patterning. The system even encompasses a secondary influencing feature of the personality, called a "wing," which we can equate with the subtle persuasions of your Essence's family of *belonging*.

It may be that Gurdjieff and his forebears when formulating the Enneagram system were "channeling" into a vein of knowledge deep within their subconscious minds. The relative popularity of the system over the last century suggests that Seth's families-of-consciousness metaphor to explain human intent is a more recent interpretation of the knowledge.

Channeled guides categorically state that there is no such thing as a true coincidence. A coincidence, they say, emanates from your Essence self as a means by which your inner self can get your ego-self's attention. There is always a meaning associated with coincidence, although for your conscious-mind to fathom exactly what the meaning is can prove a formidable task. For me, the coincidence of coming across the Enneagram system, with its nine basic types, suggests a greater meaning of the value of the system.

Do the families and enneatype descriptions match up?

Some characteristics do in fact transfer across the systems admirably, but by no means do the groupings completely match. However, if we bear in mind the myriad combinations involved in the expression of intent, the subtlety of enunciation, the overlapping nature of their hues, and the varying of the family brought to the fore in respect to the circumstances, it is hardly surprising to find such a looseness of fit.

Again, our desire to delineate and categorize physical things does not decode too well when dealing with the nonphysical psyche. Enneagram theory nonetheless remains a valiant attempt to fathom the complexity of intent when expressed through the human psyche.[61]

Exercise 3: Finding Your Alignment. The aim of the exercise is to make you consciously aware of your family of alignment. When you've repeated this exercise a few times, you should have a reasonable idea of which roles you are naturally inclined to adopt and/or what form of activity consistently brings you enjoyment and fulfillment. The notes and doodles you make will offer clues about your intentional leanings. You will need to have your work journal and pen handy for making notes and sketches. (Go to Appendix VI.)

Chapter 6

Your Spiritual Self

When examining a complex concept such as the Self, the tendency is to break it down into its constituent parts. Unfortunately, such a reductionist approach loses sight of the intrinsic *wholeness* of the concept under examination. We ostracize Consciousness, which is the invisible and essentially indivisible component that permeates every concept, construct, or creation. We often forget that Consciousness is the crucial cohesive force that forms any number of parts into a more meaningful *gestalt*.[62] Seth tells us that although there may *appear* to be various parts or layers to the Self no definitive boundaries exist between them. Furthermore, he reminds us, because Consciousness is all pervasive, there are in fact no definitive boundaries "between what is self and not self."[63] This statement becomes easier to comprehend when we accept that the reality before us is of our own creation—a reflection of our current overall perception of our Self.

We shall now examine the nonphysical aspects to our Selves by using... reductionism! Why? Simply because this methodology is the one our ego-selves are most used to and therefore find most understandable.

Areas within Consciousness

Considering that *your consciousness* is an expression of the oneness of Consciousness, we must ponder whether individual consciousness exists outside of the physical realm. Does your overall *Self* span both physical and nonphysical dimensions of existence? If it does, what part of the Self exists in the nonphysical dimension, and do we have any idea what's going on there?

To help answer these questions, we need to consider the concept of *areas within Consciousness*. (Seth uses the term

Frameworks and other channeled sources use terms such as *regional areas* and *planes of existence* to describe places of existence outside the physical dimension.)

Be aware that there are no divisions, no *places* within a *space* as we are used to, no levels, and no hierarchy, just as no divisions exist within the Self. Rather, you have areas within Consciousness *where the attention of your consciousness (awareness)* may focus. For example, your consciousness uses your ego-self (while you are awake) to focus its attention on the physical world. When you're asleep, your consciousness has opportunity to focus its attention on other planes of existence that your ego-self would have difficulty interpreting.

For ease of understanding, here are the four areas within Consciousness we are most directly concerned with. The boundaries between them blur, overlap, and are highly flexible. Importantly, we need to accept and allow for the reality of such areas if we are ever to understand the complexity of our Selves:

The Objective Area. An area where Consciousness expresses itself in a manner that conforms to "inner universal laws" (*natural principles*). We call this area the *physical dimension* and summarize its description as the space-time continuum. Seth refers to physicality as *Framework 1*.

The laws of physics are our interpretations of how the natural principles affect this area of expression. We perceive this dimension through our five physical senses (and any enhancing instrumentation). We assume *cause and effect* to be a physical law within this area because we perceive *time* as a linear construct. Importantly, our thoughts, beliefs, dreams, and emotions all influence our perception of the Objective Area.

If we reflect on exactly *how* nonphysical energies come together to manifest in the physical realm, then *quantum fields*, postulated under quantum theory, may be as close as physics has come to mapping an area of interface between the Objective and the Subjective Areas within Consciousness.

The Subjective Area. An area within Consciousness closest to and aligned with the Objective Area. Conventionally referred to as the *spiritual realm* or *nonphysical dimension*, metaphysical guides also call it the *electric universe* or *electric field*[64] (suggesting that the only tangible form within it is of an electromagnetic nature). It is a *subtle field* within Consciousness containing many layers and properties, not the least of which are properties of an alternative electromagnetic nature. Seth refers to this area as *Framework 2*.

Our concept of time does not operate in this area, yet potential physically perceived *things*, destined to manifest in the Objective Area, "begin" their construction here. This area bridges between all areas within Consciousness and is the dimension from which *Source Energy*[65] originates.

You can perceive the nuances of your own existence (other aspects to your Self) in this area through *altered states of consciousness*[66] such as dreams, meditation, prayer, and other manipulations of your *inner senses*.[67]

The Subconscious Area. (Explored in *Chapter 9*.) An area within Consciousness concerned with projecting the vitality of Consciousness into the physical plane. You can access this area through investigative psychological techniques such as hypnosis, meditation, visualization, and various other mental exercises presented in metaphysical literature and in this book. The portal to this subconscious domain is within your *Mind*.[68]

The Transitional Area. (Seth's *Framework* 3.) An area within Consciousness where your Self creates certain psychological structures, so your physical self can operate within the Objective Area. You can imagine this area to be within your "portion" of the collective Subconscious Area.

After physical death, following a brief awakening in the Subjective Area, your ego-self and *personality*[69] come to the Transitional Area to reorientate to existence outside of the Objective Area.

Compartmentalizing Consciousness

Seth uses a metaphor to help us understand how Consciousness forms our nonphysical Self: He breaks Consciousness down into units, which he calls *Consciousness Units* (CUs), and their progeny, *Electromagnetic Energy Units* (EEs).

Seth describes CUs as "the smallest psychological unit of individual consciousness which finds physical fulfillment in the formation of matter."[70] CUs are not *particles*, as they are not physical, and they possess and retain their own identity despite their propensity to combine with other CUs. *Combinations of CUs* begin to "slow down" their energy frequency as they become EEs. EEs then remain within the Subjective Area until their energy frequency is further slowed to within physical electromagnetic frequencies.[71]

Our propensity to divide, map, and categorize our reality, along with determining cause and effect, is an inevitable consequence of our ego-self's condensed perspective within the time-based confines of the Objective Area within Consciousness. In the Subjective Area, the nonphysical aspects of our Selves use a totally different organizational system, based on *associations*. The connections between ideas, thoughts, images, feelings, and emotions take precedence in the system over logic and rationale. The Subjective realm is all about the interconnectivity of Consciousness and the *durability*[72] of connections in an environment free of linear time constraints and thus of cause and effect.

In the Subjective Area your nonphysical Self utilizes mental associations to organize an infinite number of *probable* events, based on their electrical potential, into a schedule for physical manifestation. Importantly, such subjective organization is meant to *complement* the objective machinations of the intellect.

Identifying your identity

Let's take a moment to briefly visit the Subjective Area within Consciousness. Close your eyes intermittently as you continue to read and try to imagine a place of "no-thing-ness."

Imagine you are floating in a deep blue sea of clear, transparent space. Nothing is above, below, or around you other than the deep, deep, inky blueness. As your awareness drifts casually about this ethereal location, you begin to sense a rush of energy around you. You can feel an invisible breeze. You can even sense that this energy in motion is *aware of itself*, as you become conscious that *your awareness* is part of this vast sea of e-motional *vibrational tones*.

This movement of energy is the very *breath of Consciousness—electromagnetic energy units*, or EEs. They rush about with a crackling intensity and a determination to slow down their vibrational frequency in readiness for physical manifestation.

Within the Subjective Area, wavelets of energy formed by CUs begin to combine resources to produce the beginnings of your Self. This is not to do with EEs yet. The newly forming *identity* is a cooperative gestalt meant to broaden the experience of individual CUs, and it is safe in the knowledge that each unit within the complex maintains its own identity and individuality.

To conceptualize this *unit identity* maintained within a *gestalt identity*, a useful analogy would be the cellular structure of a living organism. Cellular biologists, in particular those involved in the burgeoning field of *epigenetics* (the science that studies "the molecular mechanisms by which environment controls gene activity"[73]), teach us that cells maintain their own identity and purpose within the body.

The cell membrane, far from being the point where the cell separates from the whole, is actually the surface of transformation, an electrochemical interface that keeps the cell and the whole body informed of the *psychological*, as well as physical, environment. Cells are aware of their environment and are conscious of their importance to the living whole. Each individual cell is conscious of the collective cooperation required to maintain the organism.[74]

In a similar fashion, Consciousness Units combine by instinct, with a collective ambition, to form the identity of your *Essence*.

The identity of each CU within the whole of your Essence is not lost in this process. They agree to come together to form a more complex expression of Consciousness, which builds its own overseeing identity (along with its own awareness of self), for the purposes of cohesion and durability. With your Essence formed, your physical birth can be formulated in accordance with extraordinarily complex psychological considerations, not the least of which is the slowing of CUs and EEs to vibrational frequencies conducive to physical manifestation. Such frequencies make their presence felt in the *quantum field* (a "place" postulated by Quantum Field Theory), where the Subjective and Objective Areas within Consciousness come together.

Let's play God for a moment

To further your understanding of how and why CUs come together to form your Essence self, let's momentarily adopt the position of Consciousness (or God, if you can't yet relinquish the term). Imagine *your* mind is the mind of Consciousness/God. As it is difficult to imagine being everywhere at the same time, let me suggest you place your Self on a bench in a vast *causal field* of ripened grain nodding gently in the soft summer breeze.

As Consciousness, you are aware that you are a limitless source of energy. You are in a constant state of becoming—of self-actualizing—and you exploit this growth and development of your Self through endless acts of creation. While in this exalted position on your comfy bench, consider now the individuated portion of your Self that you are about to create (*that would be you, the reader!*) with your marvelous little individuated units (CUs). You have decided upon a *human expression* of your Self. As such, you want it to be able to explore various dimensions of experience, with a focus upon the Objective Area you created earlier that everyone's talking about.

To do this, you first construct the nonphysical "tissue capsule"[75] required to maintain the integrity of your creation's existence—otherwise known as the *Essence body* (explained below). As you form the Essence body, you incorporate psychical characteristics that will reflect the nuances of intent you wish for it to explore. From this foundation, you can begin to create the necessary conditions for this part of you to enter your Objective Area.

One psychical condition you've concocted for this imminent person-to-be is the concept of *time*. Time is a very clever twist to your own principle of learning through experience. Essentially, in order to contrast the simultaneous conditions in the causal field that you are familiar with, you've integrated a subtle dimension—albeit a psychical one—to the *perception* of physical reality by your human expression. In creating the perceived physical dimension of the human being, intentional actions are drawn out in the materialization process—all action, any experience, any progression of an idea—is more readily distinguishable, *more open to examination*, and *more observable* by the incorporation of the elasticizing property of time.

You, God, are slowing your vibrational frequency—Source Energy—down to an extent whereby an experience, and the learning it contains, is more open to thorough examination through the medium of objective realization.

Return now to your own mind. I know, it was nice being God for a while, but don't let your ego-self get too carried away.

Towards the physical

Your physical birth originates in the Subjective Area and emanates from a cooperative mass of CUs that comprise the identity of your Essence self. We can condense the complex body of CUs that make up all the nonphysical aspects to your Self into four core elements:

Your Identity. The psychic gestalt with its own identity, created by the coalescing of CUs, is independent of the physical domain and is, from your ego-self's time-based viewpoint, immortal.

Your identity, which you occasionally sense as being the "I" of who you are, is a constantly adjusting artifact within your *subconscious*, which considers your development and experiences within your lifetime. Attachments to other identities or Essences do not occur without your identity's consent.

Your nonphysical, originating identity is inviolate—meaning that nothing can extinguish it once it has formed.

The identity your ego-self uses to describe who you are is usually a narrowly confined list of physical attributes and achievements relating to your physical experiences, with little inclusion of any psychological or spiritual understandings.

Your *inner self* takes care of your identity's cohesion via the *inner senses*, which entails maintaining the integrity of *your* identity along with the identities of the cells, molecules, atoms, EEs and CUs that all cooperate to make up the entirety of your individuality.

Your identity comprises a psychic bank of intentional plans, abilities, and purposes that your physical ego-self can draw upon at any time.

Your Essence self. The total configuration of energy relating to your Self in the Subjective Area within Consciousness. More commonly termed "soul," metaphysical literature suggests various other names for your nonphysical self: *Source* (Abraham), *Source Energy, Entity* (used by Seth), *Oversoul,* and *Higher Self* (Omni). Your Essence maintains a unique vibrational signature at its core—your identifying *tone.*

Your inner self. The channeled literature refers to this aspect of your nonphysical self as *source self, inner ego, inner being,* or even *entity* or *essence.* I keep to the term *inner self* as much as possible to provide consistency.

Your inner self employs the *inner senses* to translate essential data on the integrity and condition of your overall Self for your physical self (ego-self, *conscious-mind,*[76] and personality) to assimilate. Its main concerns are to do with maintaining the foundations and overall stability of your Self.

You can regard your inner self as the emissary of your Essence self, a soul from your Oversoul, an agent of Essence whose mission is to maintain communication with your physical self on matters pertaining to your Essence and the Subjective Area within Consciousness.

Your inner self maintains a focus upon how your physical self expresses itself in the physical world and uses a number of subtle devices to help steer you along your path of intent, such as emotional messages, intuitional feelings, dreams, inspiration, and synchronous or coincidental events.

Your subconscious. *Your* subconscious is a personal portion of *the* Subconscious Area within Consciousness. It is your mental gateway to the myriad realities of that area.

Your subconscious encompasses the *psychic gestalt* of your *Mind,* which is your inviolate portion of the indefinable energy formation called the psyche.[77] It is a place of sorts where your inner self is able to communicate and interact with your physical self.

Your subconscious utilizes both your inner senses and your outer physical senses. Within your subconscious area, various zones handle the complexities involved in maintaining and supporting your physical self.

Your subconscious maintains a vast library of knowledge and information pertaining to the entirety of your Self—not the least of which is your originating identity or Essence self. It also provides an access to far deeper wells of knowledge relating to our species, and even to the workings of Consciousness itself.

Figure 1 presents a graphical representation of these nonphysical aspects to your Self. The perforated lines symbolize the nonexistence of any true, firm boundaries. The spheres with a "P" at the center of the structure represent the individuated personalities of other lifetimes. The personality and its continuance within Essence is a subject covered in *Chapter 8*.

Exercise 4: Accepting Your Inner Self. (See Appendix VII.) This simple EFT exercise helps to familiarize your ego-self with your inner self and begin a trust and appreciation of your inner self's capabilities. You will need to have the basic EFT guide to hand for reference (see Appendix II).

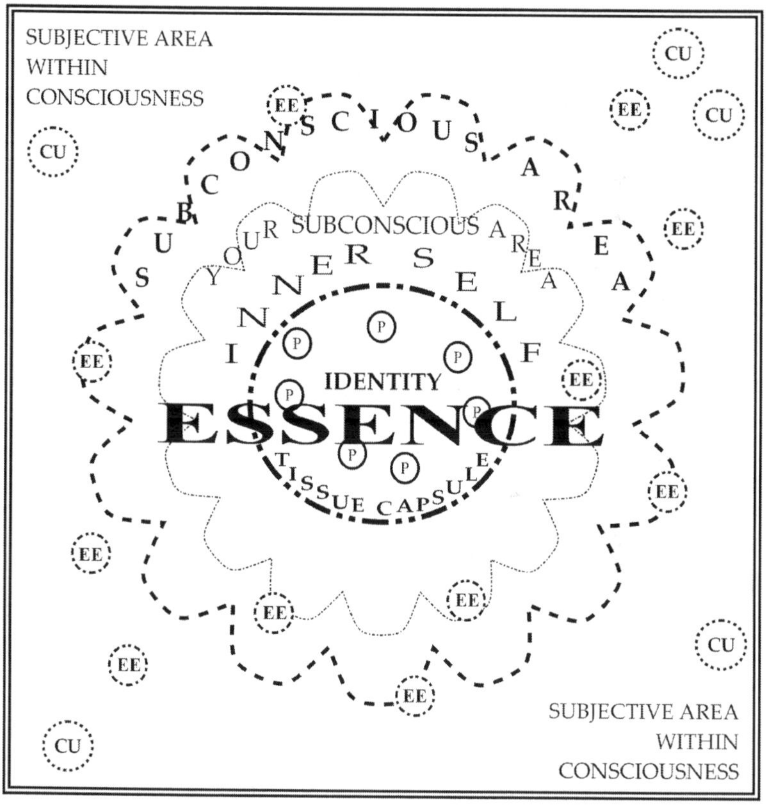

Figure 1. The fundamental elements of your spiritual self

Part II

Being Truly Sensible

Chapter 7

Your Physical Self

Now that you are familiar with a metaphysical depiction of your *spiritual* self, let's look at the basic structure of the physical you, or more precisely, your core psychological elements for functioning in the physical dimension.

Just as Consciousness individuates itself to get to know itself better, your Essence self, as a child of Consciousness, does the same. Your *physical* self is a further iteration of Consciousness's never-ending quest for Self-knowledge.[78] Your Essence self, for reasons of its own expansion and educational needs, chooses a broad yet definitive intentional path of learning for your physical self to explore.

Let's get physical

Most adults are familiar with the purely physical aspects of producing a physical body. Two contrasting sets of genitalia come together in a generally messy encounter, sperm swims to egg, egg *accepts*[79] the sperm, and, following a scientifically acknowledged miraculous gestation period, a baby is born.

According to Seth, there is no specific point in linear time when the individuated portion of your Essence (*soul* if you like) enters the physical form. The birth of your physical body into the Objective Area within Consciousness is an obvious observable event; however, the birth of the psychological structures that complement your physical form is a gradual process that from our time-blinkered perspective "begins" before even our parents are born.

A common understanding is that a baby is born with a *tabula rasa*—a "blank slate" for a mind. The assumption stems from 17th-century English philosopher John Locke, who maintained that a baby has no innate mental faculties and only learns through experiences via the five physical senses. Sigmund Freud formulated his psychoanalytic theories on this assumption, and the behavioral psychologist B.F. Skinner cemented the blank-slate idea into the modern worldview in the 1960s. It remains there, despite later research about how people acquire language, by Noam Chomsky for example, that has demonstrably refuted the premise.

As Steven Pinker points out in his book *The Blank Slate*,[80] blank slates don't *do* anything, yet paradoxically young minds evidently *do* a lot of learning. The importance of learning to the human experience is clear, and one can witness the phenomenal rate of learning in the very young. Therefore, certain faculties *must* logically be present in the new mind for learning to occur.

To grasp your newborn psychological state as presented by our metaphysical guides, you need to realize your life begins *before* physical birth. It begins within the Subjective Area within Consciousness, where linear time does not feature in the creative process of birthing a new personality. As your Essence starts to individuate, it not only organizes a path of intent for the new personality to align with, but it also deliberates upon which physical environment is best suited to its educational aims.

Your Essence has many factors to consider regarding your physical birth, including your parents (yes, you pick them as much as they pick you!) and other familial issues, cultural and geographical relevancies, the linear time period, and various other psychological elements that will set the stage for your lifetime's learning experience.

Far from being a blank slate, your newborn self is primed psychologically with self-expanding information from its spiritual origins. To use a little slang, you have form before you are formed!

In addition, you are indeed born with a predisposition for language. The physical apparatus for speech reflects a subjective template within the psyche that prepares you not just for speech but also for all the psychological complexities language embodies.[81]

According to Seth, as one's life is being prepared for birth, many such patterns within the psyche come into consideration—even one that readies our adult form in later life, albeit within highly variable parameters.[82] Such ideas become easier to comprehend if we spend a little linear time contemplating what simultaneous time might be like in the *spacious present* of the Subjective Area within Consciousness.

Your inner self is your spiritual self's vanguard, pioneering the new enterprise of the physical you. It helps set the stage for your personality's adventures. A new life, driven by the intent of your Essence, is set into physical motion.

Your physical self then begins with three basic psychological elements at the forefront of a vast and largely unexplored complex named the *psyche*. These prominent portions of the psyche form the basis of your *Mind*:

- ***Ego-self***
- ***Personality***
- ***Conscious-mind***

It is important to remember, as Seth states, that "the personality and the ego are not the same."[83] I refer to this tripartite assembly as the *physical self*. We also need to remember that the physical self is a gestalt of extraordinarily complex psychological components. This trio is the barest minimum set of components for understanding your physical self's psychology.

Your ego-self

Perhaps unfortunately for some philosophers, we do need an ego-self. It forms from conception onward in conjunction with your physical body. From the beginning of your physical existence, your Essence self entrusts your inner self with laying the egg of your ego. As you physically grow and psychologically mature, your ego-self breaks free of its protective shell to take up the responsibility of directing your actions within physicality. The onset of puberty signifies not only physiological changes but also the start of a psychological development that involves the ego-self establishing its own personal identity and independence.

You can think of your ego-self as a necessary by-product of the individuation of your Essence self—*only required for the period of a physical lifetime.* Your inner self breathes life into your ego, but when your ego-self takes up the reins it is free to make its own choices, despite the ever-present umbilical cord of communication between it and your inner self (*a cord that has become severely constricted in most of us*).

A computer analogy might help. If we liken our physical body to that of a computer, with its various bits of hardware inside, our ego-self is the operating system (Microsoft's Windows, for example), which enables our computer body to interact with its environment. Your ego-self allows you to *operate* within the *system* of physicality. As with most new computers these days, other software comes preloaded—a word processor for example—comparable to our preloaded capacity for language.

In the main, your ego-self develops through a combination of hereditary and environmental factors—that is, through *nature* (genetic inheritance along with innate mental predispositions), as well as *nurture* (physical experiences that are *intent*-ionally managed at a subconscious level by your inner self).

Please don't imagine that your ego-self has no free will or that your life is predetermined. Free will exists for your ego-self when selecting an action related to your path of learning, and your ego-self is even free not to stay on the path at all. *(The latter option would be the sign of a strangled, if not severed, cord.)*

The primary reason for Consciousness to introduce the ego-self into its human evolutionary experiment was to allow the

conscious choice to bring one of myriad *probable* realities into physical manifestation. The ego-self has been given license to create its own reality—which is an enhancement in expression over acting out of pure animal instinct.

Bearing this risky evolutionary venture in mind (risky as suggested by our current collective reality), let's examine more closely what the ego-self's function is.

It's all about perception

Your ego-self is a psychological structure for ***interpreting*** what you ***perceive*** in the physical field.

Your *perception*, however, is far more than simply physical-sense data. It incorporates the outer-sense information along with information available from the Subjective area within Consciousness, which includes how you view and interact with your Self, the physical world, and others who share the physical experience—your overall worldview. Your perception includes and employs the sum total of all the energies and functions that constitute your Self. These are the subjectively and objectively oriented structures of your consciousness, along with the creational keys of your *dreams, thoughts, beliefs, feelings, emotions,* and *impulses* your Mind entertains.

So, when your ego-self interprets what you perceive, it filters the abundance of information through the *intellect*, a facet of the conscious-mind that discriminates between information it regards as important to the ego-self and that which is unimportant. Your ego-self's beliefs *about* what it perceives compromise the intellect's discrimination.

Because your collection of beliefs (stored in your subconscious area) heavily influences your perception, what the intellect sees as important is reliant on the level of emotional charge the information carries. Some sets of beliefs are more powerful than others because of a greater degree of accumulated emotional energy.

So, your beliefs and the emotional energy accrued to them have a crucial governing role in your ego-self's decision-making.

The ego-self's beliefs with their related emotional charge, together with what the intellect *interprets* to be real, are of course personalized. But everyone creates his or her reality and perception of reality through these elements. Ironically, using these filters to make sense of reality and establish independence from Essence blinds the ego-self to the broader and more flexible understanding of the inner self. That's why young children, who haven't yet begun to develop their ego-self, often seem more authentic than adults.

Essentially, our ego-self's *job* is to use its perception of the physical field to decide what actions to take. However, it is not often consciously aware that its perception is the vital instrument through which we manifest a reality.

Chapter 8

How You Get a Personality!

Your personality

According to Seth, your ego-self's *purpose* ***"is the manipulation of the personality within the physical universe."***[84]

Seth explains that the "manipulation" involves the ego-self "impressing" its interpretations of the physical environment upon your highly malleable personality. As previously mentioned, the ego-self uses the intellect to determine which physical information is most important (that is, most *impressive*) for your personality to recognize and incorporate within its form. The intellect is meant to be as objective as possible in this determination but is often thwarted by the prejudicing influences of rigidly held beliefs. In other words, your ego-self's manipulative hands are restrained by the gloves of its beliefs.

Moreover, the ego-self is apt to introduce narcissism to the process, in that it imagines the personality to be a *rival* identity to its own. The ego-self seldom recognizes that it and the personality are part of a larger psychological construct (*physical self*), which in turn nests within the broader identity of your Essence. Your personality is inherently fluctuating, which the ego-self views as unstable and a threat. Consequently, your ego-self attempts to shape your personality into a more permanent and stable portion of itself. It arbitrarily makes a unit of itself, a unit we call the "I" of who I am, a separate identity than is in actuality but a collection of beliefs charged with the fear of change. Despite your ego-self's paranoid attentions, your personality's identity remains securely encapsulated within Essence.

It is because of the ego-self's delusions of Self-grandeur combined with a nagging awareness that it began life as a *blank slate* that we even entertain the notion of a blank slate to describe our newborn selves. When we consider that our ego-self, the director of our life's operations, is at best confused and more likely unaware of its *own* purpose for being in physicality, it is not surprising that few of us have a clue as to our life's *overall* purpose.

As history has shown, the remedy for the ego-self's plight, particularly if it has progressed into pathological proportions, is not to reinforce its self-imposed sense of separation by scolding it for the errors of its ways. Instead, we need to awaken the ego-self to *its* actual purpose and integrate it back into the *overall* purposeful drive of the Essence self.

The ego-self is born with a fabulous potential for manipulating not only the personality but also the reality it perceives. Its intellect is highly adept at sifting vital information from what has been created in the physical plane and relaying the juicy bits back to the nonphysical, inner aspects to your Self. When the ego-self's beliefs allow, the intellect can be relatively objective when selecting physical information. Further, it can attune itself to nonphysical information relayed to it by your inner self. The ego-self is thus a valuable tool for growth.

Establishing mutual regard and respect between your ego-self and your personality is a first step on the road to an integrated, more evolved Self. This is how the contemporary philosopher and spiritual teacher Andrew Cohen describes the ego-self:

Your Best Friend and Your Worst Enemy

The ego, or individuated self-sense, is both your best friend and your worst enemy. It is your best friend because, in the most positive sense, it represents your capacity to individuate—to see yourself as a unique, autonomous entity and to bear witness to your own experience with some measure of objectivity. Individuation is what makes it possible for you to be a conscious agent of evolution, a vessel for Spirit in action. The more profound our individuation, the more powerfully Spirit can shine through us. However, ego is also our worst enemy. And this is because, for too many of us, over-identification with our separate individuality obscures the deeper and higher spiritual dimensions of our being. It is very important to understand this paradoxical nature of ego if you, as an individual, want to take responsibility for creating the future, as yourself.[85]

How do I get a personality? *(Don't read that out loud!)*
Your personality is as impossible to define as your psyche because neither is ever static. That is because they primarily exist within the constantly shifting, sometimes physical, and mostly nonphysical dimension of ***action***, which, in simplest terms, is an aspect of the Subjective Area within Consciousness.

In *The Early Sessions* books, Seth defines the personality as a "field of action." He explains that we can consider *action* to be the spontaneous means by which Consciousness can express itself through the process of materialization. Our personalities are our connection to this dimension of action.

Action is not a *force* as we tend to label such internal drives behind our own materialization; it is more a growth medium for the personality. "It is a by-product of any reality, and a part of all reality."[86] Seth also states that "action is *basically electrical*"[87] (my emphasis) in nature, but because of science's limited understanding of action being force or movement within the physical field, we are yet to develop technologies to reveal such electrical realities. When we come to understand our Selves a little better through exploration of our psyches, the discovery of the breadth of electrical realities will advance our understanding of the physical dimension.

Because action is electrical in nature and your personality is a *field of action*, it follows that you can think of your personality as an electrical field.

In a *Guardian* newspaper article (May 15th, 2011), the renowned physicist Stephen Hawking, when remarking on what death may entail, said, "I regard the brain as a computer which will stop working when its components fail. There is no heaven or afterlife for broken-down computers; that is a fairy story for people afraid of the dark." What he fails to recognize is that just because the brain—the central processing unit—breaks down and the computer doesn't work anymore does not mean the electrical grid that kept it alive ceases to exist. In death, your personality's electrical field returns to the grid to consider an upgrade!

According to Seth, your personality builds from continuous electrical signals and codes from any effect—such as thoughts, dreams, feelings, and emotions—experienced by your Self. Essentially, you *get* a personality through electrical build-up!

Your physical body superimposes itself upon this electrical ghost of a structure, yet even though they entwine they are of completely different dimensions. Your personality's electrical build-up forms an electrical pattern both within and without every cell of your physical body, yet it is *independent* of physicality.

Why do I need a personality?

Both your ego-self and personality begin their development from physical birth. Your ego-self begins with nothing other than its independence, whereas your personality has a trace of an identity from the outset, bestowed upon it by your Essence self and relayed to your personality, via your inner self and the subconscious. Because your personality has its *primary* existence within the electrical dimension, it begins life with some rudimentary knowledge, such as which of the families of intent it aligns with. Your Essence, inner self, and subconscious all have a presence within the electrical dimension, which is how your personality is privy to knowledge from each.

Your inner self, birth mother to your ego-self, has good reason to encourage the growth of your personality. Information from the experiences you create in the physical world needs to be transformed and transferred to your Essence. You need a go-between, a part of your Self that can translate data from the physical to the nonphysical. Your ego-self can't do it as its existence is reliant upon physicality—it simply doesn't get involved with the electrics.

Your personality's purpose, therefore, is to preserve this feedback from the ego-self on its interpretations of reality (including the emotional energies that underpin its *beliefs* about reality), along with all other effects from the other electrical fields of human experience (notably dreams) and get this information across to your Essence. Your Essence requires information on *all* the experiences of your life—electrical and not-so electrical—to add to its understanding of the nature of its Self.

Besides being changed by the ego-self, your personality is *forever* being manipulated and nurtured by your inner self in its nonphysical existence outside of time. Your personality is always in motion—a motion regulated by the vitality of Consciousness (Divine Love).

Your personality cannot die

Your personality, not your ego-self, has a strong association with your inner self. Indeed, Seth describes the personality as being a *portion* of the inner self. It has its own "*consciousness of self*" and is therefore aware of its role in regard to the Essence self. It knows

Because your personality is part of the dimension of action, and thus not tied to the physical plane of existence, it is the part of you that "survives" physical death. The moment of physical death simply signifies your personality's release from the physical field. It continues to exist, to change and develop, but it no longer projects itself into the physical realm.

that it is within and part of the electrical dimension of action, with its own field therein. Personality is simply a name given to this portion of the Self *that exists within all living species whether they possess an ego-self or not.*

Death for your physical self is the equivalent of permanently turning off a computer. When you turn off your computer (*or put it to sleep*), your operating system (ego-self) is unable to interact with the environment through its collection of software programs (intellect, mind, emotional body, physical body). All your electrically encoded data (personality) is still there, but by turning off your computer you've simply taken away the electrical field to which your personality belongs.

Because your personality is an electrical counterpart to your ego-self, it has all your ego-self's data (accumulated files from various software packages) copied. When you turn on your computer-self, your personality can transfer (upload) this copied data to another mainframe computer (your Essence) via the Internet (electrical dimension of action). Unlike a computer, and unrealized by most of us, turning off the computer-self cannot turn off your personality, as it continues to process information when you are asleep, *or have permanently gone to sleep.*

When it understands its survival beyond death, the personality is liberated from the ego-self's fears of physical annihilation. Then you can more readily turn your mental energies to improving your present physical situation.

Exercise 5: Reframing an Unwanted Behavior. (See Appendix VIII.) This is a 15- to 20-minute exercise that can quickly deal with an unwanted habitual behavior by reprogramming your subconscious mind. You will need to have the basic EFT guide to hand for reference (see Appendix II).

You need to remain aware that no definite division exists between the ego-self and the personality. Neither is there one between the physical self and the spiritual self. Your Self is one unified entity crossing the seeming boundaries between the physical and nonphysical areas within Consciousness.

Chapter 9

It's All In Your Mind

Understanding the Mind

Regarding your physical self, we've learned so far that your ego-self has a job to do—which is to use its *perception* to decide what actions to take. It has an intellect to help it out with what's important in its perception of the physical world, and its purpose is to impress upon the personality the correct elements of the physical situation (undistorted by preconceived beliefs) in its perception of the situation. Once your ego-self is (relatively) clear on what it perceives, and is readying you for action in response to a prominent issue, you then need to *deal with* the physical conditions—this is where your *Mind*[88] comes in.

A problem exists in understanding what the Mind is. A common mistake is to equate it with the psyche. They are not the same. According to Seth, the Mind is a *collective*—a quantity of psychological constructs—including several different, individual minds each playing with their own thoughts, ideas, dreams, and emotions while keeping an eye on the Self's overall intent. *Your* Mind is your individuated *portion* of the psyche at best.

We imagine that we have just one mind because we only identify with the conscious one. A brain, in the main, can only tune into one mind at a time. The collective Mind resides within your Essence. Along with your inner self—another aspect of your Essence—it watches out for your physical self as it negotiates physical existence. Your Mind's purpose, translated into your entire physiology via the brain and nervous system, is to keep you alive.

Of the minds within the Mind, **the mind we utilize in any one moment is the *conscious-mind*.**

Each one of the minds within the collective handles information and organizes reality differently. Consequently, the mind chosen as *the conscious-mind* can affect how one deals with a situation. But the ego-self doesn't realize that its use of perception in the decision-making process would be a whole lot easier if it had a more flexible approach to choosing which mind to utilize and make conscious. There are horses for courses. Depending on the situation, one mind would be more helpful to the ego-self's decision-making than another. Having a collection of minds allows one to interchange them to best express the Self in accordance with circumstances.

Due to unfamiliarity with having a choice, the ego-self tends to stick with one mind, whatever the physical circumstances. The ego-self expects this overworked mind to deal with situations it is ill-equipped to handle, which is when mental-health problems may arise—perhaps even a mental breakdown.

When we observe someone not dealing with the physical conditions appropriately, we might say, "Are you out of your mind?" or "Have you lost your mind?" Such a situation is more to do with the ego-self's utilization of a mind inappropriate for the circumstances, or the ego-self being unable to engage a suitable mind at all.

Fortunately, any one of our minds can handle *most* conditions, and we "change our minds" often through intervention by our inner self—much to the consternation of our ego-self and our family and friends!

When in a life-threatening position, your inner self instantaneously chooses an appropriate mind to deal with the situation. That's why, for example, a person after enacting a courageous deed might say, "It wasn't a question of being brave. I just did what needed to be done because I knew *how* to do it." The most appropriate mind that knows *how* to deal with such a situation jumps to the fore. If you don't have a mind familiar with the situation to some extent, or your ego-self clings desperately to one mind, you can freeze—mentally and physically.

Just as your brain sends messages to various parts of your body in order to physically deal with a situation, your conscious-mind sends messages to the nervous system about *how* to deal with it. Any chosen conscious-mind is privy to *all* the data pertaining to your Whole Self—similar experiences, other lifetimes, other purposes, challenges solved and unsolved—but it only sends your brain data that relates to ensuring your physical self's continued existence.

As we better understand the Mind and how it operates, we become *truly* more ***perceptive***, expanding our awareness into far more than just the data supplied by physical reality. Dream content would be more perceivable, for example. We would then naturally be more aware of our ability to create our physical reality. As Seth declares, this is what true *personhood* is all about.

Your Mind's subconscious area

As outlined in *Chapter 6, Your Spiritual Self*, within the totality of Consciousness there is a *Subconscious Area*. This area acts as a way station or bridging "space" between the *Objective* (physical) and *Subjective* (nonphysical) Areas within Consciousness.

Your subconscious is a portion of your Mind that acts as your personal gateway to the expansive Subconscious Area. It is somewhere where your inner self communicates and interacts with your physical self. Your *body-consciousness*[89] is a feature within your subconscious that constantly works with the highly complex information exchange going on between your spiritual self and your physical self.

Laypeople tend to interchange the terms *subconscious* and *unconscious* when speaking of levels of awareness beyond everyday awareness. Anyone at all familiar with psychoanalytic theory has come across the term "the unconscious," which Sigmund Freud used to describe a part of the psyche containing thoughts, ideas, and emotions kept out of conscious awareness.

Ignoring *positive* unconscious phenomena, Freud focused upon the malevolent aspects of this mental realm when developing his psychoanalytic theory. He deliberately used the term *repressed* to suggest that when any painful, traumatic, or socially unacceptable mental phenomena occur one blocks these out of conscious awareness. The practice of psychoanalysis originally rested upon the skills of a practitioner to bring this material to the conscious-mind for psychological healing. (Ironically, the practice now relies heavily upon pharmaceutical interventions that generally reinforce the repression.)

Carl Jung expanded upon the notion of *the* unconscious, suggesting we have a *"personal unconscious"* and a *"collective unconscious"*—the former along Freudian lines and the latter containing impersonal mental activity inherited from the collective mind of humanity.

The term *subconscious* is not a psychoanalytic term; Freud rejected it as confusing, believing that our minds are either consciously aware of information or not. His opinion was that material about to enter the conscious-mind resided within the "*pre*-conscious" rather than a *sub*-conscious.

Freud didn't realize (according to Seth) that the conscious-mind is just the one mind we have our attention focused upon. We can think of our collection of minds within the Mind as being just *below* the threshold between not conscious and conscious, poised for action in an area of our consciousness more appropriately named the *sub*conscious.

I use the term *unconscious* the same way much of the channeled literature does, meaning when the brain has shut down its main functions and the Mind is not able to express itself through a conscious wakeful state—as when a person is knocked out or in a coma. In deference to Jung, I retain the expression *collective unconscious* to mean an aspect of the psyche that contains mental activities (thoughts, beliefs, feelings) inherited from the collective Mind of our species.

It is within your subconscious area that your *inner senses* (discussed in *Chapter 10*) as well as your physical senses combine to assist your ego-self form and express your personality. Furthermore, there are other areas within this area! Areas populated by the minds that form *other* personalities—*sub-personalities*[90]—offering distinctive characteristics when given conscious expression. Suffice to say that the subconscious describes a phenomenon of the psyche that is far broader than Freud's unconscious and far more complex than Jung's double-faceted notion of psychological structures outside of conscious awareness.

Inside the subconscious library

To gain a clearer image of your subconscious area, visualize a vast campus of scholastic buildings, the main access to which is through a majestic library.[91] Your subconscious, as psychological science is now very aware, is certainly a library of knowledge and information. As you will learn, it is also the meeting ground for your inner and outer psychological formations. Let's look inside.

Imagine yourself striding up the marble steps outside this impressive building to the entrance. Between the Corinthian columns fronting your building are oak and glass revolving doors with polished brass push rails. As you push through the door, you notice three characters foolishly squeezed into the opposite partition—the one in front being pushed along by the next, who appears to have the third guy playing piggyback. All of them have resolute, if somewhat fearful, facial expressions as they leave.

Once in the reception hall, you see a dozen or more people sitting in large, comfortable armchairs or generally milling about, each similar in physical appearance to yourself, but their dress and mannerisms reflect clearly different personalities.

Various large oak tables are set in rows for study purposes. A reception counter is in front of you across the hall, with a genderless, robotic librarian behind its much-polished oak top. To the librarian's right, perched precariously atop the counter sits a very distinguished and wise-looking woman. To the right of her, similarly sitting on the counter, is a figure that again mirrors your physical features yet is ghostly transparent. You detect a pulsating electrical hum emanating from this character.

Stepping inside the library denotes leaving physicality. The people in the reception area are your *other minds*, waiting for the call to be made conscious. The librarian is the custodian of this subconscious archive, who does as instructed with computer-like efficiency. The librarian's sole purpose is to feed information into the library's electrical database and retrieve information from it when instructed to do so. Like the fictional character, Lieutenant Commander Data from the television series *Star Trek*, your subconscious librarian makes no judgments, forms no opinions, and is incapable of dishonesty or deception.

The three characters who just left the building are the three portions of your physical self, on a mission to deal with a current challenge in the physical realm. Your *ego-self* pushes *the conscious-mind* in front of it, as it balances your *personality* on its back and shoulders. The wise and compassionate lady sitting on the counter is of course your *inner self*, the overseeing, noninterfering benefactor to the library. And the ghostly (not ghastly) electrically humming one is your *body-consciousness*.

Behind the librarian is an arched entrance to a corridor that leads far back into the library and to other buildings and areas on campus. Above the arch, a sign reads *Information on the Self*, and if you peer down the corridor, one entrance indicates *Other Lifetimes*; another, *Probable Selves*.

The librarian sits at a computer console surrounded by visual display monitors. One of these monitors has the label *Body's Physical Systems* affixed to it. Readouts of all the autonomic systems of the body appear on it, from heartbeat to blink rate. You notice that your body-consciousness is staring at this monitor the whole time.

Another monitor sits next to where your inner self is sitting on the counter. It is turned outward, for the convenience of anyone at the counter wishing to see what may be upon its screen. Away from the librarian's counter, shelves stretch around the room and fill the walls from floor to ceiling. Each is laden with ancient dusty tomes. An occasional window interrupts the swathe of shelving, and on the south-facing wall to the right a set of French doors allows a glimpse of a densely planted garden outside. Above the doors, a sign reads *Garden of Beliefs*.

Take a moment to read through this visualization again so that it becomes a reinforced image of your subconscious area *within* your Mind. Or...

Exercise 6: Art Exercise--Depict Your Subconscious Library. It can be a sketch, a painting, a collage—whatever you find easiest to do. Just include as much of the description elements as you can and add as much detail as you like to make the scene an inviting one. Creating a physical picture of your subconscious library is the best way to retain the image in your mind. (See Appendix IX.)

You should retain the fact that the subconscious is *not a mind* or part of a mind, as when inappropriately referred to as "the subconscious mind." Nor should you equate it with Freud's "the unconscious." It is not a scary place as Freud might have you believe—albeit, granted, the body-consciousness figure is a bit weird. It is instead a part of the psyche where all the players involved in the game of your life can discuss strategy. It is a welcoming, comforting environment made so by your inner self's benevolence. You can trust your inner self will see to it that you come to no harm while in this place of psychological inter-*action*.

The ego-self's folly

It's a sad fact that at present we have a poor understanding of our subconscious area and no real idea as to its purpose. Our ego-self fears entering the subconscious library because of one or more adopted beliefs. They grow from the seeds of scientific materialism, which rejects its very existence; from ill-founded Freudian notions of a noxious *id*, where ghastly gremlins lurk; and from religious doctrine that suggests the subconscious lands are the badlands of the psyche—populated by despicable devils aiming to drag your soul off to Hades.

Because of our fears, Western psychology's expeditionary parties have made little progress in exploring the subconscious, let alone *utilizing* it.

Most of us understand that the subconscious contains a great store of information on our life's physical and mental experiences. Many are aware of methods to access the subconscious, such as *clinical hypnosis* or *mindfulness,* which appear to quell the ego-self's fears and allow repressed feelings and emotions to come through.

Eastern meditational practices have expanded our use of the subconscious for what it is—*a psychological facility*—but the practices and exercises highlighted in the channeled literature are designed to exploit more fully the possibilities. Seth and several other metaphysical guides offer them as tools to help us maintain our mental and emotional balance as well as facilitate psychical exploration through altered states of consciousness.

Most of us negotiate the subconscious in a slapdash fashion. We usually enter our subconscious library through ego-driven necessity rather than through adventurous enquiry. Furthermore, our ego-self will usually only venture into the library timidly because it is unsure of how to act in such an unfamiliar environment.

Because of your ego-self's reluctance to linger too long in this uncharted territory, it immediately puts its habitually chosen conscious-mind under pressure. It wants your conscious-mind to quickly snatch any information on what to do so that it can make a hasty exit. Your personality, incidentally, unbeknownst to your ego-self, *does know* how to utilize the action potentialities of this place, and will often jump down from your ego-self's back and nip off to the Garden of Beliefs to find out what energies might come to bear because of any action your ego-self decides to take.

Your ego-self is only aware that in this library there is information available to it on how to act. It simply instructs the conscious-mind to ask the robotic librarian, "What do ***I*** (as sole authority on the Self) *normally do* in this situation?" Your ego-self remains by the revolving doors, looking out for any hobgoblins that might assault its illustrious persona, nervous that your personality may return from the Garden of Beliefs laden with creepy crawlies. It regards the other characters within the room as separate to itself, unaware that some of them are *other minds* that can interchange with the conscious-mind it has habitually adopted as sole agent. Your ego-self regards your inner self as irrelevant and is oblivious to its loving influence.

At the librarian's counter, the conscious-mind describes the physical situation as perceived by your ego-self and asks the preset question. The librarian feeds the data into the computerized archive, thus updating energy readings on relevant information packages.

The answer, chosen *electronically,* appears on the monitor perched on the counter. It holds the largest amount of electromagnetic charge when all the Mind's thoughts, beliefs, feelings, and emotional energies are accounted for.

Unpromisingly, because of the structure of the question ("What do ***I*** *normally* do?"), the answer arises from analysis of information solely confined to the ego-self's currently limited perception. The answer's electrical charge is thus only the accumulated energy from the retained actions of previous experiences, the retained *thoughts* in relation to those experiences, and the emotional energy attached to *beliefs* about them. Unfortunately, because the inner self is often ignored, its highly pertinent contribution (involving energy configurations on far broader levels of your Self) is left out of the equation.

We already know from Seth that the ego-self is well equipped to handle the physical environment. However, it needs to *perceive* "correctly" (that is, as unimpeded by its screen of beliefs as possible) the physical situation and relay its interpretations as succinctly and as clearly as possible to the subconscious librarian for input into the psyche's database.

The ego-self should be at the counter with its conscious-mind, making sure the information transfers correctly before the subconscious computer analyzes its content. The ego-self should then have the librarian tap the inner self's phenomenal skills and energies to help assess the situation and formulate an answer that considers the entire Self's needs. The ego-self should also make a point to know which of its minds is the most appropriate for subsequent action. Perhaps one day the ego-self will have evolved sufficiently to confidently ask the inner self for input directly! Here is what Seth has to say about ideal circumstances for information exchange within the subconscious library:

> It is the communication between the very areas of the self which is so important here, as in many other matters. It is possible for the ego to realize its position as but one part of the whole personality, while it still behaves in a directive manner toward physical manipulation.
>
> This is the ideal circumstance, for when this is the case the ego listens to the inner self, and then directs its energy outward in a way that is beneficial for the whole framework.[92]

With such behavioral alterations adopted, answers to the modified question "How is it best for me to act in this situation?" may turn out to be unexpected or even ridiculous—to the ego-self. It will then need to trust in the computational wisdom of the combined psychological characters that make up the entirety of the Self.

An answer that clearly *frustrates* the ego-self indicates that the ego-self's interpretation of what it perceived—the information it fed into the subconscious computer—was compromised by an intellect shackled by beliefs. A mature ego-self will recognize this to be the case and act on addressing the beliefs that generated the frustration.

A graphical representation of the Self

Figure 2 offers a graphical representation of the structure of your Self as described in the Seth material and other metaphysical teachings. It shows the basic psychological elements discussed in *Chapter 7* that form your physical self, rising from its originating source (your Essence or spiritual self, discussed in *Chapter 6*) through the varying "levels" or areas within consciousness.

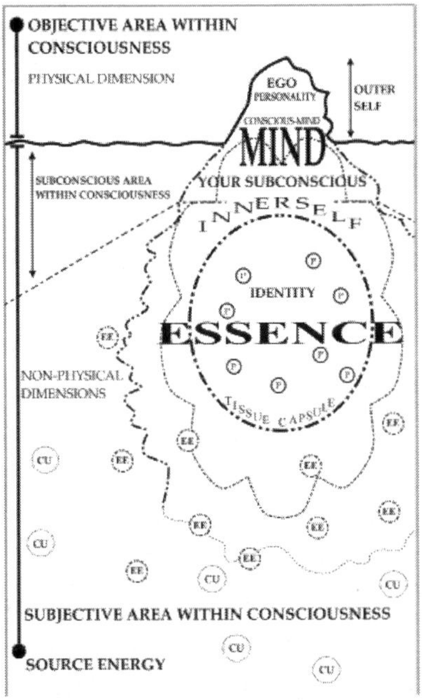

Figure 2. The Self

The figure modifies the classical iceberg model of the Mind proposed in psychoanalytic theory. Unlike with the psychoanalytic model, the Mind bridges the illusory boundary between physical and nonphysical and forms an area within the Self, rather than the Self being a part of it (as in Jungian theory). The Mind acts as the psychological agent of consciousness, *choosing* which quantum waves of Consciousness out of the subjective ocean of probabilities to collapse into physical matter.

This iceberg depiction of your Self is kept afloat by the ocean of Consciousness from which it emerges. Notice the Consciousness Units (CUs) and the Electromagnetic Energy Units (EEs) in this ocean as they, just like water molecules turning into ice, slow their vibrational frequency to become solidified—*through you*—in the physical realm.

As you view *Figure 2*, bear in mind that every aspect of your Self, psychic *and physical*, from your inner self to the cells of your body, is aware of your intent and purpose. Your ego-self, looking out onto the physical world, may well ignore such knowledge in its bid to separate itself out as *the* Self; however, rest assured that it retains access to this knowledge when persuaded to engage the inner senses.

A healthy, well-integrated Self requires open communication between all aspects and areas to the Self. Your ego-self simply needs reminding occasionally of its place within the gestalt of your Self. It has the director's role in the movie of your life's experiences but should remember to listen to the producer, your inner self, so that its directions benefit the totality of your Self.

Parallels in Jungian theory on the Self

Whereas metaphysical teachings use the term *individuation* for the separating of Consciousness into smaller expressions of itself, in Jungian analytical psychology the term describes a process whereby the various aspects to the physical self become integrated into a healthy whole, otherwise known as the *true self*.

In consideration of this duality of meaning, you might want to regard my depiction of the "individuation of Consciousness" as simply a description of how your Self comes into existence. This book, and the others in the trilogy, will hopefully assist you in becoming your true self, in Jungian terms.

(Note: In the following condensed presentation of Jungian psychology, the terms in parentheses are my ideas of metaphysical analogues.)

In Jungian theory, the *collective unconscious* (humanity's collective *sub*conscious) is a *repository of archetypes* (far-reaching psychical store) that organize, direct, and inform human thought and behavior. Jung regarded "the Self" to be one of our archetypes. His archetypal Self represents a coherent whole, unified consciousness (a reflection of our Essence self) that includes the *unconscious* (the subconscious area) of an individual. The Self, according to Jung, is realized as the product of *individuation,* which in the Jungian view is the process of *personality integration* (integrating the ego-self's characteristics with the personality's abilities and functions).

What distinguishes Jungian psychology is his idea that there are two centers of the personality (Self), an ego-self and an inner self, each with their own personality. We can equate Jung's dual personalities with the two centers of intent emanating from within the Self. That is, the personality's—and subsequently the ego-self's—family of *alignment* and the inner self's family of *belonging*—the Essence's family to which the inner self is an emissary.

Jung describes the duality by saying the *ego is the center of consciousness* (at the center of our physical self, which includes the personality). The Self (Essence) is the center of the *total personality,* which includes consciousness (our individuated consciousness), the *unconscious* (the subconscious area), and the ego (this part of the physical self). The Self is both the whole and the center, while the ego is a self-contained little circle off the center but contained within the whole.

Jung situates the ego-self with its personality twin (Seth says they are not quite the same) within a *total personality* at the center of our being—what I've described as the Essence self.[93]

Your inner self constantly monitors and affects the Jungian individuation process. Part of the integration deals with bringing your physical self's thoughts, beliefs, and behaviors in line with your overall Self's intent and purpose.

Jung's *archetypes* within his *collective unconscious* do not necessarily conform to the families of human intent, but we might consider them to be generalized personifications of the primary expressive elements of particular families. For example, someone who follows career pursuits involving the nurturing of a family unit, other people or animals, the natural environment, or the needy (in accordance with the Borledim/Nurturers family of intent) might embody Jung's "earth mother" archetype.

Jung also conceptualized the "supraconscious-mind,"[94] which we can liken to *the* Subconscious Area within Consciousness, as opposed to *an individual's subconscious area*. The concept refers to other *frameworks of consciousness* (a Sethian term) or deeper levels of awareness within the Self, where one engages with the mystical and transcends everyday experiences. The Jungian Self (Essence/inner self) emerges from the supraconscious, orchestrating the individuation (steering one back onto the paths of intent) from a perspective that surpasses concerns of the ego-self.

The resemblances between Jungian psychology and metaphysical ideas suggest that Jung may have intuited such information during meditation. Certainly, he would appear to have been deeply in touch with his conceptual inner senses. Some evidence suggests he gleaned a great deal of information on the nature of the psyche from dream recall. Albert Einstein, incidentally, was another genius who took his dreams seriously.

Chapter 10

Coming To Your Senses

In *Chapter 6, Your Spiritual Self,* I mentioned the *inner senses* as the means by which your inner self translates vital information from your spiritual self's broader view of an experience for your physical self to use in its decision-making.

When we perceive the reality before us, our familiar five outer senses report the *result* of the creation process to us. Our inner senses, on the other hand, are profoundly involved in the process itself. Our spiritual selves utilize them to bring our mental imaginings into physical reality. By developing *conscious* management of our inner senses, we gain a tremendous advantage in the creation of our personal reality. We can move from merely looking to five-sense data and habitual thoughts and beliefs when planning how to act, to a mind-expanded state offering a far broader perspective on the choices available.

Before your ego-self begins fantasizing on the possibilities available to you, be aware that for them to work at their best they require a mental environment attuned to the *natural principles*—the universal principles that oversee the way any expression of Consciousness (that includes you and me) creates and sustains something in the physical realm.

Because our inner senses are so important to the creation process, nested as they are within the workings of our spiritual self, our Essence self keeps a cautionary grasp of their reins and understands the most favorable conditions for when to introduce them to the ego-self. To keep your ego-self more open to their introduction it would be prudent to be well-versed in the natural principles before attempting to engage fully with your inner senses.

From laws to principles

I deliberately introduced the natural principles early on in this book because of their importance to *conscious* creation. The sooner we can assimilate them into our everyday actions and mental outlook, rather than simply understand them intellectually, then our mental environment becomes *naturally* more open to the intuitive knowledge provided by our inner senses. I derived the natural principles from the information provided by Seth and other metaphysical teachers, on the most fundamental laws and principles that underpin all that exists. Indigenous wisdom, philosophical enquiry, religious doctrine, and even investigations into quantum mechanics all contribute in some way in confirming the validity of the natural principles.

We know that the physical dimension of reality conforms to the laws of physics. What we don't know, say our metaphysical friends, is that natural universal laws *underpin* our physical laws. These natural laws transcend our usual understanding of the word "law" and are more appropriately called *principles*, a set of values by which Consciousness itself adheres.[95] That is, they are not a set of mandates presented by some almighty being; they are simply *how Consciousness works* within our physical and nonphysical worlds—something Sir Arthur Eddington may have sensed when writing in the early part of the 20th Century:

> I believe that the mind has the power to affect groups of atoms and even tamper with the odds of atomic behaviour, and that even the course of the world is not predetermined by physical laws but may be altered by the uncaused volition of human beings.[96]

For "uncaused volition of human beings," think *the natural universal laws* as expressed through human consciousness.

Seth refers to the natural universal laws as "the basic laws of the inner universe,"[97] naming ten such laws between sessions

44 and 59 in *The Early Sessions: Book 2 of The Seth Material*. Their inclusion in his legacy was to help us understand that there are deeper principles that promote and underpin all reality creation in the physical dimension. He states that "the laws of the inner universe apply to ***all*** camouflage [physical] universes, and ***all*** consciousnesses on any plane must follow the basic laws of the inner universe."[98] Here's a summary of Seth's laws of the inner universe, which I prefer to call *principles*:

1. The first principle is the existence of **Consciousness** itself. Consciousness is an ever-present property of any dimension or plane of existence. Consciousness instills itself within *all* creations, giving each creation *self-awareness* to some degree. As Seth remarks, "There is no case where this is not so."[99]

2. Consciousness uses the universal **principle of creation** to expand and evolve through experience, which is its intent. It creates an infinitesimal number of theaters or playgrounds, some physical (as we might perceive them) like our own world, some nonphysical or other dimensional, to our way of thinking. Creation is the principle by which idea constructions (and thereby our desires) manifest in the physical realm.

3. To help Consciousness explore the complexities of this principle of creation, it formulated the universal principle of *value fulfillment*—also referred to by Seth as **Divine Love**. Divine Love, as you may remember from earlier, is a principle through which all creations can reach fulfillment of their individuated expressions while also aiding other creations in their own expression.

4. For Divine Love to work efficiently, Consciousness requires the universal **principle of cooperation**. It gives rise to the myriad structures we observe within the physical world. The less complex structures, such as atoms and molecules, apply this principle when forming more complex, multifaceted gestalt structures present within inorganic matter, as well as living organisms.

These cooperative structures form their own identities, without the identities of the less complex structures losing theirs. By cooperating, the particulate structures (for example, atoms and molecules) gain in their ability to express themselves through mutual regard and joint endeavor, acting within the universal principle of Divine Love. Cooperative structures are an expression of the principle of creation inherent within the universal principle of Divine Love.

5. When Consciousness creates a physical or nonphysical reality, it requires a further universal principle by which to transform its energy. Scientists have not yet realized that Consciousness, or *Source Energy*, can transform from a nonphysical state of existence into a physical one. We may think energy has created itself from nowhere—thus breaking the empirical law of physics (energy can neither be created nor destroyed)—but the universal **principle of energy transformation** supersedes this law.[100]

The following path of transformation, derived from Seth and other channeled information on how energy converts from nonphysical expression to physical expression, may intrigue the physicist in you:

Consciousness ≡ Energy > CUs > EEs > QFs (Quantum Fields) > space-time continuum.

This transforming sequence is essentially about slowing the vibrational frequencies of energy to within those of the electromagnetic spectrum we call *light*. Energy *transforms* itself across all dimensions of Consciousness, and this universal principle is continuously occurring.

6. In transforming energy into our dimension of physicality, Consciousness employs the dimension of *time*. You can view this fourth dimension of our physical realm as the way by which we can more thoroughly examine our experiences. Time draws out an experience into all its nuances of expression, just as each frame on a film reel captures the detail of an action.

Our personal understanding of time is implicitly involved in the process of perception.[101]

From the viewpoint of Consciousness, time is an interesting (and probably amusing) psychical construct. From its perspective, only one *moment point* exists, which enables Consciousness to express itself both outside and inside the dimension of time. Seth refers to the moment point as the *spacious present*. The concept of a spacious present, or one moment point, helps in our understanding of **another universal principle: spontaneity.**[102]

Consciousness behaves in a spontaneous fashion; when time is not a factor, it cannot be otherwise.

7. Given the spacious present and lack of any real concreteness about time, you may wonder how anything might *last*. What would give something *continuity*, not least in the nonphysical realms of Consciousness?

Continuity is our mind's time-confined interpretation of the next universal principle. Because we view things through the spectacles of time, we assume that physical things continue to exist because of it. They don't. Time does not control the continuity of existence; the universal **principle of durability** does.

The length of *duration* of a physical construction is in

direct proportion to the construct's embodiment of the universal principle of Divine Love and its ability to sustain the universal principle of energy transformation.

Death, or cessation of focus upon the physical dimension, occurs when durability ceases to operate for the physical construct.

8. Consciousness also incorporates the universal principle Seth describes as the **capacity for infinite mobility**. Because we are individuated expressions of Consciousness, our inner self can utilize this principle in transcending any psychological barriers to our experience.

9. Changeability and transmutation is a universal principle that expands upon the principle of energy transformation, in that energy has the capability to not only transform into any cohesive structure in our physical dimension, but also change that structure within the spacious present (i.e., at any "time"), should the need arise. It can do this because energy *is* Consciousness and vice versa.

In other words, *any* creation contains within it, at a molecular level so to speak, knowledge of the inner universal principles and can thus act upon them instantaneously. This explains why so-called miraculous events happen, such as instant remission from chronic illness (also referred to as *spontaneous* remission).

Your inner self exploits this inner principle when utilizing one of the inner senses called *diffusion*. The principle and the inner sense combine to bring about materialization of the Self within the physical realm.

10. The final basic law of the inner universe named by Seth is that of **quality depth**. It's a particularly difficult concept to understand (and you were doing so well!), as little in physical terms demonstrates its existence. Its primary influence is upon the psyche. As the inner principle of cooperation plays out in the observable universe, with structures joining together to enhance their expression of value fulfillment (Divine Love), so too is this process mirrored in "pyramids of psychic comprehensions"[103]—the psychical equivalent of obtaining value fulfillment through cooperation.

Quality depth is a psychical space for all idea constructions and psychic action to enjoy and expand through infinite dimensions. It is a space driven by the winds of Divine Love.

Seth's laws of the inner universe are notoriously difficult to understand, and although he mentions other inner laws, along with "laws of attraction," he doesn't elaborate on them. Besides what other channeled guides call the *Law of Attraction,* the above summary should provide you with an outline of what Seth considered the most important universal principles affecting the use of your inner senses.

The Law of Attraction

Although Seth doesn't enlarge on his *laws* of attraction, Abraham (channeled by Esther Hicks) and various other channeled sources go into detail for us on this universal principle. Now commonly referred to as the *Law of Attraction (LOA)* in the Mind/Body/Spirit community, this phrase, the *Power of Attraction,* and the *Power of Magnetism,* are all used in the metaphysical literature.

Seth does remind us repeatedly that when it comes to reality creation "you get what you concentrate upon."[104] This axiom sums up what the LOA is all about when we consider the various explanations given by other channeled sources.

However, the LOA is far more complex than this saying suggests. The mechanics of manifesting our reality is not quite as simple as concentrating upon what we want and applying some positive thinking. The LOA is, though, a crucial factor for us to understand in the creation process.

We can think of Divine Love as a feature of Consciousness that helps us fathom the reasons behind *why* we create our physical reality. Without it, there would be no *form* of physical existence for us to perceive through our senses—whether inner or outer senses. The principle of the LOA, on the other hand, helps us to understand *how* we create our reality.

Since the turn of the millennium the LOA has gained notoriety as *the* mysterious rule or law governing the creation of our reality. Many in the Mind/Body/Spirit movement have highlighted it as such since it came to prominence with the release of *The Secret* in 2006.

I'll let you into a secret of my own. The LOA isn't a secret at all, it's simply one of the universal principles that we've lost from our conscious awareness for some time—along with the other principles that underpin our physical laws. It is important that we become consciously aware again of the LOA, however, it would be naïve to assume that a superficial knowledge of this universal principle, in isolation, is all that's required to overcome life's challenges and become a master of conscious creation. As Alexandra Bruce helps to point out in her book *Beyond the Secret*, when taken out of context, extracted from the other interweaving natural principles, and without due deference given to Divine Love which explains the why of creation, knowledge of the LOA is unlikely to provide you with *the* answer to your creational woes.

The metaphysical descriptions of this universal principle underpinning how we create our reality are generally succinct but none-too enlightening—for example, "all that is like unto itself will be drawn to it" (Omni) and, "you are the attractor of everything that comes into your experience" (Abraham).

The general idea is that we each incorporate a psychological power that behaves in a similar fashion to a magnetic field.[105] You are essentially a magnet, drawing to yourself, not iron filings, but the *probable reality*[106] that, within the moment point of now, is the best vibrational match to the tone of your personality.

Let me explain! Energy has electro-*magnetic* properties. Thoughts are an electromagnetic energy form and they, along with everything else in physical and nonphysical realities, attract other forms of energy of a similar vibrational signature. The LOA allows all forms of Consciousness (including you) the ability to experience the Self. The reality you perceive to be "out there" is actually a reflection of the accumulated electromagnetic energies you build through your thoughts, beliefs, feelings, and emotions. In other words, what you perceive to be real—the reality you draw to you—reflects the energies contained within your Mind, mirroring the tonal frequency of your personality in that moment point.

Bashar (channeled by Darryl Anka) puts it this way:

> What you put out is what you get back. The energy you give off based on your beliefs—your emotions, your behavior—the [tonal frequency] you give off is what determines the kind of reality experience you have. Physical reality doesn't exist except as a reflection of what you most strongly believe is true for you. That is all physical reality is—it is literally like a mirror.
>
> If you are looking in a mirror and you see your face with a frown on it, you know that you don't go over to the mirror and try to force the reflection to smile—you must smile first. There is no way to change the reflection without you smiling first.
>
> But, you can also conversely understand that when you decide to smile the reflection has no choice but to return the

> smile, because it doesn't have a mind of its own.
>
> So, the idea to understand is that physical reality very much is really like a mirror—it will not change until you do first. But if you do, it has no choice but to follow suit because it is only a reflection of what you have put out.[107]

The LOA is the universal principle that explains how you attract to yourself one of innumerable probable realities available to you in the moment point of now—the *spacious present*. The thing to remember about the LOA is how important it is to monitor the thoughts you entertain, as they will attract similar thoughts, which gain energy in their assembly and thus become closer to physical manifestation. Thoughts alone though do not create your reality. If this were the case, we'd all have killed each other in a truly brief period!

If your accumulated thoughts run contrary to the universal principles, then you will eventually encounter a challenge within your life. The more your thoughts are in accordance with them, the fewer challenges will arise. If you encounter difficulties when you come to exercise your inner senses, you are again likely to be acting against one or more of these vital universal principles. I therefore devised the *ten natural principles* as an encapsulation of the universal principles in a comprehensible form to help you create an ideal mental environment for exercising your inner senses while in the act of conscious creation.

Conscious creation is a difficult thing to master if you are not conversant with the natural principles describing *how "things"* ***really*** *work* and are unpracticed in the use of your inner senses. Let's now examine these tools by which you form your personal reality.

Chapter 11

Exploring Your Inner Senses

Your inner senses—in tandem with the natural principles

We rely upon our five physical senses and their extensions (scientific instrumentation) to provide us with information about our physical reality. Occasionally though, we become aware of information that does not appear to come from our physical senses. We generally assign such occasions to a mysterious *sixth sense,* a gut feeling, or a moment of intuition, all too often dismissed as inconsequential by an ego-self that only trusts the physical senses.

Your inner self uses a variety of ways to wrestle your ego-self's attention momentarily away from the physical senses. Feelings (as opposed to emotions) are its primary attention-grabber, signaling to your conscious-mind that your inner self has information to share. Dreams (including daydreams), impulses, moments of inspiration, and "coincidental" or synchronous events are other ways it makes you aware of important subconscious information.

Like the way your outer senses determine nuances relayed by physical objects (color, smell, taste, etc.), your inner senses determine the *vibrational tones and frequencies* pertaining to the object (or event) found only in the subjective area within Consciousness. Your inner self relays this *inner* information to your conscious-mind so you can expand your perspective, casting light on the *subtle energy* detail. Essentially, your inner self, if your ego-self allows, expands perception for you to make better informed decisions. The inner senses connect *what you have just created in the physical realm* with how it relates to the bigger picture of your life's overall intent known to your Essence self.

Seth describes nine inner senses in Chapter 19 of *The Seth*

Material by Jane Roberts; you can find further elaboration in *The Early Sessions: (Books 2 and 3) of The Seth Material*. My own interpretation of Seth's inner senses is available as a free download document on my website (cwejohnson.com) entitled *Your Inner Senses*.

Seth informs us that although your physical self has the capacity to receive and include most inner-sense information, there are some senses that reach into areas of knowledge that your ego-self would have difficulty handling. This difficulty arises through lack of awareness and thereby lack of use. Many of us don't yet acknowledge our inner self's counsel, let alone *consciously* utilize it.

The Western world's general dismissal of inner knowledge creates a psychological condition not unlike schizophrenia[108] within us. A schism exists between our inner self (thereby Essence self) from our ego-self (thereby the conscious-mind)—which necessitates caution as we begin to heal the divide and allow for *conscious* manipulation of our inner resources.[109] Diligently working away in the subconscious area, your inner self constantly organizes inner-sense information about probable realities available to you for manifestation. Your ego-self *filters* these probabilities through the act of perception—essentially, through its belief systems. Due to our schizophrenic condition and lack of belief that we are involved with the creation process, we create most of our realities *un-**intent**-ionally*; that is, with very little truly informed and deliberate steering from our ego-self.

Right now, this may not be so bad, as Seth states we could not manage the abilities that fully utilized inner senses would afford us. We therefore need to take things slowly, initially stimulating just a few of our inner senses. Reestablishing the connection to our inner world may be a lengthy business for some, arduous work for most, and not lacking in anguish or even trauma for a good few. We need to persuade our ego-selves gently and compassionately that the inner senses are invaluable for creating preferred realities.

The current shift in consciousness affects an individual in many ways, not least by a growing awareness of his or her inner senses. The burgeoning phenomenon of channeling in recent years is another indication that Consciousness is awakening people to the depth of personal and collective reality.[110] Reconstructing a conscious connection with the inner self, at an individualized pace with a good heart, is vital. So, don't lose patience.

Primarily, trust that your inner self will guide you in this. Begin by slowly, carefully, and regularly employing the exercises and suggestions presented within this course. If you become frustrated with your progress, remember that your inner self knows what your physical self is capable of handling and when. Use the Basic EFT routine (Appendix II) to dissipate any feelings of frustration.

You may see frustration as a prelude to anger, so stop doing what makes you frustrated. Remember, though, that the ego-self is always keen to maintain the status quo, so it will use the feeling as its excuse for not changing. Frustration is a signal, from your inner self, that you are criticizing yourself or doubting your creational abilities. You may perceive yourself to be not good enough, not clever enough, or lacking the necessary skills. No, you are not lacking skills. Everyone has the same inner senses, you just lack using them. Frustration demotivates you, so make sure you address this feeling, using EFT, whenever it arises.

Although Seth outlined nine inner senses, the more recent information from Elias[111] suggests, for ease of understanding, that we can sort them into three groups according to sensory quality.

- **Empathic.** *Relating* to empathy—but more accurately, to sense, understand and *merge* with the "being-ness" of things.

- **Conceptual.** To fully connect and merge with concepts and ideas.
- **Time-based.** Relating to the perception of time.

The inner senses all work together and overlap in their actions. There is no hierarchical structure to them as they are all equally important.

Empathic inner senses

The empathic senses allow you to instantly *know* the *being-ness* of any structure within your field of perception. Without losing a sense of your own identity, these inner senses permit you to expand your conscious-mind to perceive, incorporate, merge, and thus intimately interact with the *vibrational signature*[112] of the other structure's identity. Employing these inner senses in the perception of another organic structure, such as a tree, an animal, or another person, stimulates a far greater appreciation and compassion for that expression of Consciousness. Where another person is involved, empathic inner senses bring an instant knowing of various elements pertaining to his or her Essence self, including feelings and emotions affecting the person's psychological climate.

Use of such senses does not imply any form of takeover of another's Essence.

According to Seth, our Essence selves possess *energy retaining capsules* to ensure structural integrity. Nonetheless, they are still able to connect with each other under certain circumstances managed by these empathic inner senses, without compromising the inviolate identities involved. Seth refers to such energy boundaries as "*tissue capsules*." Terms that you might be familiar with that are also attempting to describe this containment field, or protective sheath, are your *astral body*, or *subtle body*. The "skin," or outer portion of your astral body can contract and expand to enable exploration of other realities associated with our physical reality. It enables us to experience projections of consciousness, as in lucid dreaming or out of body experiences (OBEs).

Not surprisingly, we call those who regularly engage these inner senses *empaths*—people who can read the vibrational tones of another person, animal, structure, or place in nature. An accomplished empath might use these senses to experience the being-ness of a mountain, a butterfly, or even a pebble from the beach.

Our inner selves regularly employ empathic inner senses to understand others, but not to the extent that the inner selves might, due to the aforementioned difficulty of the ego-self with inner-sense abilities. The senses invariably act subliminally, with very little of the information gathered made available to the subconscious area of your mind, let alone the conscious-mind of your ego-self.

Conceptual inner senses

Concepts and ideas have electromagnetic energy patterning properties of their own. As with empathic inner senses, conceptual inner senses offer a type of mergence. Rather than merging with the vibrational tone of a physical structure, these inner senses bring you a *direct knowing* of the broadest expression of a concept or idea. They enable an assimilation of the multidimensional energy patterns involved.

When we utilize conceptual inner senses, they take us far beyond intellectual analysis. Thought processing is not involved. Conceptual inner senses send information directly to the conscious-mind through *impulses* and moments of *inspiration* specifically designed by the inner self to bypass intellectual involvement. It knows the purity of the information cannot be sustained once your ego-self starts thinking about, rationalizing, and judging the content.

When you engage these senses, it's possible for you to play a musical instrument in the style of a certain musician or paint a picture in the style of a particular artist. The Brazilian medium Luiz Antonio Gasparetto is a living example of an individual able to tune into one or more of the conceptual inner senses. He produces works of art in the style of several well-known artists—Pablo Picasso being one. Albert Einstein would be another example, albeit in the field of science, of a person highly attuned to his conceptual inner senses. As he poignantly remarked, "The true sign of intelligence is not knowledge but imagination." Using your imagination is a way of exercising the conceptual inner senses.

Conceptual inner senses are not exclusively human; all living organisms can exercise one or more of them. They provide the deepest awareness of the basic *natural principles* that power the vitality of the universe—*creativity and cooperation,* for example. Through these senses, organisms can access packages of inner universal knowledge, in a manner pertinent to the organism's ability to manipulate energy within its own area of expression.

For example, a spider utilizes a conceptual inner sense to access information about creating its web. In doing so, it downloads, if you will, data held in archives of the subconscious area within Consciousness.[113]

Further, recent scientific research into dolphin communication may reveal this animal's ability to engage the conceptual inner senses. Researchers use hand signals to tell the dolphins to "be creative"—essentially asking the creature to come up with its own behavioral display rather that any specifically learned one. Enthusiastic cetaceans are all too keen to carry out such a suggestion![114]

Time-based inner senses

Our time-based inner senses offer us the opportunity to better understand the construct of time and how it relates to other dimensions of reality. These senses reveal to us the importance of the *natural principle of spontaneity* and put us in touch with *natural time* (how the natural rhythms and cycles of Consciousness control the sequencing of events in the physical world), which helps us to develop the virtue of patience, another natural principle. Furthermore, they open the gates to other time frameworks and dimensions.

Exercising time-based inner senses brings about a greater appreciation of your whole Self and can subtly lead to discovering the other inner senses. Playfully exploring them makes switching between your inner realm, with its expressions *outside* of time, and your outer realm, with expressions *within* linear time, easier.

Time-based inner senses, when combined with empathic and conceptual inner senses, can enhance your perception of the *being-ness* of a structure (living or otherwise), or the energy pattern of a concept or idea. The perception is thus brought into the *spacious present*, where the separation of past and future does not exist. The notion of cause and effect becomes a moot point, with realization that both cause *and* effect are codependent in the initiation of an action.

Inner senses related to time are prominent in the dream state. Many of us, after pressing the alarm clock's snooze button, have lengthy dream events—seemingly of an hour or more—that take only five minutes of linear time. Such events remind us of the flexibility of time.

Precognition and *past life recall* relate to time-based inner senses. If you can grasp the concept of a spacious present, then you can see that "past-life recall" should be "other-life recall," or maybe even "probable-self accessing." With practice, engagement with time-based inner senses may bring you the richness of a long life in the past or future and in a relatively fleeting period of linear time—much like a long dream packed into five minutes.

An evolutionary awakening

Our shift in consciousness has everything to do with awakening to our inner senses. However, an assimilation of the natural principles into our worldview is necessary for us to consciously utilize the inner senses without making our reality any worse. Before we can enjoy the benefits of a mind with an information processing system that incorporates the inner senses on a regular basis, we must create the right mental environment collectively and individually.

If you struggle when exercising your inner senses in pursuit of a preferred reality, rest assured it is not because your inner senses don't work properly. In contrast to your outer senses, the keenness of your inner senses does not rely upon a physical information relay. Your inner senses won't falter like your hearing or eyesight might. Lack of success will be due to either your beliefs damming the flow of creative energy, or your chosen actions contradicting the natural principles governing creation. Remember that your inner senses *must* obey the natural principles. Your inner self, though, can always enlighten you with information gathered by your inner senses on errant beliefs or dubious actions interfering with your creativity. The solution to any problem with your creativity lies in examining the beliefs you hold.

The inner senses provide a gateway to a much broader understanding of your Self and how you create your reality. You can utilize them to uncover psychological and emotional factors that not only impede the full expression of your personality, but also prevent you from engaging fully with your life's intent and purpose. They also allow you to understand your connection, or otherwise, to family members and other individuals of importance in your life.

Awakening to our inner senses will reenergize our interactions with others. The natural principle of *cooperation* will come to the fore as the concept of competitiveness becomes better understood in its association with our survival mechanisms. The inner senses take us beyond empathy into a deep understanding and acceptance of the differences we express in our world—an understanding that *allows* for differences rather than judging them.

By awakening to the creative potential of your inner senses, you can ease your personal transition through our current momentous period in human evolution.

This is how the Sethian scholar Lynda Dahl sums up the inner senses in her book *Ten Thousand Whispers: A Guide to Conscious Creation*:

> When we consciously use the inner senses, we transcend physical reality and play in the universe unfettered by restrictive beliefs. We can enter other realities, clearly communicate with our inner selves, develop telepathic, precognitive and clairvoyant abilities; and sense the workings of the universe. We become aware of our multidimensionality, aware that physical reality is a very small portion of our existence, and aware that we have at our disposal an incredible tool to use in everyday life to consciously manipulate physical reality to our liking.[115]

Exercise 7: Elias's Clarity Exercise. This entire exercise should only take three or four minutes to complete. It may appear deceptively simple, but it is in fact, initially, quite difficult to do. Elias suggests you spend a week, with two to three run-throughs each day, practicing this exercise. (See Appendix X.)

Chapter 12

Feelings and Emotions

I hope *Chapter 11* will have convinced you of the reality of the inner senses and their importance to you—particularly as your personal shift in consciousness becomes more apparent. Learning to recognize and utilize your inner senses *consciously* will provide you with invaluable insight into the changes happening within your psychological structuring as you strive to ease your passage through humanity's collective shift and begin to consciously create and co-create realities of preference. Creating the right mental environment—essentially one that reflects the natural principles (begin with compassion, at the very least for your ego-self)—on a sustained basis, will hasten the awakening of your inner senses.

Now, it's all very well having an intellectual understanding and classification of the inner senses, but *how* do we become consciously aware of information relayed by them? What sensations should we look for in the body/mind as we navigate our way through new experiences, unfamiliar places, and meeting new people?

The briefest answer to these questions would be through the sensations of your feelings and emotions. However, one thing that needs to be very clear is that *feelings are different from emotions*. Feelings *and* emotions are energy forms that help you express yourself in the physical world. Their energy is neither positive nor negative as we are wont to describe them.

Crucially, most feelings act as a mechanism for *initiating* action, whereas emotions are a potential energy resource for *concerted* action.

Ignoring and suppressing our inner senses has led to a confusion in the terminology and misunderstandings when we attempt to describe the experience of becoming consciously aware of information that does not appear to come from our outer senses. Adding to the melee of confusion, unbeknownst to most of us, is the preference we hold for *the way in which we process information*—whether received from our outer or inner senses.

Before we get into distinguishing between the distinct types of feelings we have and the emotional energy that can follow them, it would be sensible to review the diverse ways, or "routes," by which we can process information, as they have a commanding influence on our *interpretation* of that information.

Information processing routes

According to Elias, the initial energy patterns of information, gathered and graded by our inner selves, flow through four distinct energy-processing centers. Each center gives birth to *thoughts and feelings* for the conscious-mind to digest. These energy-processing centers relate to the bioelectromagnetic energy centers we know from Eastern traditions as the *Chakras*.[116]

You can receive and transmit information through *any and all* of these four processing routes. However, you will prefer one of the four, a predetermined (by your Essence self) aspect of your personality that marries with your personal expression of intent. Like your adopted families of intent, your information processing preference serves as a layer of distinction in the construction of your personality.

Below is Elias's list of the four information processing centers and the distinguishing features of the information each of them deals with:

1. Crown Chakra. This energy center processes information of a philosophical nature. Issues related to truth, freedom, reality, existence, concepts, and causality flavor the thoughts initiated by this center. The ***conceptual*** inner senses relay this type of information.

Its focus is upon the intellect and thought-based processing rather than feelings-based. Information enters this center through *impressions*[117] (Seth talks of "mental enzymes")[118] that are *almost immediately translated*[119] into thought patterns.

A personality that favors the Crown chakra processing route trusts in thought and is suspicious of feelings, particularly if they invoke emotions. As they process information almost entirely through the action of thought, avoiding feelings and emotions, psychological challenges can ensue. The ego-self may develop a truncated relationship with the rest of the Self. It does not understand how to process the energy signatures of feelings and emotions and will at best misinterpret their messages. Ultimately, much valuable information pertinent to full expression of the personality is lost.

This doesn't mean such personalities cannot correctly process feelings and emotions at all, but understanding and utilizing them will be a constant challenge.

2. Throat Chakra. This energy center processes information relating to our interactions with others. This covers a broad spectrum of exchanges within Consciousness that span both the nonphysical and physical realms.

Interactions are "energy exchanges" that occur within and between our Essence selves; between our Essence selves and various layers within Consciousness; and between our outer selves and physical *others*—from rocks, trees, dogs, and spiders, to children, adults, communities, and countries.

The Throat chakra deals with mental enzymes concerned with *collectivity* and "bringing things together." Information travels into and out of this center on a bed of *sensations*—a subtle form of feelings, not overly imbued with emotional energy. This center thus produces more of a mix of thoughts and feelings, and is again associated with our ***conceptual*** inner senses although there is openness to the ***empathic*** senses that include emotional energy.

The primary physical structures associated with processing this type of information are the pituitary gland, hypothalamus, thalamus, thyroid gland, and thymus gland.

Personalities that favor this processing route are relatively rare. They lean towards further processing to be thought-based but bring into consideration feelings and their inclusion in deliberations.

3. Solar Plexus Chakra. This center is involved with processing information concerned with artistic expression. As you can imagine, this subject matter covers another broad spectrum. Associated with our ***empathic*** set of inner senses, the priority is on *feelings* when first translating the *psycho-electric data.*[120]

Information arrives on a bed of pure feeling, expressed later with an emotional intensity that links to those feelings. The center still generates thoughts, and they play their part in further processing, but the focus is upon feelings and any emotional energy that may adhere to them. Personalities that favor this route to physical expression *trust* their feelings and the expression of their emotions.

Feelings are energy forms that signal information from our inner self is available for processing. Our personal feeling-tone within us initiates the inner self's capture of these signals for initial processing through our *body-consciousness*[121] and this energy center. Feelings are a language of the *electric field,*[122] a way of communicating within our Self.

Personalities that prefer this way of processing information are apt to pay attention to their emotions. However, because of beliefs and our confusion over feelings and emotions, this doesn't mean that such individuals have an easier time of processing information.

Physical structures allied to the solar plexus center are the stomach (hence that *gut feeling*), the gallbladder, the liver, pancreas, small intestinal tract, and diaphragm.

4. Base Chakra. This center processes information pertaining to our spiritual self. Information received relates to our physical self's relationship to nature, to our Essence self, and to Consciousness itself. One's capacity for translating this information will reflect one's desire to connect. Religions are born of our desire to connect to the spiritual realm, each telling their own story of how we can achieve connection.

Empathic inner senses are again integral to the relay of this information. The center's physical presence is around the base of the spine. Apart from processing spiritual information, it also functions as an anchoring station for all energies contributing to the physical self.

The receiving mechanism, the bed on which this information lies, is one of *feeling* again, except this is a feeling that does not form a direct link to emotional energy. We may sense this feeling as a form of direct insight, or direct *knowing*. Thought is not directly involved with the feeling, but we can generate a peculiar *quality* of thought after processing this feeling.

You might regard the feeling as a direct awareness of the natural power of Divine Love.

Prominent religious figures, such as Mother Teresa of the Catholic Faith and the Dalai Lama, are examples of personalities that exhibit a preference for processing inner information via this energy center.

Remember that these four information processing styles are *all* included within your personality. You have chosen a preferred style, but by listening to the feelings and emotions presented by your inner self, you can become receptive to the others.

The dominant processing routes are the Crown chakra, reliant on thought as a path to expression, and the Solar Plexus chakra, reliant on emotions. Perhaps contrary to what we might expect, according to Elias, most people prefer to process information through the Solar Plexus chakra. This is because, of all our inner senses, it's the Empathic ones that hold our attention—just as with our outer senses, sight, followed by hearing, take precedence.

In summary, most of us process information either through our thoughts or through our emotions and allow these energies to dictate the expression of our personality. Personalities that choose the Throat and Base chakra routes to expression are far less common amongst us.

Feelings are different from emotions

Now that you are familiar with the information processing routes, let's explore the differences between feelings and emotions as described in the metaphysical literature. First though, it is important to remember that feelings and emotions have one thing in common—they are both *independent* electromagnetic energy forms.

Feelings are an integral part of how your physical self functions. They are part of the mechanics of how you express your Self in the physical realm. An emotion, on the other hand, maintains an existence in the electric field and is not a part of your physical expression unless you invite it to be so. As with thoughts, emotions do not require a host mind to exist and you can choose to entertain them in your mind or not.

Feelings alert the conscious-mind to information or knowledge about to transfer *directly* from the inner self and/or body-consciousness. In short, they are a signaling mechanism. The transfer may seem instantaneous, or when the signal is of the ***emotional-signal***[123] variety, a momentary delay occurs for purposes of conscious acknowledgement. We are yet to understand the significance of the delay, although according to

Elias, it is a crucial moment of choice between ***re*-acting** to the impending information or taking more considered action.

Emotions are not signaling mechanisms. They gain conscious awareness through the preceding emotional-signal, as they usually, not always, enter processing through the solar plexus chakra route. Feelings are very often a stimulus to act, with the emotional-signal type of feeling informing you of emotional energy held in readiness should you do so.

Recall the *Touching Your Tone* exercise from *Chapter* 3. Its aim is to put you in touch with your Essence self's unique energy identity within Consciousness, its *vibrational signature* or ***feeling-tone***.[124] Your feeling-tone is not a feeling as such. It is a facet of your Essence self that allows you to identify the feeling-tones of other energy forms. Acting as a form of language to yourself, its interpretation depends upon the beliefs you hold and which of the information processing routes you favor.

An emotionally-focused person (Solar Plexus Chakra route) tends to translate the feeling-tone information into an *emotional-signal feeling*. For example, if Mrs. Solar Plexus is looking to move to a new home, and on entering a prospective property, senses something about the place, the tonal information she's sensing is immediately translated into a recognizable emotional-signal—sadness, joyfulness, or perhaps a feeling of oppressiveness. As an emotional-signal feeling is different from the feeling-tone itself, information from the feeling-tone can become unclear.

We need to tune into our feeling-tone and get familiar with its qualities before we can sense its messages without distortion. When you accomplish this for yourself, it will become an incredibly useful instrument for everyday interactions. You'll be able to recognize the vibrational signatures of other individuals, places, and objects. With practice, this quiet inner voice will be as loud in your conscious-mind as the voice of your ego-self.

In case you are equating a feeling-tone message with an ***impulse***,[125] note that they are different forms of communication from your Essence. The distinction lies in the *nature* of the communication. Information offered by your feeling-tone is to do with the *identification* of other vibrational signatures. Impulses are direct *instructional* prompts for you to direct your physical actions in a certain way.

Feeling-tones aside, we constantly equate the *feeling* of an emotional-signal with the emotion that follows it, which is why we believe such *signals* to be the same as emotions, thereby confusing the two differing forms of energy and distorting the information contained within them.

Feelings associate with the body-consciousness, emotions with the personality

Another factor that distinguishes feelings from emotions is the way in which the inner self handles them. The inner self will only send feelings to the conscious-mind after it has consulted the body-consciousness. This is because the layer of the Self that *feels* feelings and generates a high proportion of them is the body-consciousness. The inner self and body-consciousness work in harmony to offer the conscious-mind the *information* contained within feelings and ***the strength of any feeling*** indicates the level of importance your inner self puts upon the information in transmission.

Emotions, on the other hand, *belong* to the personality. They are the connective forces that bind the spiritual self to the physical self. Therefore, the inner self will work with the personality when dealing with emotional energy.

The personality is the portion of the Self that manages and channels emotional resources. It is responsible for holding emotional energy from immediate release and does so under instruction from the inner self—usually with a regard for overall health. It will also hold emotional energy when instructed by the ego-self—often delusive instruction formulated from fearful beliefs.

If your personality holds an emotion's energy to it, it does so for a reason. Any subsequent release of this energy becomes a *significant event* as the emotional energy has gained *important psychological meaning*. This meaning changes the emotion from its pure energy form to an energy form *with a communication*.[126]

The strength of any emotion, following an emotional-signal type of feeling, indicates the level of importance your inner self assigns to the *psychological communication* carried by the emotion.

Feeling inspired

Most feelings are to do with relaying information to the conscious-mind as instantaneously as possible. An experience that virtually all of us have enjoyed that illustrates the immediacy of feelings is feeling inspired. When we ***think*** about it, inspiration is an experience that often puzzles us—in the sense that we wonder where the idea came from that accompanies the feeling. We may assign it to an active imagination, but we will intuitively know that it came from our inner self to *inspire*[127] us along our life's intentional path.

Remember that in the subconscious library the inner self hands over its collection of information to the body-consciousness for translation into physical energy terms. The body-consciousness then filters the patterns through the energy processing centers, giving preference to your center of choice. Your inner self, though, can override normal procedure for psycho-electric messaging and will do so if it feels the message is important enough, or may suffer distortion in translation. It may thus instruct the body-consciousness to relay the information through an energy center more attuned to accept and express it. In the case of inspirational information, this would be the Throat chakra center. This center produces a mental *sensation* that precedes thought processing in the conscious-mind.

Although the body-consciousness can itself generate a feeling and relay it immediately to the conscious-mind (think sitting on an angry wasp), the inner self is almost always collaborating with the body-consciousness when instigating the feeling of pain—whether psychological, emotional, or physical in nature. Physical pain is of course a direct communication to the conscious-mind that we should act immediately.

An enduring physical pain, along with emotional and psychological pain, communicates that your beliefs need serious review and adjustment.

Many of us dismiss feelings (even pain) as unimportant, even though we constantly receive numerous kinds of feeling signals. They come as sensations through the Throat chakra; a sense of awareness of our internal state (emotional-signal) through the Solar Plexus chakra; and feelings akin to intuition, but more profound, signaling a direct awareness of the vitality of Divine Love, through the Base chakra. We can also throw *impulses* and *impressions* into the mix of energy forms that vie for attention in our conscious-minds.

Please note that if you ignore a negative feeling it is likely to persist, escalate in intensity, and eventually become mentally, emotionally, or physically debilitating.

Dealing with a "negative" feeling

If you sense a negative feeling when talking with someone, it can mean your Essence self is sensing that their feeling-tone does not resonate with yours, or your inner self and body-consciousness are generating an emotional-signal. An emotional-signal implies that you are allowing his or her negativity (expressed thoughts and beliefs) to grow in your mind. Know that a negative emotional-signal is asking you to act in one of two ways.

The first way is simply to accept that their expression has a detrimental effect on how you feel in the moment, so don't allow his or her ideas to concentrate in your mind and disassociate yourself from the conversation. If the feeling is overwhelmingly oppressive, end the conversation; if not, just change the subject. Trust in this feeling and appreciate that each person chooses the thoughts they wish to share, albeit usually without conscious awareness of the feelings they can generate in others. Your inner self is essentially asking you to use *your* conscious awareness of the feeling-tone or emotional signal. It wants you to maintain good feelings about your Self, so choose whether to accept the thoughts and ideas on offer, or to politely end the conversation.

Furthermore, it's not your job to insist that others accept your own thoughts and ideas because they make *you* feel good. Trust and appreciate that the thoughts you are offering in return produce a positive effect on you, but others are free to take them or leave them. You do not need to defend that which makes you feel good. If you find yourself doing this, then know that you are denigrating your inner self by not trusting in its guidance—good feelings are indications from your inner self that you are in tune with who you are and your personal intent.

The second way to respond to a negative emotional-signal is to explore it. If the feeling has roused an emotion, then know that your inner self is asking you to examine your beliefs. You don't need to begin a belief examination immediately when you sense an emotional charge, just appreciate the fundamental message, and resolve to investigate it when you next have a quiet moment for yourself.

Remember that your Garden of Beliefs (explored in *Chapter 15*) contains ***all*** beliefs, but not all thoughts. Perhaps you need to realize that the negative thoughts another person offers have already grown in your garden into a belief and you are unaware of this, or you are denying its existence.

See where the feeling takes you. Is the person expressing thoughts that generate an emotional-signal that has an emotional charge attached? Are you sensing anger, hate, guilt, jealousy, envy, or any other negative emotion? If so, and you find yourself rising to the emotion, perhaps embracing it, or finding it difficult to dismiss, then you have an awareness of a belief within you that requires attention.

Feelings, followed by emotions, shadow your beliefs.

As Bashar (Darryl Anka) remarks, "There is no such thing as a feeling without a point of view [belief] that creates the feeling."

Work with the feel of your feelings

According to Elias, it is important to us from an evolutionary perspective to begin recognizing and interpreting the variety of feelings we experience as they originate from our spiritual self—which means they always contain information or instruction for our physical self's benefit and expansion.

We can begin this expansion by getting in touch with our feeling-tone. Practicing this connection will help us to listen to and trust our inner self's guidance mechanisms—feelings, impressions, and impulses. This in turn will move us into trusting our Self and letting go of fear.

We're used to working with the outer sense of touch and distinguishing between the feel of various physical surfaces. Integral to any personal shift in consciousness is to become used to working with one's inner senses and discerning between the feel of one's feelings. We lazily sort the nuances of our feelings into either good or bad sensations. We then don't fully appreciate the good ones in case they might be sinful, and don't investigate the bad ones because we're scared to go there. Ironically, bad feelings are *good,* in the sense that they have the potential to teach us more about our Selves and the reasons as to *why* we don't feel so good!

Important inner-information speaks to us through the signals of our feelings and the voice of our emotions. You can count on the fact that if the information is not important, we wouldn't get the feeling. If it wasn't *especially important*, it wouldn't have emotional energy backing it.

By attaching information to an uncomfortable feeling, your inner self is suggesting that before your conscious-mind can come to a considered response, it needs to check with your personality for any emotional involvement. If present, the emotion's intensity reflects how imperative it is that you attend to your beliefs. An emotion can *scream* at you at times. It does so because it is in your Garden of Beliefs that you will find the reasons behind any form of negativity you are experiencing.

You will find the reasons amongst the roots of your beliefs. Uncovering them may require some digging but bringing them into the light of awareness can substantially alter the landscape and thus the disposition of your personality.

Chapter 13

Getting All Emotional

Emotions are an element of your expression that you have chosen to be the method, so to speak, of your expression within this particular physical dimension. This is not to say that other physical dimensions do not incorporate emotion, for some do, but within this particular dimension, it is one of the base elements of your creation of expression.[128]
Elias

Clearly defining emotions

Emotions always come with a communication. They are born as a subjective communication to an objective awareness—a message from your spiritual self to your physical self's conscious-mind. Your personality, in collusion with your inner self, instigates the communication. Within any situation, if an emotional-signal feeling invokes an emotional response that carries a negative tone (anxiety, anger, sadness, guilt, anything that makes you feel bad), the communication's essential point is that you carefully consider your actions, if not in the moment, then as soon after acting as possible.

Information encapsulated within a negative emotion provides the most precise documentation of what you are creating in the moment and how the creation interferes with your overall intent.[129] It is therefore important for you to acknowledge and examine the entirety of the communication. Conversely, it's just as important to heed and appreciate *positive* emotions as they are indicative of your manifestations being in alignment with your desires and intent.

Our tendency is to focus simply on the tone of the emotional-signal and then assume that any accompanying emotion gives us license, as well as the energy, to *react* to the situation in a manner befitting the initial signal. If we sense anger rising within us, for example, we are likely to act in an aggressive way. Our actions focus on the emotional-signal of anger and the following emotion's energy drives our actions along while we remain in total ignorance of the message contained within.

Whether negative or positive in nature, emotional-signal feelings can consume a lot of energy, particularly if we perpetuate them. Ignoring them can perpetuate them, or we can use the energy of an associated emotion to keep the feeling of an emotional-signal going—as happens when we "worry." Because they can consume a great deal of energy, thus potentially draining the body's physical systems to a point of exhaustion, the body-consciousness will automatically subdue such feelings when need be. The conscious-mind interprets these automatic interventions as the ebb and flow of feelings.

An intervening body-consciousness offers some reprieve from negative feelings and its subduing actions also explain why positive feelings don't hang around either. Being in a constant state of excitement for example—now often referred to as being *hyperactive*—is also of course a drain on energy resources.

If you sense that negative feelings are beginning to perpetuate, then Abraham's suggestion that you deal with them as soon as you can by turning your thoughts to more positive ones is well worth considering. Omni (John L. Payne) reminds us that, "Emotions are the result of thought; they don't spring up without there being a sponsoring thought."[130] By refocusing your thoughts, you *consciously* help your body-consciousness with its energy management. If emotional energy has taken the feeling to an intensity that makes it difficult for you to change your thoughts, then you must, when calmer, pay attention to the emotion's communication and act upon it. Such diligence will then make it unnecessary for your inner self, personality, and body-consciousness to generate this emotional-signal again!

In a bit of a mood

Moods seem to ebb and flow, so are they the same as feelings?

Well… yes and no!

Moods certainly come and go, and although they are different from feelings, they do focus upon the emotional-signal type of feeling.

Your mood is a measure of the collective tone of the emotional-signals waiting in your subconscious for the attention of your conscious-mind.

You can think of your mood as an indicator of your personality's *emotional climate* (Abraham's *"Emotional Set-Point")* in any one moment. Or, if you will, the *atmospheric pressure* within your personality's Garden of Beliefs.[131] Rather than ebbing and flowing like emotional-signal feelings, your moods have highs and lows that indicate the strength and polarity of the emotional-signals gathered within this subconscious area of your Mind. Alternatively, you can consider your mood to be an assessment of the accumulation of emotional-signals foisted upon your personality by the ever-dubious conscious-mind.

However you conceptualize them, moods reveal a subconscious stage of preparation for future actions and give a good indication as to how you will allow energy to flow through into action—heavily or lightly. A heaviness of mood slows your physical actions, lightness speeds things through. Of course, the heaviness or lightness of your overall mood also gives you conscious indication of the mean positive/negative value of your personality's emotional-signal collection—where your current mood falls on a continuum that ranges from ecstasy to despair. A sense of neutrality or quiet contentment is what you're aiming for.

If you gauge your mood to be both heavy and negative—a "bad" mood—then negative emotional-signals dominate, which set your thoughts on a track that leads to an emotional outburst, or another form of energy release. As Abraham suggests, begin to change your mood by changing your thoughts.

Moods are about emotional-signals, not emotions. Emotional-signals always precede emotions. They give us the opportunity to prepare ourselves psychologically for the incoming energy surge of the emotion. They allow us to *choose* whether to invite the energy into our experience and offer a chance for us to consciously manage the energy's distribution.

Your emotional-signals can lay dormant in the subconscious, in readiness for when your personality and inner self decide for them to trigger their associated emotions. As the Dalai Lama remarks in his conversation with the psychologist Paul Ekman, "We cannot find a Tibetan word that captures the concept of 'mood' accurately. There is a concept of 'latent emotions' in Buddhist psychology."[132]

Ekman states that he believes moods "must be a byproduct of something else," whereas channeled literature suggests that the build-up of emotional-signals produces moods. Because emotions *follow* emotional-signals into our experience, emotions do not produce moods. The energy aftermath of a released emotion will sustain a mood to some extent, although this is because other emotional-signals associated with the emotion naturally become attracted to the psychological state that has just occurred.

Ekman also remarks that he would like to see moods banished, and in reply to people asking about *good* moods, he suggests they are a delusional state, closing off potential problems. Good moods are not "useful" from a Darwinian perspective.

Metaphysics suggests this attitude is a discounting of the Self. All experiences, whether expressed physically or psychologically, positively, or negatively, have meaning and are therefore useful.

For the reasons stated above, moods—emotional-signals—are an important part of our psychological life. Their design is to assist us in the *use* of energy, as we allow emotional energy to flow into the physical dimension through our Selves.

Emotions are not reactions

Regardless of how positively we label them, ***all*** emotions act as carrier waves of communication from the radio station of our inner self to the receiver of our physical self's conscious-mind. Emotional-signals ask that we bring our attention to the communication of an emotion and tune into the message it contains.

An emotion offers a precise communication. The message encompasses the *vibrational equilibrium* of our Essence and its inner systems—*in the present moment*—and what thoughts and beliefs, if any, are influencing this equilibrium. In essence, the communication tells us what we're psychologically doing to our self—right now. It can identify the core belief system, if not the specific belief, within our subconscious that is manipulating us in the moment; and it can tell us precisely what pattern of thinking has been stimulated.

An emotion is not a reaction to the circumstances; it is informing you of all the factors that go into creating the circumstances.

In the case of so-called negative emotions, what we are doing to our self psychologically is belittling or criticizing our self. Elias refers to this as "discounting" yourself in some way.

Embarrassment, for example, is to do with *judging* yourself because of concern over how another person perceives you. Anxiety relates to *self-doubt*. Doubt signals a lack of trust in yourself. Disappointment is to do with discounting your creational abilities.

Elias informs us that if we look more deeply into sadness (the emotional-signal) and sorrow (the following emotion) we find sadness signals the loss of a preferred creation from our reality. This could be a cherished object, an abandoned idea or concept, a beloved animal or plant, or of course, a fellow human being. When the loss appears to have obvious permanence, as in physical death, the signal of sadness may evoke the emotion of sorrow. Our mental blurring of the differing energies of the signal with the emotion leads to confusion over their information content.

The signal of sadness also implies that we perceive a limitation of our choices. When we are just dealing with the emotional-signal, there is recognition of loss, but the underlying communication is suggesting that if we employ the emotion of sorrow, we may enter into some type of denial of our self and our creative abilities. This may relate to actions we've taken, to our future choice of actions, or to our *freedom* to act. Remember that anger and anxiety are emotional states which also carry the message that we are subconsciously perceiving a limitation of choice. Sadness contains this subconscious information, but when sorrow comes into the reckoning, a greater subtlety of meaning emerges—largely missed by most of us.

When sorrow enters the picture, part of the message comes from your Essence self. It is *feeling sad* for your physical self! Your Essence is sad that you are not using the sorrowful experience to learn more about your co-creative abilities. In the case of the death of a loved one, it is sad that you do not understand that physical death is not the end to that person or creature's existence, or their influence upon your creations. Sadness is the signal that the loved one was of value to you in the co-creation of your reality. It is a signal designed to bring your Mind into a state of *appreciation* (an expression of Divine Love) of the value of the other's contribution to your life. Sadness is thereby the feeling that has you recognize and appreciate that in *cooperation* (a natural principle) with this other person or creature you were able to co-create mutually beneficial experiences.

The fact that the other no longer chooses to *directly* participate in your physical reality appears to your ego-self to put a limit on your further choices in life, when in fact the event signals an opening of choices, more self-empowerment, and more clarity in relation to your Self. (Imagine that the person exiting the physical domain is saying, "I trust that you don't need my help anymore in the creation of your reality. You'll do simply fine without me or with someone new.")

Grieving is a natural process that releases the ego-self's feeling of sadness along with dissipating the emotional energy that follows as the ego-self comes to terms with the ending of the co-created physical experience. Crying is a physical symptom of that energy release.

Positive feelings, on the other hand, such as happiness, generate the message that you are validating your physical self. Joyous emotion can also lead to tears as the emotional energy confirming your love of life flows through you. Excitement is also to do with validation, even though the emotion of surprise sometimes tinges its coloration.

There are a vast number of emotional communications. Once we begin to recognize that emotions are energy resources that always carry a message from our inner self and *are not a reaction to the circumstances,* our freedom of choice on how to act ***in*** the circumstances opens to us. Many of us assume that we have little power of control over our emotions. We readily recognize feelings to be part of our psychological makeup, but emotions appear to be forces "outside" of us—independent organisms akin to viruses and bacteria whose energies will help us either resolve a situation or make matters worse. Emotions are indeed independent forms of energy. However, they are still very much a part of us, intimately interwoven into our psychological structuring and our ability to express our Selves. Again, they are interwoven in the life force of this physical dimension of existence.

The origins of emotions

Mainstream science assumes that, like our consciousness, emotions are a by-product of brain function. Scientific research does indicate that areas within the limbic system of the brain, particularly the amygdala, in conjunction with the endocrine system and autonomic nervous system, play a key role in emotional expression.

The channeled literature suggests that these physical systems, particularly the pineal gland of the endocrine system, are indeed "crossing points" for the not-so-physical electromagnetic energies to gain physical expression.

Beginning with René Descartes' early fascination with the pineal gland, through to the discovery of their chemical representation in the body (the "molecules of emotion") provided by Dr. Candace Pert, the emergence of emotional intelligence (EI) in the 1990s as a personality measure, and the more recent work in epigenetics on how our emotions affect cellular structure, emotions are slowly establishing themselves as a topic of interest in the scientific world. Perhaps motivated by a resurgence of interest in emotions, Charles Darwin's *The Expression of the Emotions in Man and Animals,* first published in 1872, is again available. The work illustrates the evolutionary significance of emotions to the more complex levels of consciousness in the physical world.

From the metaphysical perspective, emotions originate for a wide variety of reasons. Many of them are encouraged into physical existence by a sponsoring thought triggering an old emotional-signal feeling. The personality can initiate their appearance, or they can materialize as a sudden rain shower visiting your personality's Garden of Beliefs.

Emotions can only gain physical expression *through* us—and

as they take this route to manifestation, they cannot avoid flowing through our garden of beliefs. The personality, though, is quite capable of steering and managing the emotional rainwaters as they flow through into the ocean of reality. The ego-self, however, can all too often be a hindrance to the personality's emotional flow management. The roots of a belief system that the ego-self refuses to address can dam their progress, forming stagnant pools of energy that can sustain habitual thought patterns and behaviors.

When not part of our psychological makeup, just as with thoughts, emotions exist as electrical forces within the *electric field*.[133] As the emotion comes into the physical world through our conscious awareness, it requires translation.

Seth tells us that the translation of energy and information contained within the emotion involves a sophisticated system of interrelationships. Think again of the characters in your subconscious library and imagine the relationships between each of them. They may all be speaking the subjective language of Electric-land, but each character has their own interpretation of the meaning of the emotion as well as their own regional dialect to describe it!

For our ego-selves to understand an emotion's full meaning through the objective languages that describe only our knowledge of the physical realm, our inner selves rely heavily upon metaphor and symbolism as ways of blending the disparate tongues. As biological scientist Lloyd Fell poignantly remarks in his book *Mind and Love: The Human Experience*:

> George Lakoff and Mark Johnson have shown us that: "the essence of metaphor is understanding and experiencing one kind of thing in terms of another."[134] In other words we can think of one thing in terms of another and utilize this meaning bridge to jump our train of thought onto another track: to change the direction of our thinking and thereby change

what we are experiencing. ... So, metaphors are not merely to beautify our language; they actually define our reality, shape our thoughts, our plans and our expectations, and form the basis for our actions.[135]

Translating emotional language

Metaphors continue to act as the bridge of knowing that spans the physical and nonphysical worlds of our being. Up until the advent of quantum mechanics, yet still somewhat mesmerized by the perceived linearity of time in the physical domain, science had concentrated its efforts on explaining actions and events through cause and effect.

Quantum Mechanics—which shows that events can occur simultaneously, thus doing away with time as it crosses space—heralds a new understanding of other *fields* of existence. Fields of existence, not least quantum fields, begin to appear that require explanations that we can only possibly understand using metaphors. Once we have a grasp of the concept through metaphor, we can then go about rewriting and embellishing our vocabularies.

Albert Einstein, after providing us with the definitive mathematical metaphor for the physical field ($E = mc^2$), also sensed that we require something else to explain the actions of physical bodies—another field of action, a "subtle force," was at work in nature. *New Scientist*[136] quotes him as taking inspiration from the work of James Clerk Maxwell (1831–1879) on electromagnetic fields and his subsequent equations in formulating relativity theory.

Other notable field metaphors to help us understand our dimensions of existence come from the physicist David Bohm (1917–1992), who proposed an "implicate order" to explain the fields of existence outside, but not separate from, the physical dimension—which he named the "explicate order"; and the biologist Rupert Sheldrake offers "morphogenetic fields" to explain *A New Science of Life.*[137]

Metaphors are the medium of explanation for concepts that are new to us and contain great subtlety of meaning. Quantum theory has taken science into a land where metaphors ease our understanding of the language of subjectivity. It revolutionizes scientific thinking and is a progression from not so long ago when Seth remarked:

> The trouble has been that your scientists see or perceive electrical and chemical systems, for example, *only in their relationship with the physical system* [my emphasis]. They do not realize that these systems exist in universe actualities of their own. And the electrical and even chemical systems play a much larger part within the physical system than matter plays within their systems. They could both exist without the world of physical matter, but the world of physical matter could not exist without them.[138]

Emotions act as the driving energies behind our actions and they inform us of the nature of our subjective world—*in the present moment*. To some degree, emotions are metaphors in themselves, a stage in translation of the information captured by our inner senses. They are, Seth tells us, "the outer extensions of our inner senses."

Abraham suggests that just as your outer physical senses interpret the vibrational signature of physical matter *in the moment,* your emotions act as your inner sensors of your emotional climate in relation to your experience in the moment. They indicate to your conscious-mind the present state of your vibrational offering. Emotions also indicate to you whether you are allowing Source (universal energy) to flow through you unimpeded.

Emotions affect communication and time

Because emotions are integral to our communications, we are not particularly good at communicating without them.

Who hasn't sat through a presentation or speech where the presenter makes it exceedingly difficult for us to remain attentive because there is no emotional involvement in its delivery?

We absorb information more readily if it comes with emotional energy. Whether delivered with passion or aggression, it is the emotional energy that grabs and keeps our attention. Humor—immediately recognized as being associated with positive emotion—makes additional information that much easier to absorb because positive emotion relaxes the ego-self's normal defensive posture.

Without emotional energy, there is little lasting information transfer. Emotions connect us to the underlying electrical encodings of an experience or physical event. This is why we more easily remember events that were very humorous or emotionally upsetting. As with the physical sense of smell, which can connect us to the information of a place and revitalize memories of experiences in that place, emotions connect us to the psychological conditions and information surrounding an entire physical experience—thus *similar* experiences can evoke memories of the originating event.

We are all capable of recalling an experience or two where time appeared to speed up or slow down. For example:

"The experience was so joyful the time just flew by."

"I was in a rage, officer, everything happened in a flash."

"The more excited I got that my team were winning, the slower the clock ticked down to the final whistle."

"The fear seemed to take over; everything seemed to go into slow-motion."

Such experiences mess with our concept of time, reminding us of its non-uniformity—they show us that time is in fact a *mental construct* that we use to understand the progression of an experience.

Boredom is a feeling, a special type of emotional-signal, that tells us time is dragging so slowly because we are not exercising our imaginative and emotional talents. Our conscious-mind is devoid of thoughts, feelings, and emotions. The stream of emotional energy flowing through our garden of beliefs has reduced to a trickle—we have become psychologically and physically inactive.

The futility of denying, rejecting, or repressing emotions

Seth categorically states that ***energy cannot be retained—it must be released***. We cannot, therefore, retain the energy of emotions within us. We must release them, one way or another. We might build a psychological dam to hold back the waters of emotion as they flow through our garden of beliefs, but eventually they *will* express themselves in the physical realm. This being the case, we do need to understand how we can *consciously* manage their energy. Better we manage them, than wait for the dam to burst.

Seth advises that emotions, like thoughts, have their own *structure*. Now, we are naturally adept at manipulating structures.

As previously mentioned, science is beginning to discover that emotions have an electrical and chemical structure. They also have a psychological structure. Seth informs us that when the electric field of action forms an energy structure (like an emotion or a thought), it *commits that form to act* and we *cannot stop* the form's act of expression. This being the case, we must look to manipulate their structure in our mind (where emotions and thoughts appear first on their way to manifestation) so that we might influence their expression. We are starting to do this in relation to our thoughts; our challenge is to do the same with emotions. The *conscious* manipulation of the energies of emotions is central to our psychological awakening. It is an essential ingredient of our shift in consciousness.

Within our personal area of the psyche, to *deny* an action—let's say an emotion (energy in motion)—automatically changes the path to expression of the emotion *and the person's own expression of their personality*. Similarly, any attempt to *reject* an emotion affects our own psychological structures the most, not so much the emotion's structure. And because of the committed nature of energies and actions in the psychological realm, it is therefore also impossible to *repress* an emotion. We can though, and do, create *an action of repression*—which we assume to be "repressing" the emotion. This *independent* action of repression is the energy form that affects and thereby changes the original structure of the emotion—while at the same time affecting our psychological structuring.

Denying, rejecting, or repressing an emotion is thus psychologically detrimental. The characters within our subconscious library (inner self, body-consciousness, personality) do not produce such acts of avoidance. They are always looking to supply us with information on *why* such detrimental acts occur. It's our ego-self that generates such actions. In other words: denied, rejected, and repressed emotions will express themselves, if in a somewhat warped fashion, despite our ego-self's futile efforts to rebuff them. Importantly, they will often do so in an unruly, defiant fashion, outside of the direct control of the ego-self.

The ego-self imagines (somewhat arrogantly) that it can stand apart from action. Because of its preoccupation with the objective physical realm, it has "objectified" action to such a degree that it believes it has the power not only to manipulate the energies behind an action, but also disallow them a path to expression if it so chooses.

The ego-self's refusal to accept an emotion usually involves one of two actions of its own. Either it will attempt to return the emotion to the subjective world of the subconscious—hand it back to the personality so to speak—or it will attempt to set it further apart from itself by a constant disregard of its existence. Either action is born of ignorance of an emotion's commitment to action.

The acceptance and non-acceptance of actions such as those offered by emotions illustrates that the ego-self is *itself* a series of actions, a collection of "approved" actions selected from the many that it perceives. According to Seth, our ego-self, *"on the whole,"* develops from actions chosen as characteristic of its own nature, actions that resonate with our personality's tonal frequency *in the moment*.

Actions, by their nature, change things. Therefore, the nature of our ego-self changes as it constantly accepts and rebuffs actions. This means actions or emotions our ego-self chose as acceptable in the past may become unacceptable and subsequently denied entry into its collection of approved actions later in life. This in itself can lead to psychological discord as the former action, once accepted and "positioned" within the pattern of actions forming the ego-self, finds itself fighting for its place within our ego-self's identity.

The future of human emotions

According to Elias, we can *feel* without emotion (as with feeling your feeling-tone), but emotions *only* come with a feeling—the emotional-signal feeling.

Creatures, for example, do not entertain emotions. They *do* have what we might recognize as feelings, including sensing and reflecting emotional-signal type feelings in humans (pets especially), but as they do not have the mental capacity to reflect upon the objective world, emotions (from our perspective) are not a part of their being. Essentially, from a psychological perspective, creatures remain within the subjective area within consciousness while maintaining a physical expression. They act on *instinct*[139] and feelings that are not of the emotional-signal variety, which means there is no translation of communication required before they act. Without an *objective* awareness, a self-reflective conscious-mind, the communications of emotions are not necessary.[140]

Before an ego-self evolved as part of our psychological structuring, feelings served as they do for many life forms—as the stimuli to action. Objective awareness and a self-reflective conscious-mind heralded the need for a means of communication between the spiritual self and the physical self. Our collective shift in consciousness brings a further evolutionary step to the expression of our physical self. It is a realization, in every sense of the word, and appreciation that emotions not only provide the energy to drive our outer physical actions, but also *inform* us of our inner motivation and psychological health.

In the coming years, we move from ego-self-awareness to total Self-awareness. We progress from the ego's reflections on its little-self, prone to misconceptions, fears, and habitual reactions, to a *Whole-Self*-reflective ability.

Our Self-reflective focus will be upon reading the communication of emotions and acting upon these instead of focusing on only the *emotional-signals* that precede them. We will come to realize that emotions are the life force of this physical plane, as they are integral to its expression *through* our Selves.

It is primarily because our conscious-minds are under instruction from our ego-selves to ignore incoming information associated with feelings and any subsequent emotions, that we remain in abject confusion as to their true nature and importance to our well-being. Until we fully understand them, we will continue to react to certain situations rather than respond to them in a fully informed, objective, and self-developing manner.

Anger, for example, is a negative emotion that contains the message from our inner self that at this moment, as our conscious-mind assesses the situation, we cannot see a choice as to how to act. We *re-act* to the emotional-signal of anger by utilizing the emotional energy that follows—usually in an aggressive manner—and then allow ourselves to think such behavior is "normal" for the situation. We lose or ignore the emotional communication, the element that can prevent us from reacting the same way in similar situations, and the anger persists as a force that closes our choices—choices that are always to do with following the healthy path of our intent and purpose. We *always* have choices; anger tells us that we cannot *see* the choices because of a belief we hold.

We need to train our ego-selves to allow emotions to flow through us with acceptance. They are, after all, *energy in motion* (E-motion), they will pass, and others will replace them. When our ego-self attempts to hold onto them or rebuff them (usually because of fears), they are made stronger and less manageable. Seth advises us that, "the validity and strength of emotions cannot be overestimated." They are a representation of the vitality of the universe, just one stage of translation away from the energy of Consciousness itself, as it seeks expression and experience through you, the individual. This vitality: "has been tinged psychologically in its entry through the subconscious, but that is all."[141] Here's a concluding quote from Seth on feelings and emotions:

> Yet the soul is above all a fountain of energy, creativity, and action that ***shows*** its characteristics in life precisely through the ever-changing emotions.
>
> Trusted, your feelings will lead you to psychological and spiritual states of mystic understanding, calm, and peacefulness. Followed, your emotions will lead you to deep understandings, but you cannot have a physical self without emotions any more than you can have a day without weather.[142]

Part III

Belief In Your Self

Chapter 14

Think About This

The physical reality you create for yourself is the result of a production process begun in the nonphysical realm of the psyche. It's a process that involves a turbulent mix of key elements—intent, feelings, emotions, thoughts, beliefs, loves, wants, and desires—and the intensity of these energies within your Self.

Hopefully, now with a better understanding of what's involved with intent, feelings, and emotions we can move on to clarify how ***thoughts*** and ***beliefs*** contribute to the reality production process.

Here's a thought

We already know that Consciousness wants to know itself through experience, and one way in which it can do this is to explore the possibilities of materialization—create physical, objective, realities. Materialization, though, does not confine itself to what we consider the one reality, the physical dimension we are all familiar with. It involves other realities, other planes of existence that intermesh with one another. Now when it comes to materializing a life form within a physical dimension, such as a human being, a whole bunch of other fields of reality (not least several *electrical fields of action*) interlink with and project themselves into the physical construction. Our physical body exists within the physical field, but the materialization of *our* consciousness (individuated as it is from Consciousness) involves various other "bodies" existing in a variety of fields of expression.[143]

To ease any confusion, I'll keep the number of "electrical fields of action" to the one phrase—*electric field*—and the various bodies involved in our materialization to two basic ones—our physical material body and our *electrical body*.[144]

Our physical body, then, comes with an electrical body, a subtly layered energy structure that science is beginning to detect and describe—the electromagnetic energy body (popularly known as the Chakra system[145]), and the *human aura*,[146] for example.

Long-standing thinking attributes our aura, or auric field, with qualities similar to an electromagnetic field. In the 1840s and 50s, the magnificently named Baron Dr. Karl Ludwig von Reichenbach, while investigating the similarities, declared that what he termed the "Odic force" differed from electromagnetism in a significant way. He found an inversion of the magnetic polarities within this force. Contrary to the familiar principles in magnetics of like repelling like and opposites attracting, within our Odic force like attracts like.

The good doctor described this Odic force as an "emanation" present in most things, but particularly living things. We can but reflect on whether von Reichenbach's discovery may have been an early scientific recognition of Law of Attraction mentioned in metaphysical literature.

Electric fields of action

Our physical body's survival rests upon our electrical body. Our body-consciousness regulates its health and thus our physical health. Our subconscious area is the place of contact between our physical and electrical body. By exploring the subconscious, we can become aware of and appreciate other fields of realities and the subtle forces contributing to the entire process of reality creation.

Often, the information that enters our subconscious from the electric field requires translation. There are various "languages" within the electric field, each with their own grammatical laws, which need decoding by our physical self. Dreams for example (the "language of our psyche") exist as a field of electrical reality, with a symbolic language we are all aware of but have a tough time translating.

Deciphering information from the electric field is *usually* where the brain and its specialized neural cells come in. Our brain is our main decoding center—the central processor if you will. It is the physical place where information from the electric field transforms into human instruction.

Neurology, however, has shown us that electrochemical actions occur at the cellular level in the brain and the rest of the nervous system. Neural cells (neurons) are found in various other places in the body, not just the brain—the heart, spinal column, and gut, for example. A nerve cell passes electrical or chemical signals to other cells (neural or otherwise) through its synapses. We can imagine these actions to be jumping the divide between electrical reality and physical reality. Recent research has discovered that there is a further form of electrical communication happening within the brain's cerebral cortex—*ephaptic coupling*.[147] This phenomenon reveals a separate connection of electrical *fields*, something different to synaptic transference, which may help to explain the brain's phenomenal powers of coordination when processing information.

Neural networks, at least in the brain, thus appear to span the *electrical fields of action* mentioned in the metaphysical literature. Such literature informs us, however, that *all* the cells in our body, not just neurons, are constantly involved with passing information throughout the physical body *and* instantaneously transferring data throughout and across our various other bodies of expression required for materialization—electrical and otherwise.

Thought—a psycho-electric pattern from the electric field

Seth describes a thought, in its *purest* form, to be a "psycho-electric pattern" that begins its existence in the electric field. When the psycho-electric pattern enters our mind, its energy transforms into what we recognize as a thought. Transformation begins when our inner self presents the pattern's information to our body-consciousness in the subconscious library. Our body-consciousness holds together our physical body's functions along with those of our electrical body. It also transforms and translates, communicates and coordinates—along with initiating the transfer of information from the electric field to the physical field. Thought is thus the result of a projection of psycho-electric data into the physical realm via the processing systems governed by our body-consciousness.

Who's doing the projecting? (You might ask.) Well, *you* are—more accurately, your inner self is. Your inner self, able to operate in the electric field, filters out psycho-electric patterns that it wants to bring to your physical self's attention. To do this, its first step is to gather them together and give them over to your body-consciousness. Your body-consciousness begins to process this electrically coded data by assigning it to the four information processing routes described at the start of *Chapter 12*. After this initial processing, which creates *thoughts* and *feelings*, your body-consciousness presents these energy forms, thoughts, and feelings, to the conscious-mind for translation and interpretation to continue.

Independent thought

According to Seth, once a psycho-electric pattern becomes a thought (by entering human consciousness), it takes on its own identity, it becomes an "*independent* electrical action," an "energy sphere," measurable in terms of "an intensity" within the electric field from which it originates.[148]

Because a thought exists in the electric field (and is thus *unconfined* by linear time), it is possible for a thought to be available to our (*and any other*) inner self, *at more than one moment in time.*

This crucial factor in a thought's independent nature, its independence from time, can affect reality on a personal and on a societal level. From the personal standpoint, if our mind doesn't *nurture* (essentially think the thought more than once) a particular thought at a certain time, we can regard the thought as being "returned" to the electric field—in other words, it's not lost or dead, because it still exists regardless of whether it is in a person's mind or not. In the electrical field where it lives, it can "wait" for a time when physical conditions are more conducive to its psychological unfolding in our physical self. Thoughts and other energy patterns (dreams, for example) we have assigned to the electric field for processing later, we should regard as psychological *markers*, or, "more probable" probable realities for our future experience!

On a societal level, this crucial factor provides an explanation for how similar thoughts are "taken up" by different people's inner selves at separate times; or indeed, by different people at remarkably similar times, particularly if their concentration focuses upon a specific field of thought.

The 19th and early 20th Centuries saw the birth of many inventions that are difficult to attribute to any *one* person's thinking: photography, radio, pneumatic tires, and cinematography to name a few. The most obvious example of such synchronous thinking might be the birth of evolutionary theory with Alfred Russel Wallace and Charles Darwin—two scientists with a claim to have had the same thought, or idea, "first."

This is a hugely important property of thought. A thought, produced by our physical self's processing systems from a psycho-electric pattern, can live within many dimensions of existence because it gains an electrical signature—an *identity*. It does not require a human mind or brain to maintain its existence. I remind you that patterned energy with an identity is *inviolate*, and from our point of view in this time-based physical realm, immortal. A thought's lifetime (more accurately *durability*[149]) relates to the level of electric charge enjoyed at its birth—this also applies to its durability within your own mind, within your subconscious library if you will. It is worth noting that any emotional energy present at a thought's birth *amplifies* the strength of this charge.

Richard Merrick, the exponent of *Interference Theory*,[150] when referring to the brain as our main thought processor, remarks:

> After all, as our brain thinks, quantum mechanics tells us that the electrons making up our thoughts are constantly taking quantum leaps in and out of this space-time.
>
> As quantum physicist Evan Harris Walker suggests, "our brain may be acting as a kind of quantum receiver with our thoughts under the influence of non-local quantum effects."[151] So, while the body and brain may be harmonic like everything else in the Universe, our mind must resonate beyond space-time.
>
> All joking aside, human beings might simply be semi-autonomous, biological robots under the remote control of a Higher Self. Given our current understanding of physics, it is really not that farfetched to think that we could be guided by impulses transmitted and received via quantum leaps from some other realm. Our concepts of free will, creativity and personality might well be a glimpse into this other realm, resonating through to us from space as subtle patterns in the liquid crystal antennae of our brains.[152]

Thought's contribution to the creation process

Readers of the Seth material and many familiar with the New Age movement will be aware of the phrase "thoughts create reality." Seth says this many times, but it's simplistic to assume that it's *only* your thoughts that create your reality. To take this one expression out of context and concentrate solely upon changing your thoughts to accommodate your wishes will not guarantee success. The reality you have before you is the result of a multidimensional information processing system, one which includes your thoughts, beliefs, feelings, emotions, desires, personal intent, energy processing chakras, and inner and outer senses—all organized at a subconscious level under your inner self's guidance in the formation of your *perception*.

It's not difficult to grasp that we create our thoughts. What we are only just beginning to understand is that our thoughts are very real energy forms that *contribute* to the creation of our reality. Once a thought has gained its independence by traversing the human mind, it takes on certain qualities. Its identity and electrical intensity give it a vibrational signature. This vibrational signature exudes a force that radiates outwards. It is a force with electromagnetic properties like the electromagnetic field we are familiar with, but dissimilar in respect of polarity attraction and repulsion. This unique force invokes the inner universal Law of Attraction. It is this quality of thought which contributes to your personal reality creation process—it gets the creation ball rolling for you. As Abraham remarks, "Nothing can occur in your life experience without your invitation of it through your thought."[153]

This quality of thought directly affects us because it means that thoughts of a similar signature or resonance draw to each other in our mind, while differing signatures repel each other—birds of a feather, as it were. It is this attraction and rejection process that helps build and shape our personality. Our personality thereby attains a *climate of attraction*, created by the electrical fields of our thoughts—as well as those of our beliefs and emotions. Abraham refers to this as our "*Emotional Set-Point*." Importantly, rejecting new thoughts becomes a habitual action of our conscious-mind as it will resist thoughts of a differing climate to that of our personality. This is why it can be extremely difficult to keep a truly open mind.

Our thoughts also affect others, as every thought we create produces energy fluctuations in the aura surrounding our physical body. Our inner senses notice these fluctuations, giving us a *feeling* about another's mood. Ultimately, we are each constantly influencing everyone else through the connected subtle fields that produce our expression in Consciousness. Every iota of energy we transform (under the inner universal law of *Energy Transformation*), such as a psycho-electric pattern into a thought, affects everything else.

Habits of thought

Because we create them, we tend to nurture thoughts as our own, as we might a seed or bulb planted in the garden of our beliefs. We create habits of thought, rerunning certain ones repeatedly—a practice that can lead to problems if the blossoming thought presents a distorted view of ourselves. Any thought or thoughts given too much attention can grow to dominate the personality.

Cognitive Therapy (addressing how we think), devised by Aaron T. Beck in the 1960s for treating depression, marked the beginning of mainstream psychology's recognition of the importance to our health of the way we think. Cognitive Behavior Therapy (CBT, a more comprehensive approach) is now the most preferred form of intervention for dysfunctional thinking. Since the turn of the millennium, an intervention named "mindfulness-based cognitive behavior therapy," which combines *mindfulness* meditational practices from the Buddhist traditions with CBT, has gained prominence.

Imagining that our conscious-mind simply needs to expel negative thoughts and introduce positive ones remains a one-dimensional solution. Our approach to attaining psychological *and physical* health needs to include our *feelings*, and any *emotions* that may follow them into the conscious-mind, as well as our thoughts. Continuing to ignore all the psycho-electric energies in our mind is by itself the predominant reason for any form of ill health.

We currently believe that thought is the sole mechanism for processing information. We also believe that the only information *worth* processing is that which enters the conscious-mind via our physical senses (and technological instruments of enhancement). Feelings are another gift in the processing package we have available to us. Like thought, they begin as psycho-electric patterns of energy that our body-consciousness transforms into information for the conscious-mind to process.

Our conscious-mind needs to consider both its thoughts and its feelings when it deliberates upon how to deal with the physical reality before us. An overreliance on thought as *the* way to process information can create a psychological disturbance born of the inner self's frustration that other processing systems, not least our feelings, become denigrated.

According to Elias, it doesn't matter which of the four processing routes the information takes, we still produce thoughts; but it is the *kind* of thoughts produced that are key to facilitating further processing in the conscious-mind. Yes, the *conscious-mind* is the place for processing thought, but as yet we don't realize: a) that conscious-mind processing is a *secondary* stage of processing; and b) that we have a choice as to which of our conscious-minds we set to work.

There are minds within our collective Mind that are adapted to deal with thoughts of a specific genre—*types* of thoughts fashioned by certain *kinds* of information. We will find the entire process of reality creation somewhat easier when we eventually develop the capacity to *choose* which mind (thereby, which conscious-mind) is best suited to explore and express any newly acquired thoughts.

At present, the ego-self's habitually preferred conscious-mind often develops thought processing problems if it struggles to deal with thoughts that are of a different genre to those it is comfortable with. Furthermore, the ego-self manipulates the conscious-mind when accepting the thoughts and feelings offered by the body-consciousness, which can also be a hindrance in ascertaining *how to deal with the perceived conditions*—the information processing goal of the conscious-mind.

As Aristotle poignantly reminds us, "It is the mark of an educated mind to be able to entertain a thought without accepting it."

A final thought

There is nothing either good or bad, but thinking makes it so.
Hamlet, Act II, Scene 2

The effect of any thought on our psychological and physical systems is an exact and certain one—determined by its electromagnetic identity. This is because an electromagnetic energy system, that best functions within certain configurations unique to our Self, *saturates* our physical and psychological bodies. Thoughts can have an adverse or beneficial effect on this electromagnetic self. Our body-consciousness and our energy centers translate such effects into actual changes in the molecular structure of the cells within our body. Because of the Law of Attraction, habitual patterns of thought and their consequent effects prevail.

Regarding our health, it isn't difficult to realize that malignant or disparaging thoughts can be problematic for our physical expression—they can affect our personality and our physical body. Additionally, as we are now aware, because of a thought's independence from time, it can affect us both now and in the future. According to Seth, the truth is that although habitual negative thought patterns are the main cause of ill health, the converse is not necessarily true—ill health does not cause negative thought patterns.

On a more positive note, the metaphysical guides remind us that the more we enjoy each and every moment of our lives, less problems will occur. By enjoying life, being grateful and appreciative, compassionate and forgiving, cooperative and patient, open and vulnerable, and living as fearlessly as possible, our thoughts become *naturally* pleasant and attract similar thoughts that give rise to more beneficial circumstances. It is important for us to remember and *think* about the fact that we live in a safe universe, one that supports us. Abraham has this to add:

> You are an extension of Source Energy, and you can tell by the way you feel how much of who you really are is flowing in this moment or how much you are not allowing to flow by virtue of what you're thinking about.[154]

Exercise 8: Utilizing Your Thoughts to Feel Good. A simple and quick exercise you can do once or twice a day to have your thoughts attract good feelings. (See Appendix XI.)

Chapter 15

Things About Beliefs You Won't Believe

The thing about a thought is that as it grows in the subconscious mind it becomes a *belief* within a bed of associated beliefs, a *belief system*, in a well-established garden of beliefs.

Belief systems are at the heart of the creation process—central to the creation of our personal and collective reality.

Thought, *in itself,* does not create our reality; if it did, humanity would be long since extinct—think about it! We are yet to hand over our creative abilities to a *mechanism* whose sole function is to translate information received by the conscious-mind. We already know that constantly thinking about something we *want* to bring into reality is only rarely successful. This is a good thing, in view of the number of *unwanted* things we constantly think about. Indeed, this perfunctory property of thinking should be a reminder to us when we want to create at the collective level a more peaceful and harmonious world in which to live—that it's not going to happen just by thinking about what we prefer. Not for a considerable period at least. Thankfully, it's not thought that *ultimately* shapes and governs our manifestations—it's our beliefs that have the final say on what we bring into being.

Remember that when our ego-self and conscious-mind enter our subconscious library to widen their understanding of, and how to respond to, a certain situation, the conscious-mind, directed by our ego-self, studiously avoids any contact with our inner self—thereby missing out on her more wide-ranging and time-free (thus, *timeless*) information. The conscious-mind will tread a well-worn, direct path to the librarian's information counter. At the counter, though, our body-consciousness can slip the conscious-mind its basket of superficially processed information from the electric field—thoughts and feelings. Our conscious-mind knows what the thoughts are for, but all too often leaves the feelings in the basket because of the ego-self's mistrust of them.

Our time-oriented ego-self directs the conscious-mind to seek out the library's archival information because it is only this data that it trusts to be relevant. It regards *past information* as a prerequisite for formulating a response. Our ego-self, as *its* existence began when we were born, assumes the subconscious also came into existence on this momentous occasion. It is aware that the subconscious houses all information concerning itself. However, because of its narcissistic nature, it also assumes that this "self" information is only to do with its time spent on earth, data that its obedient buddy, the conscious-mind, need only access. The ego-self's arrogance prevents it from investigating the Essence self, with its far broader knowledge base, or the other zones of knowledge within the subconscious.

Our ego-self is thus apt to say to our conscious-mind, when the latter is in a quandary as to what to do in the subconscious library, "Now listen, there are a load of dodgy characters hanging around this subconscious area; so, as before, quickly go and ask the librarian geezer what we normally do in this kind of scenario, then we can get the hell outa here. If that weird, ghostly humming bloke bungs you a basket while you're at the desk, bring it back to me—it might just have some useful thoughts in it. We like those."

The conscious-mind must then use the limited data gathered to deliberate on how to deal with things. It is data based purely on habitual actions—*what we normally do*, and *how we normally behave*—which are the repeated expressions of what we *believe* we should do.

This ego-confined data is all the conscious-mind has to work with when assessing the current situation. Our ego-self filters the thoughts and feelings within any basket given over by the body-consciousness—usually discarding the feelings while approving thoughts that conform to already held beliefs. The conscious-mind's conclusions cause us to act, unsurprisingly, in a manner *primarily determined by our beliefs*.

It is, therefore, our beliefs and belief systems that hold the most potential (an electrical potential, incidentally) and thereby have the most influence upon our physical behavior. Clues as to the nature of our personal beliefs are evident in what we *do* and how we *respond* to a situation. Reality itself *reflects* the content of our beliefs. By noticing what we are doing, how we are responding, how we are behaving, and what information is central to the event we are experiencing, we begin to uncover the psychological framework on which our reality depends.

So, what exactly are beliefs?

Abraham succinctly defined beliefs as "thoughts you think more than once," while Seth states that beliefs are thoughts "you choose to stamp as true."

Vianna Stibal, creator of ThetaHealing™, defines a belief more comprehensively as, "The acceptance by the mind that something is true or real, often underpinned by an emotional or spiritual sense of certainty."[155] The "underpinning" comes from emotional energy present at the birth of a belief, or a spiritual *feeling* of knowing. The truth of a belief is something I'll come to later, for now, this is how a belief becomes *real*:

Once a psycho-electric pattern turns into a thought, it becomes *real* within the electric field—the playground of the psyche. As we now know, it has a charge, a vibrational signature, an identity. When our conscious-mind entertains a thought, it stimulates this charge and activates its attraction potential. Thoughts of a similar signature draw to it; electrical potential increases until the conglomeration of thoughts reach an electrical threshold and a *significantly charged* belief comes into being. A belief is thus a concentration of energy in the Mind—an established plant in the garden of our subconscious area.

Our personality is the gardener that tends our garden of thoughts and beliefs. A belief maintains the same magnetic pulling and repelling properties of thought, only with heightened potential—in an electrical sense and in terms of *likelihood of physical expression*.

As we steadily grow our assortment of psychological plants—thoughts and beliefs, watered by emotional energy—in our personality's imagined garden, an overall design takes shape. Our thoughts and beliefs present a unique canopy of foliage, a combined scent, a collective *tonal frequency* that encapsulates the essence of our garden and thus our personality.

Remember that our personality is the electrical counterpart to our ego-self. The tonal frequency of our personality therefore becomes the identity our ego-self cherishes and considers its own. Which means our ego-self's identity rests upon its collection of thoughts and beliefs. This fragile foundation (it can sense its questionability) explains why our ego-self is so fearful of any contrasting thoughts or beliefs that may affect the integrity of how it defines itself—and why it jealously guards its prized *Garden of Beliefs*.

Figure 3 is a graphical representation of a section from someone's garden of beliefs. It attempts to show how the collection of one's thoughts and beliefs create the personality's tonal frequency. A dotted line sits atop the growing foliage to signify the frequency curve of this tone. It shouldn't be difficult to imagine how this frequency curve fluctuates in accordance with the thoughts and beliefs under its canopy.

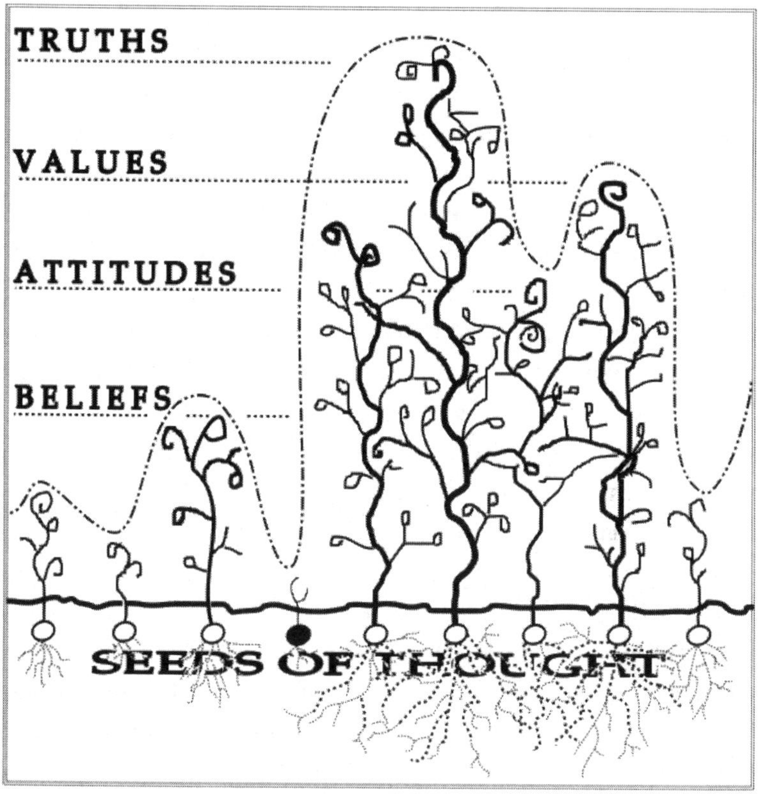

Figure 3. Your personality's tonal frequency

Because beliefs, like thoughts, exist in the electric field, their *durability* is reliant upon their electrical potential—which has nothing to do with time. Our physical self translates the *strength* of an electrical potential as the degree to which you regard a belief to be a truth—***your truth***—and its durability, in relation to time, translates as continuity—how long the belief affects your thoughts. Electrical potential builds steadily through repetitious thought patterns, but the element within the electric field that can turbo-charge that potential is emotional energy.

In other words, emotional energy is the primary force that gives life to, grows, and sustains your beliefs—*emotions water your garden of beliefs.*

Systems of beliefs

As you can imagine, we've been doing a lot of thinking over the millennia and some impressive belief structures have grown up covering a multitude of subjects. Elias (Mary Ennis) attempts to narrow down these topics to a set of ten core *belief systems* that we rely upon in the creation of our reality. Like the *families of human intent,* these belief systems have no strict delineation between themselves and their content. Topics of thought can overlap, entangle, and interweave with more than one system of beliefs, and within any one of the belief systems are hundreds, if not thousands, of subsidiary beliefs.

To aid understanding of the nature of your personal beliefs, we can take the analogy of your subconscious library's *Garden of Beliefs* (first mentioned in *Chapter 9*) a little further.

Recall for a moment the scene of the reception area in your subconscious library. You will remember that your personality likes to nip off to the garden of beliefs whenever it, your ego-self, and conscious-mind call into the library looking for information on how to act. Your personality knows that the garden contains the complete collection of your thoughts and beliefs accrued since physical birth and this is where the answers on how to act are likely to come from. To a large degree, the garden reflects the worldview of your ego-self. Aware of this, your personality takes care of it when it can; it is your gardener in residence.

Imagine your thoughts to be seeds handed to your personality by your conscious-mind for planting in this garden. Watered by emotions and nurtured by the sunshine of attention, a seedling grows into a plant—a belief. Eventually, some plants reach tree-size proportions, a size that indicates that they no longer need constant monitoring and nurturing once established within your garden.

Any gardener will tell you that you can't judge plants. A plant simply ***is***. It exists as an expression of nature—an expression of Consciousness. Your personality views the plants of your thoughts and beliefs in the same way, they exist as an expression of your consciousness. When gardening, we don't label plants as good or bad (even weeds are just plants growing in the wrong place), but we do exercise our power of choice through preference. We weed out those plants that we prefer not to have growing in our garden.

As we become more aware of the nature of our thoughts and beliefs, and begin to appreciate our personality's dutiful nurturing of our psychological garden, we become more conscious of the fact that we can choose which plants we give our attention to and thus cultivate in our garden of beliefs—we can also encourage our personality to do more than routine maintenance.

Our personality loves to be in its Garden of Beliefs. This is because it has built the garden from scratch—from the time of its own beginnings when the ego-self and the conscious-mind first began to play with thoughts, feelings, and emotions. In childhood, feelings and emotions are quickly associated with thoughts and our beliefs begin to grow—reinforced by emotional energy. In our adolescent years, we mark out the beds of our core systems of beliefs, before planting, reshaping and managing our beliefs through adulthood. Our personality becomes our loving gardener, capturing and directing the nurturing waters of emotional energy, as they flow through its garden.

Our personality creates its garden in the grounds of the subconscious to store the subjective elements involved in living an objective, physical life. The garden becomes an organic, dynamic place within the psyche that our conscious-mind *must have* for it to make sense of the physical environment. The garden is a repository of subjective information unique to our current lifetime, reflecting our physical self's identity, the *I* of who I am.

While our ego-self faces the turbulent physical world and tries to cope with an often overburdened conscious-mind, our personality does its best to organize this vibrant, if perhaps unruly, garden of beliefs. Ideally, it would prefer to manage the garden with our ego-self's assistance—after all, it is very much a reflection of our ego-self. Working together, they have the best chance of getting to grips with any beliefs or belief systems that threaten to strangle the garden's grand design.

Listed below are the ten core systems of beliefs, the ten *subject themes*, that according to Elias cover the entirety of our thought processing. All our thoughts and beliefs come under the canopy of these essential themes. They thereby underscore the reality creation process as they are the primary filters within the instrument of our perception. You can imagine them to be ten planting beds or areas in your garden of beliefs, each containing trees, bushes, and plants associated with the core theme. Their fruits, nuts, and berries contain the seeds of further thought on the theme in question.

From a therapeutic standpoint (if we are looking to do some weeding), these fundamental belief systems help us to understand and direct us to where we can find a problematic belief bush in our subconscious garden. They help start the process of addressing a belief, or collection of beliefs, that may be at the center of a reality we would like to change.

The ten core systems of beliefs

1. Spirituality. We've generated a belief system that revolves around the pursuit of spirituality. This system is an amalgamation of our thoughts on whether there is more to our being than just our presence in the physical dimension. The origin of this existential quandary stems from the *individuation* of human consciousness within Consciousness itself.

The belief system has grown because our individuation—*misinterpreted by our ego-selves to be a separation from Source*—results in our ego-self assuming it is on its own, driven by an archetypal belief that continued existence depends upon the survival of the fittest. The ego-self thus develops a profound case of solipsism. It becomes immune to prompts and impulses from the inner self that suggest it is not the entirety of the Self. Such intuitive information keeps alive the prospect of awakening the ego-self to the breadth of the Self—a presence that spans both the physical dimension and the spiritual dimension.

Much of the growth of this belief system has to do with our ego-self's acceptance of our broader Self—our physical self and our spiritual self—a unity within the Oneness of Consciousness. Religious and philosophical doctrines provide beliefs that fall into this system of beliefs and they are at the heart of our *traditional worldviews*.

2. Truth. We expend a great deal of mental energy pursuing notions of what is true, what is real, and what isn't. Seeking truth is something the ego-self likes its intellect to do.

Because beliefs can grow substantially in energy (imagine them as well-established plants in your garden), they can appear to the ego-self to be an unquestionable truth—a plant you don't mess with. Sizeable, established plants within this and the other systems of beliefs often become invisible to our ego-self as it assumes, because they are maturing and "doing well," that they require no maintenance. This means we seldom examine the health of these established plants or prune them into better shape.

This system of beliefs is the cause of many a conflict. The trunk and branches of the well-established trees of truth become thick and less flexible, unable to bend in the winds of change that challenge their strength. (See *Chapter 16* for more about "truth.")

3. Emotions. Emotions are of chief concern to the processing of information through the Solar Plexus chakra (refer to *Chapter 12*). As this is our most preferred route for processing information, and due in no small part to our ignorance of their key role in the construction of our realities, much of our thinking revolves around the topic of emotions.

Emotions themselves are independent from belief systems; they are electrical energy potentials—the vitality of our universe. In attempting to understand and explain them we've grown our thoughts into a belief system. As Elias reminds us, "Belief systems are those inventions that you create to explain what you do not understand." Think of emotions as the water that is imperative to the health of your garden of beliefs.

Alongside the energy they bring to the creation process, emotions include a communication to your conscious-mind as to the state of your overall being. The subjects of emotions and sexuality, according to Elias, take precedence in our thinking as we explore and examine the factors that contribute to our reality.

4. Sexuality. A topic, would you believe, that takes up an excessive amount of our thinking. The belief system of sexuality includes beliefs about gender—what it means to be male or female; sexual preference—which gender we are attracted to, if either, or both; and the sexual act itself—our beliefs about why, how, where, who with, and when we perform it. Overall, the belief system of sexuality generates a mass of thoughts that preoccupy our minds a great deal of the time, particularly during our reproductive years, and certainly for anyone producing inordinate levels of testosterone (usually the male of the species, but not always).

Socrates once said that at least with age (reduced testosterone production) comes the opportunity to think about something else.

An additional area within this topic that Elias brings to our attention is that of "orientations." Orientations play a significant role in our perception. They relate to sexual preference, what we conventionally think of as sexual orientation, but they go far beyond this tenuous link. Orientations are an area within the belief system of sexuality that we are yet to think about, precisely because we are unaware of their existence and thus influence upon us.

Orientations are explored in Book II of this trilogy, *Free Your Self.*

5. Relationships. This system of beliefs incorporates the many types of relationships we have, not least our ego-self's relationship with our inner self and Essence self. It isn't difficult to appreciate how this system of beliefs overgrows and entangles itself with the beliefs in the bed of Sexuality close by.

The relationships we have with our parents, our partners, siblings, other family members, our children, coworkers, other groups, other countries, our God, are all set within certain adopted codes—which are based upon socially accepted beliefs as to the particular relationship.

6. Perception. We have many beliefs about what our perception is. Some think that perception is just about our physical sense of vision, most believe that our perception is formed from only our physical senses.

Our perception is concerned with how we view and interact with the component characters within our overall Self. Usually this is to do with how our ego-self and Essence self view and interact with each other. However, it is also about how we view and interact with the physical world, and how we view and interact with others that co-create the physical world.

Importantly, our other belief systems are constantly influencing the health and growth of the plants in our bed of perception—particularly the belief system of sexuality, with its vines of *orientation* inexorably entangled.

Perception is not solely about our visual sense, neither is it limited to information processing. We construct our perception from all our inner and outer senses, all our information processing systems, all the subtle communication systems within our Self, the energy of our emotions, and all the belief systems through which we filter these reality-organizing elements. Our perception is at the heart of our worldview.

The totality of your perception regulates how you create your reality.

7. Sensing. This system of beliefs has primarily grown from our preoccupation with the five physical senses and how we might heighten them through instrumentation. Of these senses, vision has become our favorite, which explains why it has become synonymous with perception for some.

Our *inner senses* are currently subject to beliefs that discourage their use. They are as natural as our outer senses, but we currently use them either sparingly or without conscious awareness. Consequently, this system of beliefs requires some serious attention and expansion. We need to include a whole new set of beliefs in this system that consider our inner senses and how we can use them in creating a far better-informed reality creation process.

8. Science. The belief system of science provides us with an excellent foundation for knowing the physical universe. The map or description of what it means to be a physical expression of Consciousness is virtually complete. For it to become more complete there needs to be a realization that to know more of the physical domain we must expand our exploration into the nonphysical, spiritual realm. According to Seth, practiced use of the inner senses will eventually achieve this.

Most scientists do not believe we have inner senses capable of increasing our knowledge of the physical world. This belief flies in the face of evidence that many scientific breakthroughs are a result of the inner senses at work. Accessing the information obtained through the inner senses happens naturally (or otherwise) in altered states of consciousness—dreaming, daydreaming, meditation, moments of inspiration, impulses, and synchronous events, are all incidents of altered states.

The success of scientific endeavor since the renaissance period has seen this bed of beliefs become quite a feature in our collective garden. This dominant system of beliefs features considerably in our modern worldview. Some of its plants are beginning to resemble the hardy perennials of religion found in the Spirituality bed. We need to be careful not to create a "religion" of science, as it will only perpetuate a system of beliefs that attempt to *explain* our inherent spirituality rather than truly embrace it.

9. Physical creation of the universe. This system of beliefs has grown up from our fascination with our own creation and that of the universe. The belief systems of Science and Spirituality (specifically religious doctrines) provide us with inadequate explanations—they each have their own myths on what happened "before the beginning."

10. Duplicity. Deliberately left until last, this system of beliefs does not even attempt to confine itself to one bed within our garden of beliefs. The plants that associate with its theme are generally creepers that grow amongst the other beds, often smothering the more established shrubs and trees.

According to Elias, this belief system grows from our notions on duality. Contrast, or difference, is a primary constant within our physical world. Without contrasting elements within our reality, we would not be able to make choices on what reality we would prefer to create! We need to know what we don't want to create and what we do want. Elias names this belief system Duplicity, because there is more to it than just deliberating over what we prefer.

The plants of Duplicity incorporate a degree of deceitfulness. That is, the perfumes of its plants seduce us into thinking that because we observe a contrast, we also need to make a judgment about the contrasting elements. This is right for me, so that must be wrong. I must make the *right* choice here. Your belief is wrong, my belief is right. The system lures us into being judgmental—virtually all the time. This judgmental aspect leads to conflict, both within our minds, and in the physical environment.

Its strength within our belief systems stems from a lack of trust in our physical selves and our ability to make choices. Duplicity is at the center of our difficulties when it comes to recognizing and addressing our problematic or unhealthy beliefs.

A prerequisite for us to move to a new level of consciousness is to come to terms with this system of beliefs. Before we begin any re-landscaping projects in our garden of beliefs, we must identify and deal with its all-pervasive, insidious creepers that smother our other beliefs and stymie our choices.

Life is about making choices. A choice is often a duality of preferences. Our work is to choose that which we prefer for ourselves and allow that which we do not choose to remain available to others. Another person may need to choose the alternative to learn more about what not to choose! There need be no judgment involved in choosing.

The theory of evolution—a confusion of beliefs

To illustrate the process of how a thought grows into a belief and eventually a "truth," let's look again at the Darwin/Wallace example of synchronous thinking mentioned in *Chapter 14*.

The theory of evolution came about through Darwin and Wallace having remarkably similar thoughts on how living forms might have evolved over time. (A *theory* is a belief about something arrived at through contemplation.) It was just a case of who would be able to express their *growing* beliefs first through publication. History reveals that Darwin pipped Wallace to the post, but it does not reveal *why* and how their rivalry affected the theory itself.

From information provided in another channeled book by Jane Roberts, *The Afterdeath Journal of an American Philosopher: The World View of William James*, we can surmise that it was the greater strength of the electrical potential behind Darwin's beliefs that propelled his work into physical reality ahead of Wallace. Events suggest that a secondary train of thought triggered another set of beliefs within Darwin that in turn attracted and accrued a considerable amount of emotional energy. This emotional energy superimposed itself upon the electrical potential of his beliefs on evolution, thus helping to power them into physical expression.

The extra charge projected his theory into the physical realm, but most importantly, the secondary set of thoughts and beliefs associated with this crucial energy *distorted the vibrational signature and thus the* ***integrity*** *of his thoughts on evolution* (remember all thoughts are electrical actions that interact with and affect other thoughts). The distortion, or electrical interference, gave rise to *a heightened potential for misinterpretation* when Darwin's collection of thoughts eventually achieved manifestation through publication. The entangled thoughts and beliefs that instigated the interference stem from the rapidly growing shrub of beliefs about *competition*.

Darwin had written up and developed his work on how species come into being through natural selection twenty years before 1859—the date of first publication of *On the Origin of Species*. He was planning to publish a far broader work but was diligently refining it and searching for the definitive explanation as to why organisms mutate.

T.R. Malthus's *An Essay on The Principle of Population* provided Darwin with a solution to this puzzle. The solution, though, had become inexorably bound to another philosopher's interpretation of Malthus's work (Herbert Spencer) who is reputed to have coined the phrase "survival of the fittest." Darwin's explanation of natural selection—the "randomly occurring variations in offspring" being favored in a changing environment both for survival and for the formation of new species—became interpreted to mean that the struggle for life revolves around the elimination of the unfit. This "modern" belief of the time gained considerable growth in the human psyche during the industrial revolution.

Survival of the fittest became the catchphrase of a belief now nestled within a system of beliefs within the human psyche; a collection of beliefs that erroneously suggest that as we are separate from others, we must therefore be *in competition* for life's resources.[156]

Wallace, another fan of Malthus, sent Darwin his own paper outlining a theory of natural selection. In the face of this competition, "Darwin was appalled."[157] It sparked a chain of thinking in Darwin's mind that had him agonizingly nurture this modern belief within himself and led him to project these thoughts on human competition into his seminal work. In *The Afterdeath Journal of an American Philosopher,* William James remarks:

> Darwin's considerable achievement in perceiving the interrelationship of creature, species, and environment was entirely misinterpreted. His cataloguing of effects led him to perceive only competitiveness, and made him blind to the basic cooperative ventures existing between species and between creatures and their environment.[158]

By the fifth edition of *Origin,* Darwin was using the expression *survival of the fittest* as a synonym for what he originally described as natural selection. This expression, the catchphrase of his thoughts on competition, ignited the potential for misinterpretation of his work. Darwin's emotions rushed him into publication. A more patient and more cooperative stance with Wallace (they did at least give a genial joint presentation of their works to the Linnaean Society in 1858) may have seen a more robust and purer expression of his beliefs on the origin of species.

Had Darwin exercised the natural principle of cooperation back then, we may not have had to endure the fear generating belief that life is all about the survival of the fittest. The concept of *competition*, which should be about an appreciation of excellence, not as a determiner of the fittest, may not have come to pollute the Western mind. Perhaps we would not have come to believe that we live in a hostile world, where every living thing is hell-bent on preserving its gene pool.

The theory of evolution began as a thought, grew into a belief system of heightened electrical potential, before becoming a "truth" by which we perceive our reality. This classic example should be ample illustration of the immense potential (electrical or otherwise) of our thoughts and beliefs.

When thoughts become beliefs, they move from being mechanisms for interpreting information, to a tool that *manipulates* our perception—perception being the overall psychological instrument that forms our reality. Beliefs and the systems that develop from them are not an artifact of our Essence self, they are psychological *tools*, peculiar to our physical selves, meant for the construction of our physical reality.

Your beliefs don't just grow from your thoughts

Apart from growing an electrical potential from the seed of a thought, we can acquire beliefs through various other means. In the main, they come as "gifts" from others. Wrapped in the paper of communication, they take the form of seedlings ready for us to plant and nurture in our personality's garden of beliefs. Our primary caregivers present us with some fundamental beliefs on physical survival, but we receive beliefs not just from our parents and family. Everyone and every experience can submit a belief for consideration. Moreover, it is everything around us that nurtures and reinforces the growth of our beliefs—because we draw to us events that conform to our beliefs.

Emotions govern the speed by which our beliefs establish themselves in our psychological garden. Whether it's fear of punishment for not eating our greens that has us believe coercion is a precondition required of eating vegetables; or that endorphin-enhanced blissful comfort we experience when chomping into a chocolate bar that has us believe eating chocolate will dull the emotional pain—emotions play a key role in belief development.

We gather beliefs even when we are not aware of it because the wrappings of communication distract us from the underlying belief on offer. Messages masked by the technological wizardry of communication devices capture our thoughts and get us to believe in something without any direct experience to work with. Gone are the days when we only acquired beliefs from our immediate family and friends. But then again, from the big picture perspective, perhaps the superficial, emotion-free, social media generated beliefs we acquire are a first step in our understanding of the true nature of beliefs—that they are transient displays of energy which we can consciously manage in the reality creation process.

Continued accrual of electrical charge raises a thought's potential to a belief and above that, as potential increases, beliefs begin to grow into stronger psychological entities. A belief can grow into an *attitude,* which in conventional terms is, "a belief by which a man acts by preference."[159] It can then become a *value* we hold (a more *durable* belief) and then mature into a *truth* (a core belief in which we trust)—which we do not *believe* are beliefs! Notice that each of these terms embodies an increasing degree of *emotional strength*. An indication of how *true* a belief has become in someone's garden of beliefs is seen by how vehemently they will defend it in conversation.

A little more about beliefs

Because our ego-self is caught up in the belief that the progressive sequence of our observations is dictated by linear-time, it naturally assumes that there is an observable sequence of psychological events that precedes the physical creation of our reality—something must come "first" at least, and if such a sequence exists, how can we consciously manipulate it during the creation process?

So far, we've learned that the overall adjudicator controlling what we bring into our reality is our *perception*[160]—formed from (amongst other things) our feelings, emotions, thoughts, and beliefs. What we need to remember is that these four primary aspects of perception are independent energy forms, "living" in an electric field of existence unconfined by the construct of time. Such energies live within "simultaneous time," Seth's *"spacious present"*—ready to express themselves in physical reality "when" the time is right for us—which is what makes the present moment, the now, so powerful and important when it comes to *consciously* creating our physical reality. Indeed, the present moment is the only "time" worthy of our attention. When we think of a sequence and try to work out what comes before something else, we are thinking in a linear-time, cause and effect, fashion—which is futile, as feelings, emotions, thoughts, and beliefs are "outside" of linear-time. They are both cause and effect. Consequently, any sequence of *when* these energies engage is not the issue—it is the cooperative merging of their independent natures that sets the *natural time*[161] of their *e-mergence* onto the physical plane.

When our conscious-mind, ego-self and personality head out of our subconscious library into the physical world armed with a plethora of energies and information on what actions to take next, they do so with everything primed to fire at the same "time." This said, it is possible to discern a pattern of psychological events that appear to be sequential, and it is to this pattern that certain channeled guides would have us focus if we are to consciously control the creation process.

Glimpses of this sequence come from various metaphysical guides. Omni (John L. Payne) advises us that "thought precedes emotion." Seth states, "Your thoughts will activate the appropriate feelings."[162] Abraham concurs with this (which is why Abraham's fundamental message dedicates itself to addressing the way in which we think), and Elias states that the feeling of an emotional-signal precedes an emotion.

From such statements we can surmise that a thought can *begin* the creation process. A thought can invigorate a feeling, an emotional-signal, which can then usher in the energy of an emotion. So, if we're experiencing an emotion, it has appeared in our reality (not always, but most of the time) because of our thinking. Psychology is now recognizing the importance of our thoughts and emotions to our overall state of well-being, which is why the practice of Mindfulness[163] has come to the fore in the West since the turn of the millennium.

Elias and Seth agree that emotions and beliefs engage at the same time—in unity. Because of this, we should not regard emotions in themselves as *reactions* to what we perceive—the reactionary element is the belief, not the emotion that fires with it. Elias and Seth remind us that our emotions, along with our *imagination* (the forming of our ideas and thoughts), "*follow*" our beliefs. Here, I've interpreted "follow" to mean that the vibrational signatures of a thought or emotion will naturally be attracted to the resonating frequency of a belief we already hold that has accrued similar energies—the energy of new thoughts and emotions thus *following* the accrual of energy behind the resonating belief.

Exercise 9: Art Exercise—-Depict Your Own Garden of Beliefs. Under the subtitle of *Systems of beliefs* at the start of this chapter I use an analogy, the *Garden of Beliefs*, to help explain the interrelationship between the thoughts, emotions, beliefs, and "truths" we sow and grow in the process of defining our personal worldview.

As a relaxing exercise you're asked to spend two or three hours drawing, or painting, or creating in some artistic way, your own garden of beliefs. Allow your imagination to provide the guidelines. Some ideas will come to you as you read through again the *Systems of beliefs* section.

Creating a pictorial representation of your Garden of Beliefs provides you with a visual reference for when doing a meditative exercise to clear a belief or two. (Go to Appendix XII for more instruction.)

Chapter 16

Ain't That The Truth

It ain't what you don't know that gets you into trouble. It's what you know for sure that just ain't so.
Mark Twain

The danger of truths

When a belief becomes a truth within your mind, beware. It can easily hold back your progress in understanding the reality of who you are and what your intent and purpose is for this lifetime. As an example of beliefs holding back our progress in understanding our collective reality, we can look to the once held scientific belief in *phlogiston.*

The belief in phlogiston, held by chemists from the late 17th Century until the late 18th Century, halted the discovery of the naturally occurring elements—particularly oxygen. Phlogiston, a belief cultivated by the thinking of Johann J. Becher (1635–1682) and nurtured by the thoughts of Georg E. Stahl (1659–1734)—who devised the term—was an "air" that carried the properties of fire. Understanding of the physical elements in the 17th Century began with the premise (belief) that they came under classical definition—they were of earth, air, fire, or water. Thoughts about *fire* gave rise to the belief in phlogiston to explain how things ignite and burn.

It was the French father of modern chemistry, Antoine Lavoisier (1743–1794), who eventually showed that phlogiston did not exist. It was neither a substance nor a principle for combustion. His discovery of oxygen and hydrogen put paid to the belief in phlogiston.

This example of a scientific belief holding back our understanding of the physical world should be a reminder to us all that if we hold too firmly to our beliefs and don't examine them regularly, we slow the evolution of our understanding of not only our physical environment, but also the nature of our Selves.

> Believe nothing, no matter where you read it, or who has said it, not even if I have said it, unless it agrees with your own reason, and your common sense.
> *Buddha*

Our truths are simply beliefs

A truth grows from a belief we hold with a great deal of supportive energy. That energy accrues through many thoughts associated with the belief and an abundance of emotional energy amassed through experiences that appear to verify the reliability of the belief. So, it's not as if there is a set of unquestionable absolutes or unchanging laws that we must heed when creating our reality, it's our beliefs that dictate *what we perceive to be truths* that hold the utmost consequence for us in our creations. When we are aware that our truths grow from our beliefs, and that their strength comes from the energies of thoughts and emotions, we can observe and manage them in a more relaxed and objective fashion. If necessary, we can reassign our energy, dissipating energy supporting inappropriate or fearful beliefs before redirecting it to propagate positive, life-affirming ones that encourage our creativity, appreciation, and spontaneity.

Surely though, I hear you ask, our mystics, scientists, philosophers and intellectuals have found something in either our physical or psychological worlds—a law, a fact, a constant—that we can categorically call a truth and rely upon its consistency when creating our reality? Surely there's an ultimate Truth, one with a capital T, to reassure us?

Before I answer such questions, consider this metaphysical definition of a *truth* provided by Elias:

> A truth is an absolute—a constant facet of Consciousness that exists throughout all expressions of Consciousness. "Regardless of how it may be translated or interpreted, it ***is*** in itself—and therefore is also a truth. It is a basic element of consciousness."[164]

A truth, then, needs to be something that isn't simply a facet of the physical dimension, it needs to exist in some form in all other "areas" or "levels" within Consciousness. The speed of light for example, a scientific law, is only a truth within our physical dimension, but on other levels of Consciousness it doesn't even exist. These are the *facets of Consciousness* that exist across all expressions of Consciousness:

- **Consciousness.** The ultimate Truth with a capital T. Described by Seth and other metaphysical guides as *All That Is*.
- **Energy.** The vitality of Consciousness.
- **Reality.** The myriad individuations, physical or otherwise, of the creation process employed by Consciousness.
- **Tone/Vibration.** The vibrational signature of an individuated product of the creation process.
- **Color.** A vibrational constant within the expressions of Consciousness.
- **Divine Love.** The natural power that provides the impetus for all creative actions within Consciousness.

The relativity of truth

To answer the previous questions, we need to understand the principle of relativity. Relax, not the *theory* of relativity, just the principle of relativeness.

According to metaphysical teachings, *there is only one absolute Truth*—which gets a capital T to match its capital C—Consciousness. The above truths emerge from this one Truth in order that Consciousness can express itself across all dimensions. This makes the above list of truths, after Consciousness, *relative to it*. They are one rung down on the ladder-of-relativity if you like, they don't get a capital T, but from our perspective in the physical realm, *to all intents and purposes*, they are the truths our reality relies upon.

Your consciousness, for example, which falls under a *"Reality"* on the above list, is a truth *relative* to the absolute Truth of Consciousness.

Another step down the relativity ladder are the *natural principles* (described in *Chapter 4*) and the *Law of Attraction*[165] (see *Chapter 10*). These are the truths relative to how Consciousness creates and sustains our physical world—of which we are a part.

Over the course of human history many philosophical enquirers have been looking for *the* Truth (God, the God particle, a Grand Unified Theory, a Theory of Everything)—*within our collective belief systems* (described in *Chapter 15*). Unfortunately, because our beliefs are a subjective psychological construct pertinent only to *our* human consciousness and its expression, they do not necessarily comprise any of the above listed Truth and relative truths, even though, ironically, belief systems do have an element of *the* Truth within them, as no-*thing*, even the thing of a belief, is separate from Consciousness. Until we accept, and thus believe, that Consciousness is the primary Truth creating All That Is, philosophical enquiry cannot progress.

Our ten collective core *systems of beliefs* are subsequently a further step down on the relativity ladder. Their truths can *only* be relative—relative to the physical dimension and the realities created therein. For example, in relation to physics, in the *science* system of beliefs, gravity is a relative truth describing how all things with mass are brought toward one another. It is a truth that *only applies* to physical dimensions—physical expressions of Consciousness. Another example is *time*, a scientifically recognized *psychological construct*, which is a relative truth by which we perceive our physical dimension.[166]

Usually, our personal *information processing systems* contain at best a translation or interpretation of the relative truths. The *feeling* of human love, for example, is *an interpretation* of the relative truth of Divine Love. Additionally, the way we perceive color as varying frequencies on the electromagnetic energy spectrum is a translation of its truth, which is, according to Elias, that it is a "multidimensional action" within Consciousness.

When we come to personal truths, *our* truths, then we must consider them as really, really relative! We might just call them "personally grown relative truths." Our truths are always relative to the amount of energy we assign to certain beliefs.

The truth of your reality

Even though we create our reality *through* our belief systems—which appear to have no real substance or consistency to them—this doesn't make our reality any less real!

Reality is just one rung down the relativity ladder from the absolute Truth of Consciousness. This means, any reality, however created, even when molded by a belief system, is a truth within the *expression* of Consciousness and has thus achieved reality for a purpose—to purify and intensify the experience. As Albert Einstein once said, "God does not play dice." Neither does Consciousness create realities for no reason.

Your reality, as observed through your senses, is your own very real and magnificent creation. You (beginning with your spiritual self) have managed to pattern raw energy (albeit through the malleable medium of your beliefs) into a *definite, solidified form* that remains stored within your Mind—and thus the Mind of Consciousness—long after its moment of being. How neat is that!

Of course, some of our creations aren't too pleasant, but we should now be aware that for us to remedy unpleasant realities we need to look to our beliefs.

Our belief systems are real to us because they are an aspect of our physical self's psychological makeup—a specially constructed medium through which we shape our creations. Their reality is their truth in our perception of physical reality, but they have only relative truth when we consider their place in Consciousness because beliefs are not a constant feature across *all* its dimensions.

Belief systems do feature and can change across *physical* dimensions though. According to Elias, we have our collection of belief systems that we use to create our reality, other physical dimensions have their own set of belief systems. In short, beliefs are a facet of physicality. As Bashar (Darryl Anka) puts it, *without our beliefs*, we would create no reality and be nonexistent. Beliefs are our templates for physical manifestations—the method by which we solidify our experiences. They are the primary filter in our instrument of perception through which we express our personalized portion of Consciousness.

Importantly, as we begin to recognize the nature of beliefs and examine them more objectively, we begin to release their hold on our actions. They are what they are, an integral part of our psychological makeup, crucial to the creation of the physical realm we have chosen to experience. There is therefore no need to judge them—beliefs in themselves are neither good nor bad, they exist as choices. Our psyche contains *all* beliefs, we choose (currently without much conscious input) which beliefs we apply energy to—which beliefs we grow in our subconscious garden—and which beliefs we express as indication of our individuated personality. What we do, how we behave, is an expression of our beliefs through the creation of our experiences.

Realities exist so that we can experience the beliefs that are creating them.

The experience of the truth of your reality is all about bringing to awareness the *relative truths* of your beliefs. Reality draws your attention to the fact that you can choose your reality! If you don't like what you're experiencing, if you prefer something else, then choose to change it—*by first reconfiguring the energy signature of your beliefs.* Always remember, though, that the heightened energy supporting your relative truths provides such beliefs with a *cloak of concealment*, making them liable to exclusion from any healthy belief examination.

Elias provides a poignant reminder of the importance of examining our relative truths, or "core beliefs," when we are addressing our beliefs:

> Now; those core beliefs may now be identified as individual truths. It is significant to be recognizing your individual truths, those beliefs that have become absolutes which you do not even question.
>
> Now; let me also express to you, in the identification of truths and your allowance of yourself to evaluate them and notice and recognize all of their influences, which they incorporate both negative and positive of, many of your truths are also interconnected with your preferences; but they also incorporate a limiting aspect, in limiting some of your choices, for they have become an absolute.
>
> But the significance of recognizing your truths is that you allow yourself to know that they may be your truths—but they are not true. In this, as you evaluate and identify and address to those truths, all of those other interconnected beliefs begin to be automatically addressed to also. Therefore, it is unnecessary to be evaluating and analyzing all of these branches of that absolute belief, that central belief which has become a truth, for the other beliefs that are interconnected automatically become addressed to also.[167]

Your personal reality asks the question, "How do you *feel* about what you've created here?" If your feelings are of a negative hue, then you know that this reality is not of benefit to you, it is an unnecessary diversion from your life's ultimate intent and purpose.

How can I better establish my own truths?

The answer has much to do with being open to as many ways of knowing as possible. The contemporary philosopher Ken Wilber, in establishing Integral Theory, promotes the recommendation that *all* sources of knowledge have something, however little, to contribute to our personal and collective standpoint. No one source can make claim to be the sole arbiter of truth, neither is it likely that any one source can be completely devoid of truth. It isn't a question of adhering to one source and discounting all others as untruthful, it's about discovering what *feels* true for you within any field of knowledge, no matter its origin.

The process of assessing what feels true, without capitulating to the ego-self's faultfinding interference, is a forgotten skill in most people. It's a process that begins with paying attention to any feeling that occurs when taking in information; for example, "I'm feeling invigorated by reading this," or, "I'm feeling frustrated by reading this."

As we now know, the *feeling* is very often the precursor to an emotion coming to the surface of our awareness. If we recognize this emotional-signal feeling to be positive—exciting, joyous, good—then we can assure ourselves that the information conforms to our inner self's guidance on what is "*true for you*." If we recognize the emotional-signal to be negative in tone—anger, sadness, fearful, frustration—then we know that the information *challenges our beliefs*.

Nevertheless, it does not necessarily mean that the information is not true for you.

By recognizing this negative feeling as a challenge, we can then go on to exercise the considerable reasoning powers of our ego-self to fathom exactly what beliefs are involved and adjust them accordingly. Importantly, we simply need to become aware that the one piece of information may irritate our current belief systems, but we don't have to narrow our choices of action to one of instant dismissal of the validity of *all* further information to come from that source. We can still choose to make note of the irritation and continue to absorb any further information that generates a pleasant, positive feeling.

As we become used to receiving information in such a manner—paying attention to any inner sense of feeling as to its substance, *as well as* employing the rationale and logic of our ego-self—we can become more confident in assimilating information into our overall perception (worldview). It is the feeling we get from our inner self that we can trust as the authority on what is and isn't presently true for us.

Learning to trust our inner guidance, while adopting an integral practice when gathering knowledge, establishes a more dependable discernment. Truth and reality are dynamic concepts, which means that what is true and real is always subjective—it is always subject to our beliefs.

Chapter 17

Setting the Creation Process in Motion

What comes first in the creation of my reality?

To make the reality creation sequence a little clearer, first imagine that the reality you wish to create is a wonderfully harmonious piece of music—a beautiful symphony. A full symphony orchestra represents the collective elements of your perception. Your thoughts, feelings, and emotions, the key sections of your perception, are the percussion, string and wind sections (respectively) of this orchestra. The symphony begins perhaps with a drum roll (a thought), before all the other sections of the orchestra are brought into the piece by the conductor. When all the sections are playing in unison, the overall sound (the combination of vibrational tones and frequencies) becomes the vibrational signature of your symphony. As with any orchestra, a harmonious rendition (or otherwise) of the masterpiece is reliant upon the conductor.

The conductor of your orchestra is the personification of your collection of beliefs.

From this analogy you can see that thoughts look to, or "follow," the conductor (beliefs), as do all the other sections within the orchestra of your perception. The conductor and the wind section (emotions) can appear to "engage at the same time," obscuring any sequence of engagement. Each symphony (reality) you create has its own score—its own *sequence* of play that your conductor interprets through his or her set of beliefs. Importantly, from a therapeutic standpoint, if the symphony is sounding disharmonious, we look to the conductor and seek to address the underlying belief or beliefs causing the disharmony.

Hopefully this illustrates the importance of addressing our *beliefs* if we are persistently creating disharmonious realities for ourselves. If we can drain energy away from the influencing belief of a disharmonious reality (by using EFT or a similar energy therapy), any negative *emotional* energy soon subsides, and we are then in a more favorable mental position for consciously creating the reality we prefer.

In *Figure 4*, opposite, I've attempted to graphically illustrate the sequence of mental maneuverings that lead up to the creation of a physical form, event, or action in your reality. These psychological prerequisites are in fact only slightly sequential (following a linear-time order), more all-at-once maneuverings that occur in your conscious-mind when thoughts, feelings, emotions and beliefs come into play. The process is as complicated as the illustration suggests! It is also largely cyclical in action, that is, the current reality (a physical thing, event or action) stimulates thoughts, feelings, and impulses, which then proceed through various stages of psychological development to produce *expectations*—which are the psychological threshold to physical expression and a new thing, event, or action. As Seth tells us, "*Expectation is the force, then, that triggers psychic realities into physical construction.*"[168]

Emotions in relation to beliefs

As mentioned in *Chapter 15,* emotions do not constitute a "belief system" although we do construct a system of beliefs to try to explain what they are. Our beliefs reside within the subconscious area of the psyche. Emotions, however, are not dependent upon the psyche for their existence and they exist regardless of any belief system. This means that it's possible to experience an emotion quite objectively, in its pure form. We might be standing on a beach looking out at the ocean when an exhilarating emotion sweeps through our body and mind. We might then utilize its energy and check in on the tonal quality of our Essence. Emotions always bring energy to act, along with notice of our overall state of being, but they don't necessarily associate themselves with a belief.

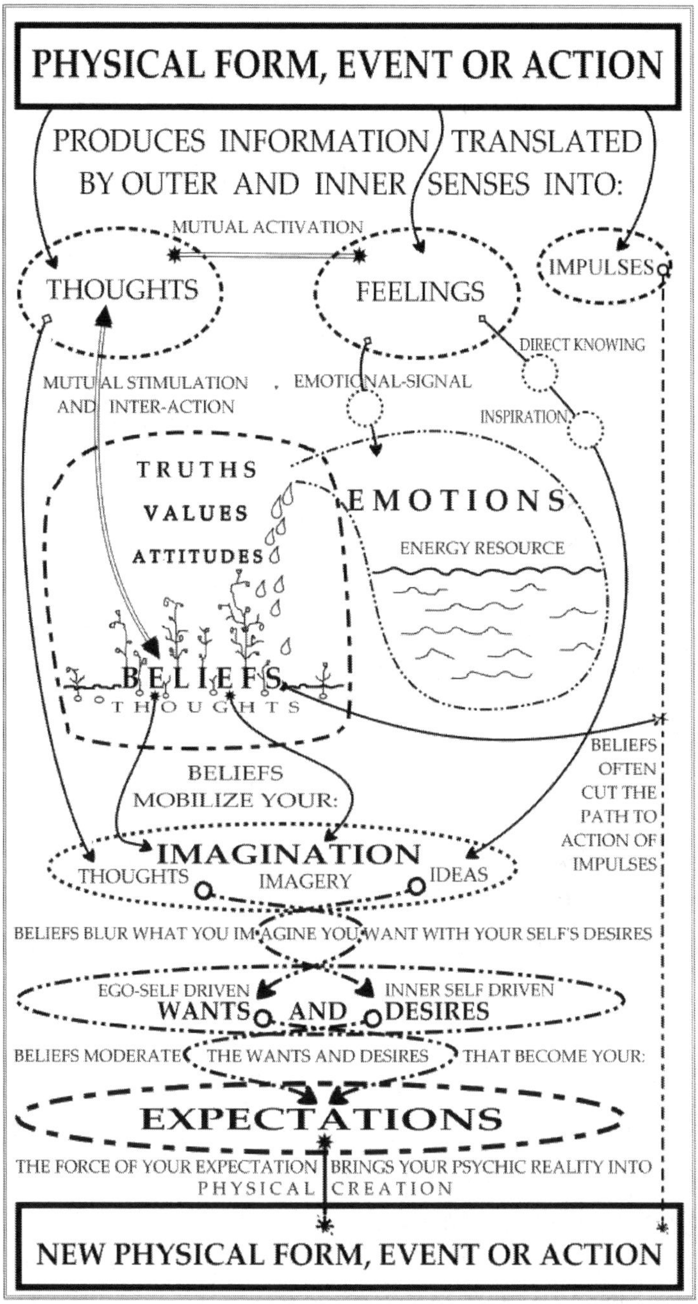

Figure 4. The sequence of mental maneuverings

In their pure state, emotions are neither positive nor negative in quality; we label them as such *as they become associated with our beliefs* during the creation process. Self-affirming beliefs will trigger positive emotions, whereas self-denying, self-denigrating, or self-discounting beliefs will trigger negative emotions.

Remember that beliefs and the core systems of beliefs we use to conduct the creation of our reality are *integral* to human consciousness. They are central to the way in which we experience and create physical reality—this is why beliefs are at the center of *Figure 4*. Emotions, in their desire to experience physical expression—as any action in the electric field seeks to do—can do so by flowing through our human expression of Consciousness. Because of this route to expression, they often become influenced by our beliefs, but at the same time they too become a fundamental component of human consciousness, offering both information on our current state of being and supplying us with energy.

If you imagine your emotions to be the life-giving waters of your psyche, they most often flow through your subconscious garden of beliefs on their way to the ocean of physicality. Other life forms, that do not incorporate belief systems in their expression of consciousness, are able to experience pure emotions more readily.

Expectation—the baking of your reality

Expectations are a compelling combination of emotional energies. According to more than one channeled guide, we cannot classify expectation as an independent emotion as it is often an amalgamation of energies constructed from various emotions. For example, excitement combined with anticipation produces a positive expectation, whereas anxiety and anticipation produce a negative expectation.

*Emotions are not the **result** of our expectations*, although an expectation that comes to fruition usually leads to further emotions being expressed—elation or disappointment, for example. To aid your understanding of how you form your expectations let's use a baking metaphor:

Think of the desired reality you're expecting to manifest as a perfectly baked, delicious cake. Your expectation is the cake mix or batter.

We begin the cake mix with the flour of our desire. This flour consists of finely ground seeds of thought that relate to our desired outcome. There can be a few lumps in this flour, formed by thoughts arising from a belief we hold in relation to our desire. Such clumps of thought can taint the purity of the flour, they represent what our ego-self *thinks* we need for a successful bake. We sieve the flour to break up and extract these lumps. Unfortunately, the only sieve we have to hand is the sieve of our beliefs. Sifting the flour through our sieve of beliefs stimulates the law of attraction, causing further lumpy clumps in our mixing bowl.

Nevertheless, we quickly mix in the salt and sugar of our feelings, the butter and milk of our emotions, and the other ingredients (the envisioned details of our expectation), followed by the eggs—the binding agent which represents the core belief systems that relate to our desired outcome. A thorough whisking ensues before transferring the batter to a baking tin and placing it in the oven—the oven of *natural time*.

In a physical kitchen, we would set the time on the oven and leave it alone. In the kitchen of our psyche, we don't. Unbeknownst to our ego-self, the time for an expectation to bake is set by our inner self, as only our inner self knows the best time for manifestation and how to compensate for any interfering factors—such as confounding beliefs (nasty lumps in the batter), the lack of an ingredient (the milk of emotional energy), or an overanxious ego-self that keeps opening the oven door to prod the mixture to see if it's ready.

Such interference in the baking of an expectation leads to a less than desirable outcome. We are likely to have a cake that doesn't quite match up to the one we envisioned, perhaps even a totally disappointing, under-baked mess.

The resounding message from our metaphysical friends when it comes to the baking stage of our expectation is, "***Leave it alone***!"

When we've done our best to keep the purity of our thought upon the reality we desire, when we've diligently put into the mix some positive feelings and emotions and been as creative as possible with our recipe, then put the batter into the oven of our psyche, close the door, and let it be. *Do not give it any attention while it's baking—and above all, don't* ***think*** *about it.* When it goes into the oven, we are, as Abraham suggests, giving it back to Source—that is, we're leaving the baking to our inner self in the kitchen of our subconscious.

Trust in your inner self's greater time-free perspective on the when and how your reality rises to perfection. You will still hear the ping to tell you it's ready. Be appreciative of whatever the outcome is. It may look a mess, but your inner self will be showing you—through the feelings, thoughts, and emotions generated—what beliefs you need to address to make the next cake of reality more to your liking.

At present, our ego-self believes that having the conscious-mind concentrate on thoughts alone will bring about an expectation's materialization. This is like asking our conscious-mind to concentrate on picking out the lumps in the batter and leave it at that. If we wish for a desire to become real, we need to make sure our sieve of beliefs is as clean and unclogged as we can possibly get it. *We do need to sift the flour of thought*, so don't think we can throw our sieve away! We need to become fully conversant with the nature of our beliefs, for our desires filter through them, and they have the greatest influence on whether our cake of reality brings us joy.

Expectations become the frameworks on which we build our realities. We each have an emotional heritage, a pattern of psychic energies that we can manipulate, just as we manipulate the "solidified" energies of physical matter. When we use the creativity of our imagination to speculate on what we desire and then back this with great expectations, almost any reality can manifest itself. We are yet to master this internal manipulation of energies in a conscious fashion, doing so is a feature of our collective shift in consciousness. Expect this to happen!

Chapter 18

Are You In Love Or In Fear?

Let's talk of love

A common notion that runs through most metaphysical teachings is that there are just two fundamental emotional states—love and fear. We can imagine these states to be on either end of an emotional continuum, with Divine Love at one end and abject fear at the other. All the emotions we label as positive or negative are gradations along this continuum.

The natural principles that describe the vitality of Divine Love (the action through which Consciousness creates) underpin our existence in the physical dimension. We translate these vital principles, or "laws of the inner universe," through our collective core belief systems. As human consciousness possesses *conscious* self-awareness, with an ability for self-reflection, Consciousness *accepts and allows* for us to exercise our free will and translate these principles *in our own way*. Distortions in translation, then, are due to the beliefs we hold within our belief systems.

Human love is our best effort at translating and expressing the natural power of Divine Love. Fear, at the other end of the continuum, is really a measure of how badly we are translating information from the spiritual, or subjective area within Consciousness—how far we are away from the Divine Love end of the continuum.

Human love

When Elias states that love is a truth, he is talking of Divine Love, a *multidimensional* quality of existence, a truth that is only relative to the one Truth (with a capital T) of Consciousness.

Human love and our descriptions of it are our *interpretations* of Divine Love.

Even though our interpretations are somewhat muddled and confused by our belief systems, they are nonetheless a creative attempt at understanding the vitality of Consciousness and making Divine Love a reality within our physical experience. Conquering our fears, which automatically leads to further understanding, and exercising the natural principle of creativity will eventually bring us closer to expressing this primal force in a less convoluted way.

The consensus of channeled advice on how we can best express Divine Love and thus enjoy its guidance both in psychological terms and physical actions is to begin with *a total acceptance of what is*. From this fundamental action of acceptance, trusting in the fact that "what is" does not exist without reason—which is to discern *what we prefer through contrast*—we might just be able to *totally* accept "what is" for what it is! The unpreferable is there to get us to act upon it being there! It's also there to get us to realize that the preferable creation we desire will entail some work on addressing one or two of our beliefs.

When we *trust, accept, and allow* that all creations are there for a reason, we begin to actively demonstrate genuine *gratitude and appreciation*—which is an expression, a natural principle, of Divine Love. Genuine appreciation of another individual is therefore the basis of human love. Genuine appreciation *allows* us to *allow* them to be who they are.

Remember from *Chapter 3*, that the channeled guide Omni stated that we have a "will to love"—because it is within the nature of Consciousness and all its expressions. Our will to love is our direct link to Consciousness and its *modus operandi*—Divine Love.

To recognize when you are being allowing and appreciative—that is, expressing Divine Love through your will to love—take a moment to review your intimate relationships, particularly those you have with a partner or any children. Notice when you *don't* appreciate the actions of a loved one, for this is when you are withdrawing your will to love from them.

Understand that this psychological withdrawal alerts your conscious-mind to *beliefs you hold about their* ***actions****—not the person*. Non-appreciation tells you to look to your beliefs *first* to see if they need adjustment in order that you can return to acceptance and appreciation. If, after examining your beliefs, their actions remain *truly unacceptable* to you (which means they are violating you or another expression of Consciousness—ask yourself whether their actions are *disrespectful* of you or another expression) then you need to make this clear to the other person if they are a key figure in your co-creations—especially your partner or a child.

This course of action is easier to understand and implement when we consider the actions of a child running across a road, less so when the actions of an adult or group of people are at issue. This is because, where children are concerned, our own beliefs are less able to interfere with our will to love them, because a subconscious hardwiring exists to reestablish appreciation and acceptance of a child as soon as possible. In addition, children have yet to lay out their own definitive core beliefs, or concern themselves with defending the beliefs they are currently cultivating. Whereas, unacceptable actions by adults invariably involve complex belief systems (religious doctrine under the core belief system of *Spirituality*, for example) and judgmental attitudes born of the belief system of *Duplicity*.

Human love and sexuality

Human love, our attempt to interpret the power of Divine Love, is often utterly confused in the minds of most of us. This is because we have two overlapping, overgrown, and entangled core belief systems interfering with the translation process. These are the belief systems that have grown from our thoughts on the nature of the two primary energy configurations driving the expression of human consciousness in the physical domain—

sexuality and *emotions*.

Our current understanding of love relies upon deep affection and attraction as its mainstays when describing it—rarely do we see acceptance and allowance in a description. We might though equate attraction with the magnetic *will to love* instilled within us, whether we are consciously aware of it or not. Or we can think of attraction as a physical reflection of the natural Law of Attraction sown into the fabric of our being by the natural power of Divine Love.

Affection, on the other hand, is a *feeling*. That is, it is an *emotional-signal* type of feeling that alerts us to the fact that emotional energy is available to us should we wish to stimulate our will to love—perhaps through an act of genuine appreciation. We can call this feeling and the emotional energy that follows "love" if we like, but keep in mind that it's natural for feelings to ebb and flow and for emotions to subside quickly. Because of this, this kind of "love" in a relationship can appear to dissolve rather alarmingly once shared actions become routine.

However, it may be worth noting that *continued acts of affection can literally reenergize a relationship*. When affection seems to be ebbing, get the emotional flow going again with a simple act that shows genuine appreciation for the other.

Furthermore, we can regard *deep affection*, often felt for offspring or another adult, as an innate ability to sustain acts of affection towards them. Sustained acts of affection, along with actions that consistently correspond to the natural principles—compassion, acceptance, forgiveness, cooperation, patience, openness—bring us closer to being in Divine Love, a pure, nurturing, unconditional love, disentangled from the belief systems of sexuality and emotions.

Sexuality represents an important way in which Divine Love can express itself in the physical realm, however, our beliefs have put enormous restrictions upon this route for expression. Our beliefs on *gender* and *sexual preference* are typical examples of such restrictions.

You may be surprised to learn that when it comes to sexual preference, this facet of your will to love attraction magnet is determined by your Essence self prior to physical birth. Your Essence self subconsciously sets, within the template of your about-to-be-born personality, whether your preference will be for the opposite sex, the same sex, or both, when your physical body reaches sexual maturity. It may come as a bit of a shock, but the greater spiritual *identity of your Essence self* enjoys bisexuality—which means your current physical self, and any physical self your Essence self creates, has bisexuality at its core.

Sexuality is a primary mode of expression for human consciousness to explore in the physical realm. Seth reminds us that too many of us equate sex with love. In the West, we have compounded this erroneous equation by imagining that apart from motherly love, sexual acts, physical intimacy, are the *only* natural way to express love. This has led us into further restriction over the use of any form of physical intimacy as we are now apt to construe this as a prelude to a sexual act. Think of the father's angst in stroking the hair of his daughter, or the cries of "get off" by many a woman who just wants to have a motherly or fatherly cuddle.

To love someone is to *allow* for and *appreciate* his or her differences. Genuine love is creative and seeks to explore—and not just the fascinating physical bits and pieces. It seeks to explore all aspects of the beloved one, including the characteristics and actions that contrast with your own. Genuine love sees and accepts these contrasts for what they are—idiosyncrasies that make the beloved special, that give them their unique identity.

Consciousness, through Divine Love, delights in the differences and contrasts because it knows that all that exists are individuations of itself—created to better know itself. Human love can bring us closer to the state of being described by Divine Love and thus the very nature of Consciousness. By adhering to the ten *natural principles*, we can get closer still in our personal quest to know our Self through the contrasts we create for ourselves.

> **In all of this, a genuine expression of love between individuals reflects a mutual allowance of each to generate and create that which they desire without restriction.**

Love your Self

There is also one important person we need to love so that we can love others, as Seth remarks in, *The Nature of the Psyche: Its Human Expression*:

> Love incites dedication, commitment. It specifies. You cannot, therefore, honestly insist that you love humanity and all people equally if you do not love one other person. If you do not love yourself, it is quite difficult to love another.[169]

The final sentence of the above quotation is a topic taken up by most channeled guides. If we cannot seem to find our will to love our Self, if we are unable to appreciate our own uniqueness, then it is unlikely we will be able to genuinely love another.

When we realize that Divine Love, the vitality of Consciousness, is all about gaining learning experiences through creative acts, *we can experience Divine Love for our Self (including our ego-self)*—through *acts* of acceptance, allowance, compassion, forgiveness, gratitude and appreciation, cooperation, and openness. This is ***the*** way to connect with Divine Love.

As we connect with it through such acts, we begin to realize that our uniqueness ***is*** our connection to the Oneness of Consciousness. We therefore owe it to our Self, and therefore Consciousness, that we express our uniqueness to the best of our ability.

We also begin to realize that as all selves are individuations of Consciousness, there can be no separation from this Oneness. As we are part of this Oneness and take up our place within this greatest of Selves, we will be able to see that to denigrate or disparage any self within this Self can only be an act of *personal self-condemnation*.

By not being appreciative and compassionate toward our Self, ***even that pesky ego-self part of our Self***, we cannot experience Divine Love, or express human love—our best translation of its action.

Abraham has this to add:

> It is absolutely imperative that you come to a place of positive vibration, which means you must adore you... The balance that you are wanting to bring into your life experience is the balance of appreciating you...
>
> And you appreciate you—not all at once on the big things—you appreciate yourself one thought by one thought, one segment by one segment, one moment by one moment, by looking for reasons to appreciate yourself.
>
> If you are having trouble in your relationship, it is because you are not liking yourself. Much as you would like to give the blame to the other for what is happening, it is your lack of appreciation for self that is responsible ***for every area of lack*** in your experience.
>
> When you are condemning the World, whether it is the political world or the religious world, or the economic world or the ecological world—when you are looking at the flaws in the world, it is not about the world, *it is about you!* It is about the way you feel about you.
>
> And so we say, friends, nothing is more important than that you establish your own relationship with you. It is our promise to you that your Inner Being adores you, but you close the door when you think thoughts of lack about yourself.[170]

In her book, *Dying to Be Me: My Journey from Cancer, to Near Death, to True Healing,* Anita Moorjani's near death experience (NDE) taught her the importance of self-love:

> You may frown or cringe at the thought, but I can't stress enough how important it is to cultivate a deep love affair with yourself... But my NDE allowed me to realize that this was the key to my healing.[171]

Moorjani goes on to say that when we realize that we *are* love; that we are, *in essence,* the Divine Love of Consciousness, we don't have to work at exercising our will to love others, "we just have to be true to ourselves, and we become instruments of loving energy, which touches everyone we come into contact with."

Self-love and self-appreciation have nothing to do with selfishness in the classical sense of the word. Metaphysical literature concurs with Moorjani when she says, "Selfishness comes from lack of self-love." Moreover, Omni makes the point that if we have issues to do with lack of *money*—which he defines as, "the physical manifestation of the energies of love and power"[172]—we will inevitably be experiencing issues to do with lack of self-appreciation and self-worth, which fire feelings concerned with fears of powerlessness.

Science on love

The "psycho-evolutionary theory" of emotion proposed by Robert Plutchik, PhD, describes love as a combination of the primary emotions of joy and trust. This is perhaps our best "scientific" translation of Divine Love.

Metaphysical literature suggests that joy begins as a feeling that can escalate in intensity to an emotion. The feeling signals that in this moment we are validating and appreciating ourselves. The emotion communicates that we are exercising a *trust in our self,* an acknowledgement that we are expressing our self freely in our choices and in accordance with Divine Love.

Abraham states that while the basis of life is freedom, *joy is the true objective of life*. Joy is the feeling and emotion that informs us that we are freely expressing our personality in alignment with our intent and purpose—the underlying objective of our physical life. Omni offers this on joy:

> Many of you have for so long held to the belief that the path to God or to enlightenment is the path of suffering. Suffering has served you in teaching you all about who you are not and what you do not want. The new teacher is joy. It is not that joy is new, but that you are only now awakening to it, for your evolution has taken you to the stage where you can feel the true essence of your soul. This is truly a new dawn, this is the return of the Christ, this is the awakening of the God/Goddess within, this is the dawning of a new age.[173]

According to Plutchik, the other primary emotion involved with love is trust. According to metaphysical teaching, the communication of joy indicates this to be the case, although trust isn't strictly an emotion, more a state of being. Trust is an expression of freedom (again, the basis of life)—a psychological state, which is allowing energy to flow freely through our Self in its *natural manner*. That natural manner accords with our intent and purpose.

An example of when we freely allow this trust in our Self to come through (albeit without conscious awareness) is the act of driving a car when engaged in conversation with other passengers. At the end of the journey, it's often difficult to recall the specifics of how we got there! What we did was move our energy from one location to another in the physical realm without concentrating our thoughts but *trusting* that we would get to where we wanted to be without anything getting in our way.

Omni's mention of issues to do with lack of money can

illustrate when this trust of our Self flies out the car window. Moving our energy to a place of financial freedom involves a complex series of beliefs getting in our way—beliefs that revolve around a lack of trust in our Self.

When our mind is in a complete *state of trust*, we should appreciate that any desires we have set in motion do not require any earnest effort on our part to bring them into reality. We simply need to remain for as much as possible within the state of trust—trusting in the natural flow of energies and allowing them to bring about manifestation in *natural time*.

The field of Biological Science is beginning to make significant progress in identifying the effects of emotions on human physiology. It is also beginning to reveal how Divine Love, albeit thought to be a combination of emotions, translates its energy into chemical expressions in the physical body.

For example, oxytocin (stored and released by the pituitary gland) is a hormone produced in a part of the brain known as the hypothalamus. First recognized as a peptide influencing uterine contractions during childbirth and milk production during suckling (think "motherly love" here), research is now linking it in humans with the state of trust just mentioned, along with feelings of *commitment*.

Now referred to as "the hormone of love," research begun in the late 1990s reveals oxytocin to be affecting synaptic strengths in the brain, producing, it appears, a "special" type of neural bonding, which is reflected psychologically by less selfish considerations and more of a recognition of mutual intent.

In *The Nature of the Psyche: Its Human Expression*, Seth reminds us that:

> Love is a biological necessity, a force operating to one degree or another in all biological life. Without love there is no physical commitment to life—no psychic hold.
>
> Love exists whether or not it is sexually expressed, though

> it is natural for love to seek expression. Love implies loyalty. It implies *commitment* [my emphasis].[174]

To round off our talk of love and its biological translations, Seth makes the point, in *The Early Sessions: Book 4*, that Divine Love is "*always* a protection"—protecting, quite literally, the integrity of all the systems of our Self—the biological, the chemical, the electromagnetic and the psychological systems.

Chapter 19

Embracing Fear

So, what of fear?

Fear concentrates the mind.

Fear signals our conscious-mind to *focus on what we are creating*. Its message is to have us *act* on what we are creating (immediately, or as soon as possible), for it does not benefit us.

We create fear for two reasons. The first reason is to do with our primal survival mechanism. Our Essence self sends a direct impulse to the conscious-mind and the body-consciousness in preparation for us to act immediately to protect our physical self. An impulse is our natural way of bypassing thought processing. We have no need to think if a lion is running toward us, just act!

Most creatures engage "fight or flight" as a suitable action; however, fear is also *immobilizing*—which is why animals can physically freeze as a survival strategy. In our case, this particular survival strategy now often translates into a potent and toxic psychological immobilization.

The other reason for the creation of fear is that our inner self needs to inform us of the psychological factors behind what we are manifesting for ourselves. Fear takes the form of an emotional-signal feeling, alerting our conscious-mind to the need for action. This emotional-signal can invoke various emotions, each with a more specific communication on what thoughts and beliefs are at play in our creation. This explains why fear is at the core of all "negative" emotions.

A matter of trust

Elias explains that if fearful emotions arise when we are creating something then we are experiencing a *lack of trust* within us. If we sense fear and there is no immediate need to act (it's not the impulse), then we should know that something is triggering a lack of trust, and trust is all to do with allowing energy to flow freely through us on its way to physical manifestation.

Although psychological science labels trust as a primary emotion, according to metaphysical sources, it's not actually an emotion but a *state of being*, achieved when our mind is in complete affinity with Divine Love. When we attune our mind to Divine Love, *through actions that reflect the natural principles*, feelings of trust emerge from within us—for our Self and for our perception of reality—in *whatever way* (negatively or positively) we are perceiving the reality. Being in a trustful state of being (attuned to Divine Love) removes all forms of judgment.

Being in a state of trust is an expression of our personal freedom to allow the natural flow of energy to move unencumbered along our path of intent. In doing so, we are trusting that the probabilities relating to our desired reality have been set in motion and their manifestation does not necessarily require any further injection of energy, such as that provided by an emotion. We trust in the natural flow of universal or *Source* energy to manifest our desire in *natural time*.

The main thrust of the Elias communications is to focus upon trusting your Self (the totality of your Self, which includes your ego-self, but not *just* your ego-self) because, "You shall not betray yourself!"

Of course, it's difficult to trust your Self when you are under constant pressure from others to trust in them. Making things more difficult is an ego-self that trusts only the information brought to it by the physical senses—which is often distorted to fit within its belief systems.

Know that when others proclaim that you should trust in the universe, this will indeed help you to some degree as it ***is*** the universe (i.e., Consciousness) that provides the ultimate state of trust through Divine Love. Remember that as you are a "portion" of Consciousness, trust is therefore implicit to the nature of your Self.

Getting our state of being as close to (Divine) trust as possible allows joyful emotions to come through. When our state of trust is waning, we move away from the power of Divine Love. Rather than trusting in Divine Love to steer the energy stream coursing through our garden of beliefs, we subconsciously begin to direct the energy toward belief beds that can produce a torrent of thoughts generating fearful feelings. Remember that feelings *consume* energy, none more so than fear, which demotivates, immobilizes, and keeps us off our path of intent.

The longer we remain off our path of intent, the more we draw divergence and conflict into our creations. The more we maintain a state of trust, the easier it is for our desires to come to fruition with less struggle. Elias:

> You are so blinded to your probabilities that you believe that the pay-off that you receive presently is the most pay-off that you may receive! What you do not realize is that as you move effortlessly in trusting of yourself, and listening to yourself, and letting go of fear, your pay-off increases![175]

The key to fear

If we are to deal with fear properly we must first realize that *we can never be a victim*. Whether we believe it or not (and I suggest you do), we create ***all*** of our reality. Recognizing this *relative truth* of our physical domain means taking on the responsibility of reality creation for our self. However, with that responsibility comes great freedom, not least from fear—as we don't have to incorporate it in our creative endeavors! Survival impulses of fear are not going to go away as they come from our Essence self, but we can eliminate much of the fear generated by our ego-self's thoughts and beliefs by carefully *choosing* what we believe and what we think about.

Ironically, accepting that we create all of our reality can give rise to a fear of the self—fears of what our self may create for us!

Remember, though, that the part of us that is doing the creating is our *perception*. When we are aware of this, and that we can manipulate our perception through addressing our thoughts and beliefs, we free up our choices and can choose actions that reinforce trust in our Self and our abilities.

It may be impossible to thoroughly eliminate fear from the human psyche as it is currently a psychological means for bringing our attention to the beliefs we hold that are distorting the purity of our physical expression. We can moderate its effects though by truly trusting and accepting our Self—particularly the physical ego-self with its idiosyncratic collection of beliefs.

We cannot ignore fear—particularly if it comes as a self-preservation impulse! However, facing up to feelings of fear need only involve noticing them, looking to the beliefs that generate them, and addressing those beliefs. As we practice dealing with fear it will become a rarity in our lives.

The difference between knowing and believing

According to Elias, *believing* always includes an element of trust, whereas *knowing* includes an element of certainty. We might think that the trust element in believing to be a good thing, but what we trust in is not always of benefit to us, or it may not be (as we're talking of beliefs here) accurate or valid.

Importantly, the element of certainty in knowing, regardless of the subject, *does not include absoluteness*. On the contrary, knowing incorporates an openness to all probabilities and possibilities in relation to the subject. The certainty of knowing is to do with the acceptance of the subject's reality (and that subject can be your Self), and acknowledging that there is no absolute, no one answer, no one expression of that subject's reality.

Believing, on the other hand, does incorporate some degree of absoluteness. This happens because *duplicity* (the system of beliefs that would have us judge everything as to its rightness or wrongness) has overgrown all our other belief systems. Duplicity has us *believe* (and thus trust) in what is "right"—thereby making our choices more absolute.

So, if we *believe* in our self, we automatically include an element of trust in our self—but this is a superficial layer of trust as it's produced through the belief systems of our ego-self. We can only *believe* in our ego-self, if you will—which is a start, but only the first step on the path to being in the *state of trust* mentioned earlier. *Knowing* our Self (both the physical and spiritual aspects), rather than just believing in our self, takes our mind and body that much further along the path to affinity with Divine Love.

When it comes to fear, it is important to recognize that each lifetime's exploration of the physical realm is an exercise in the exploration of your Self. A new ego-self and new experiences and routes of exploration come with each lifetime. These routes may be unfamiliar to your Self, but the important thing to remember is that they are paths of exploration *within your Self*. You are therefore *safe*, protected by Divine Love—you have nothing to be afraid of *within* your Self.

A straightforward way to defeat fear by Pema Chödrön

Once there was a young warrior.

Her teacher told her that she had to do battle with fear.

She didn't want to do that. It seemed too aggressive; it was scary; it seemed unfriendly. But the teacher said she had to do it and gave her the instructions for the battle.

The day arrived. The student warrior stood on one side, and fear stood on the other. The warrior was feeling very small, and fear was looking big and wrathful. They both had their weapons.

The young warrior roused herself and went toward fear, prostrated three times, and asked, "May I have permission to go into battle with you?"

Fear said, "Thank you for showing me so much respect that you ask permission."

Then the young warrior said, "How can I defeat you?"

Fear replied, "My weapons are that I talk fast, and I get very close to your face.

Then you get completely unnerved, and you do whatever I say.

If you don't do what I tell you, I have no power.

You can listen to me, and you can have respect for me. You can even be convinced by me. But if you don't do what I say, I have no power."

In that way, the student warrior learned how to defeat fear.

When Things Fall Apart: Heart Advice for Difficult Times. Pema Chödrön

Epilogue: You Create Your Own Reality

Know this at least

If you have learned only one thing from this book, then let it be that to change your personal reality, or indeed our collective reality, you must attend to and regularly address your beliefs. Beliefs are a filter to that which is possible for you and us to create.

Beliefs are a part of the matrix of human consciousness and we can't create anything without them. Acknowledging, accepting, and appreciating that the beliefs we hold dictate the manifestation of our reality will liberate our thinking and thereby our creativity. Elias:

> There are many aspects of this shift in consciousness and many actions which are associated with this shift. One of the basic elements of this shift in consciousness is to be accepting of your belief systems and rendering them neutralized—not eliminating these belief systems but rendering them neutralized—which shall enable you to expand within your objective awareness, and this shall expand your abilities in creativity futurely.[176]

Knowing that our reality is a product of our beliefs allows us to relax and enjoy the process of reality creation. Accepting that an unpreferred reality is directing us to examine our beliefs means that we can more rapidly eliminate such realities. Unpreferred realities are not likely to disappear overnight. Duality is a factor in our physical reality creations. We are still reliant upon perceiving a *contrast* so that we may choose what we prefer as we seek to perfect a natural process of creation through the natural principles of Divine Love. When we get a grip on eliminating judgment from our choosing, we should, as part of our shift in consciousness, quickly abandon creating in a reactionary, fearful, violent manner, rather than a consciously controlled one.

Now is an appropriate time

Seth speaks of the power of now. From the greater perspective of our spiritual self there is no time other than the now—the spacious present. If you want to change what is in your life right now, then you must start right now! The contemporary philosopher Eckhart Tölle explains the importance of focusing on the present when setting a goal for the future in his book, *The Power of Now*:

> If you set yourself a goal and work toward it, you are using clock time. You are aware of where you want to go, but you honor and give your fullest attention to the step that you are taking at this moment. If you then become excessively focused on the goal, perhaps because you are seeking happiness, fulfillment, or a more complete sense of self in it, the Now is no longer honored. It becomes reduced to a mere stepping stone to the future, with no intrinsic value. Clock time then turns into psychological time. Your life's journey is no longer an adventure, just an obsessive need to arrive, to attain, to "make it." You no longer see or smell the flowers by the wayside either, nor are you aware of the beauty and the miracle of life that unfolds all around you when you are present in the Now.[177]

This is another way of saying, "set the intention, with no expectations as to the outcome, live in the present, and just follow the thing that is most exciting to you in the present."

Life is a journey of experiences designed to have us know our Self. With self-knowledge comes confidence. Confidence to be who we are and share our uniqueness with others. Trust in your Self and the guidance—through feelings—of your inner self. Allow your inner senses to show you what feels right for you. Use your head and your heart—your ego-self's intellectual abilities in combination with your inner self's intuitional knowledge.

When not influenced by your ego-self's fears, the conscious-mind can follow its natural work ethic—using thoughts *and* feelings to work out what actions to take and how much emotional energy to apply to those actions. If a situation calls for immediate action, *trust* in your inner self, in association with the body-consciousness, to have you do what is necessary.

Once your ego-self becomes less apprehensive and more used to your subconscious area, by gaining familiarity through the exercises presented in this book and trilogy, you become truly appreciative of *all* your experiences, good or bad, and aware that they all contain Self-learning and a subtle guiding principle aimed at keeping you on your path of intent.

Life is about making choices and acting upon our preference. Choosing is the exciting bit about conscious creation. Just choose the most exciting option. This does not have to invite either inner mental or outer physical conflict when we realize that if our actions do not violate another expression of Consciousness in some way, then we are free to act. Conflict is an action driven by an ego-self that does not *trust* in its choices and therefore feels a need to defend them.

Pick a preference and see how it *feels*. If it doesn't feel right, choose again—never act on a feeling that doesn't feel right.

Metaphysical inspiration

According to our metaphysical friends, we are currently experiencing a "set of actions" that relate to a highly significant evolutionary development of our species—a shift in our consciousness. Existing as they do in a dimension where all actions happen in the one *spacious present*, they have an exclusive view of the probable futures available to us in the next few decades of our linear-time reality.

Noticed any signs of our shift lately? Just take a moment to think about the collective realities we would prefer not to have in our now—they highlight our need to change how our consciousness expresses itself, what beliefs we need to address so that we think in ways that reflect the natural principles of Divine Love. Think about fundamentalism in religious belief systems; think about the downfall of dictatorial leaderships; think about the turmoil in the democratic system of government; think about climate change; think about ecocide; think about the greed endemic within our corporate and financial institutions—and bearing in mind Omni's words on the definition of money, the "physical manifestation of the energies of love and power"—think about the distribution of wealth across our global society.

Lilli Bendriss, a Norwegian channeler, author, and speaker about raising human consciousness, makes the point:

> We are living in a time of great change, but there has always been change. We are simply entering a new phase. This phase involves a shift in consciousness where we will progress from the Homo Sapiens stage to the next stage of human evolution: Homo Luminous—enlightened beings.
>
> We are all playing a key part in the changes that are already in motion. The future is nothing but potential. We make our own choices about which future we want for others and ourselves. We are thinking, feeling and sensing beings, living in a sentient universe, with the power to create our own reality.[178]

In the following message, delivered in 1997, Elias offers some wisdom on dealing with personal issues, finding purpose in your life, *believing* in yourself, and *trusting* in your Self. The italicized text is where I have abbreviated some of the original text for the sake of brevity:

> You, once again, shall not betray you. You are your highest expression, and you shall always look for your highest value

fulfillment, and you shall accomplish this.

You might complain that life is all too difficult, plagued by conflict, and however much you strive to accomplish something, you never seem to attain it.

... and you may even express that you do not understand your purpose or your point. If you are allowing yourself the freedom to accept self, and to know that you have manifest to experience, and that no experience is worse or better, and that you are perfectly creating within every moment of your focus, you shall eliminate much of your conflict.

I have expressed this many times, although to this present now within your physical focus, you do not understand. You wish to be seeking out individuals that shall map your road for you, that shall express to you, "Move this way. Accomplish this. Occupy yourself with this job. Be creative within this area, and you shall be successful."

You shall be successful when you are believing in you.

When you loosen the grip of your belief systems, particularly the belief system of Duplicity that constantly has you judging yourself, then you will accomplish far more. But if you continue along a judgmental path, striving rather than accomplishing, and... not addressing to the belief systems that you hold, you shall continue within your conflict.

Do you not think that if this were not so, that throughout your ages individuals upon your planet would not have already formulated the method for complete, ultimate successfulness in every area?

You are inventive creatures. You are extremely creative. You may build machinery to explore your physical space, but you may not solve these tiny individual problems of successfulness within individuals; for no prophet or psychic may express to you a method for accomplishment, if you are not trusting of you.[179]

Where do I go from here?

Seth wasn't concerned with us believing his philosophy or turning him into the next guru to follow. He, along with many other channeled guides, simply wants us to know that we *literally* create our own reality from the energies of thoughts, beliefs, feelings, and emotions. Accepting and *assimilating* this knowledge is the crucial next step in our evolution as sentient beings. With this knowledge we can start consciously creating the realities we prefer for ourselves both as individuals and at the collective level of humankind. Individually and collectively we can set about growing, pruning, managing, and ultimately designing, a garden of beliefs that will reflect the beauty of our individuated Selves as well as the magnificence of the collective expression of Consciousness known as Humanity.

Seth was very aware of the likelihood of distortion of his ideas if we were to assign them immediately to our currently held belief systems. When he once said he didn't want us to *believe* him, he was alerting us to the importance of examining *our* beliefs, *anyone's* beliefs—as *all* beliefs should be examined constantly for their appropriateness in the formation of our personal and collective realities.

The purpose of my work is to relay this ego-self challenging metaphysical material in as clear and as acceptable a manner as possible in view of our currently held traditional, modern, and postmodern worldviews. My aim is to help create a broad yet sturdy platform of knowledge that relates to our unique multifaceted Self and the key forces by which we create our own reality—personally and collectively.

This knowledge base will not only prepare you, but also bolster your confidence, for taking the next step in attaining a fulfilling, purpose driven life—whatever that next step is for you. To better know what that next step is:

- Live in the present moment.

- Schedule some quality time alone to meditate each day.
- While meditating, allow some feelings to come into your awareness.
- Identify the feeling of excitement if it's there.
- Allow your thoughts to identify what actions, if any, you need to take in following up on that feeling of excitement.
- Stay alert for synchronous events (what we currently think of as "coincidences"), as they are pointers to your next step on your path of excitement.

If you can't feel any excitement in the moment, then be *patient* while your inner self decides on the timing of excitement arising in you. It's perfectly fine and healthy to simply feel relaxed and comfortable with your ego-self at rest and appreciate the moment of now. Being able to follow your excitement may also involve facing and resolving any fears born of debilitating beliefs. It's the work you need to do to free yourself from the habitual actions that deflect you from your exciting path of intent.

Free Your Self, the next book in the *It's About You* trilogy, focuses on our current state of being in the physical realm—from the personal and collective viewpoints. The book deals with healing and balancing the psychological and emotional energies that shape our personalities. It's concerned with clearing away the weeds and creepers in our garden of beliefs, taking stock of the beliefs we hold dear, and uprooting those beliefs that obscure our personality's original *intent*-ional design. The book is about liberating our physical self so that we can fully express our creational abilities in this lifetime. This cathartic action will reverberate through the entirety of our personal and collective Self and, as you are now aware, through the many interconnected layers of the Oneness of Consciousness.

Free Your Self takes the exercises and practices introduced in *Know Your Self* a few steps up the ladder of *living* the ideas and principles, rather than simply understanding them intellectually. They present the psychological and physical processes we need to pledge to as we consciously commit to living our life's path of intent and purpose—as Rose (Joanne Helfrich) would say, "living your *Way of Spirit*."

A final word from Seth:

> Many of my readers, or their offspring, will be involved in a new dimension of selfhood in which consciousness is fully explored and the potentials of the soul uncovered, at least to some extent.
>
> Human capabilities will be seen as what they are, and a great new period of development will occur... The species will actually move into a new kind of selfhood.[180]

Appendix I: The Ten Natural Principles

NON-VIOLATION. If you can only manage to remember one natural principle while going about your daily life, remember this one—do not violate. A violation is a deliberate act to end, harm, or undermine the physical or psychological freedom of another expression of Consciousness. **In any situation, if you're unsure of your actions, simply ask yourself, "Am I being respectful?" In harming others (what you think to be "other" than you), you harm your Self.**

ACCEPT AND ALLOW. To accept and allow is to invoke the natural power of Divine Love within you. **This is the key Principle by which to live a life filled with love. True acceptance involves eliminating judgment** while you **allow** things to be as they are. Practice discernment (this is what I prefer for myself), without being judgmental of what you don't prefer. **Crucially, this begins with the acceptance and allowance of who you are—quirks and all!**

BE COMPASSIONATE. Compassion is the ultimate gift you can give. Acts of compassion arise from the genuine acceptance and allowance of yourself and others. **Being compassionate exercises a basic kindness** and desire within you to relieve suffering when you become aware of it. This applies to your own self (self-compassion), as well as others.

BE FORGIVING. Whether just yourself or if another person is involved, forgiveness is about *appreciating* a seemingly hurtful or negative creation for what it brings to your awareness—and that of another. Appreciate the other party's hand in the co-creation for the purposes of your own, and their learning. Hurt is an important part of the craft of conscious co-creating—it brings growth for all parties concerned. Begin by forgiving yourself if you feel hurt.

BE GRATEFUL AND APPRECIATIVE. Gratitude is the creator of abundance in all its forms. When you offer heartfelt gratitude and appreciation, you expend energy and attune it with Divine Love. Source energy (Divine Love) replenishes this energy—made apparent through one or more manifestations of abundance. So be grateful and appreciative of everything you create for yourself. **Be aware, though, that genuine appreciation does not have an expectation attached. Self-appreciation enhances your creativity.**

BE CREATIVE. Creation is a quality of all existence. Creativity is a principle that emanates from the desire for Consciousness (God if you prefer) to know Itself. As you are an individualized "portion" of Consciousness, you are thus imbued with creativity. Your Essence self expects you to be as creative as possible in the exploration of your life's intent and purpose.

BE SPONTANEOUS. Expressing spontaneity instills a trust of your creative abilities. Spontaneity is the principle that keeps you in touch with your spiritual impulse **to act in the now—as the "now" is your point of power within linear time.** The impulse to do something spontaneously is a signal from your Essence self to not think (involve your ego-self's reasoning and adherence to chronological time), and trust in its guidance on when to act.

BE PATIENT. Being patient is not in contradiction to being spontaneous. Patience is not to do with simply waiting and doing nothing—**patience is an action in itself, one that reflects a deeply held trust in your creative abilities.** If you feel impatient, you are allowing your ego-self to interfere with the natural flow of your creative energies working in natural time. Impatience is a symptom of your ego-self's attempts to force an action outside of its natural timing.

BE COOPERATIVE. Cooperation is a vibrant and necessary principle of existence. Eventually we will come to know that life itself has nothing to do with the "survival of the fittest," but is instead all about the health and prosperity of the cooperative.

BE OPEN AND VULNERABLE. To be open and vulnerable is not an invitation to be hurt. **Being vulnerable is about being open to receive**—open to receive the gifts you bring to yourself through being grateful and appreciative of all you create for yourself. **It is another act of *allowing*—of loving yourself.** The best way to receive what you need and desire from life is to ***appreciate*** yourself and feel your vulnerability.

Risking vulnerability opens you to the totality of who you are, and **it opens your heart to others.** Your vulnerability allows your spiritual Essence to flow to every part of your being. Vulnerability is the "softness" through which your Essence self can enter your ego-self's shielded world. So, drop your shell of invulnerability, it is an illusory form of safety. **Welcome your vulnerability and thereby express your unique spirituality.**

For a more detailed description of the natural principles, an eBook is available on Amazon Kindle entitled *How To Be In Divine Love: 10½ Principles That Will Make You A Happy, Purposeful Person.* C.W.E. Johnson.

Appendix II: A Basic Shortcut Version of EFT

Have pen and paper to hand for making notes.

Step 1

Identify, *as specifically as possible*, the problem you wish to address.

Example: "This feeling of panic that's making my heart race, and my thoughts are all over the place, and it's making me thirsty, and I have a slight headache as well, and I'm scared."

Get the point? Really focus in on whatever it is that's troubling you, whether mental or physical, and thoroughly describe it to yourself. If you haven't produced one in your description, sense an emotion that best fits the symptoms you've described—anxiety or "nonspecific fear" would fit with the above example.

When you have tuned into the problem, particularly the emotion, assess the level of distress you are experiencing, **right now**, as you contemplate the problem. On a scale where zero is no intensity of feeling whatsoever, to ten, which is unbearable—rate your level of distress. **Write it down.**

Remember, if you are contemplating a problem from the past, or envisioning a coming event, it is not a rating of the distress you **once** felt or **will** feel—but what you feel **now—at this moment.**

Now insert your statement of the problem—remember to be as specific as possible—into the following statement—**and write it down:**

"Even though I have this... (statement of the problem)... I deeply and completely love, trust, and accept myself, without judgment, anyway."

Example: "Even though I have this feeling of panic, which is making my heart race and my thoughts are all over the place, and I need some water, and I'm getting a headache, all because of this anxiety—I deeply and completely love, trust and accept myself, without judgment, anyway."

Step 2

When you have written your statement down, put it somewhere you can read it and locate your *sore spot*. That is, go to the u-shaped notch at the top of the sternum—about where the knot of a tie would be. Come down 3 inches (7.5cms), then over to the left about 3 inches. Press and rub around this area until you find a slight tenderness under the skin. The sore spot is where you find this tenderness. **Don't press too hard,** as this is where lymph glands are situated. If this spot is too tender, try the other side (3 inches to the right of center). If neither is suitable, then use the side-of-the-hand spot (karate spot), on either hand, as instructed below:

Preferably using the sore spot, rub the area gently in a circular motion with the tips of your fingers. If using the karate spot, tap this spot (not too hard, just firm tapping) continuously with a couple of fingers. Do this while reciting the following statement, with conviction, three times:

"I deeply and completely love, trust and accept myself, without judgment, even with all my challenges and problematic beliefs."

Step 3

Now take a deep breath in through the nose and release it slowly through the mouth. Focus in on the issue you want to resolve. Go over what you have written down from Step 1 a few times and then, while you slowly read out your statement, continually tap the karate spot. You can read it a second time or embellish what you are saying if it feels right to do so—but take your time and keep tapping the karate spot while you speak everything that comes up aloud.

Example: "Even though I have this feeling of panic, which is making my heart race and my thoughts are all over the place, and I need some water, and I'm getting a headache, all because of this anxiety, and I hate it when I get like this, and it reminds me of when my mom shouted at me in the garden, and she didn't realize it wasn't me, and I hate to be shouted at—I deeply and completely love, trust and accept myself, without judgment, anyway."

Step 4

When you have finished talking it out while tapping the karate spot, follow the short sequence below of places to tap. Just firmly tap each spot (about seven or eight taps) as you remind yourself of your statement by shortening it to the primary issue—**the emotion you have assigned to it.** If you have not got a specific emotion, take a guess at which one might best suit the issue—fear, anger, sadness, guilt, grief, frustration, whatever—just put an appropriate emotion to it—and as you tap each of the spots in the sequence below, repeat your emotional word or phrase at least once.

Example (from the above example): "This anxiety," or, "This fear of being shouted at," or, "This guilt I'm feeling."

Begin at the **eyebrow spot**—tap both if you want—where the eyebrow ends at the bridge of the nose. Tap and repeat the reminder term.

Next, the **side-of-eye spot**—both sides if you want to—on the bony orbit, next to the eye. Tap and repeat the reminder.

Then **under the eye**—on the bony orbit directly under the pupil. Both spots if you like. Tap and repeat the reminder term.

Then **under the nose**—between the top lip and bottom of the nose. Tap and repeat the reminder.

Then the **chin spot**—between the bottom lip and chin. Tap and repeat.

Then the **collarbone spot**—both sides if you can, just under the ridge of the bone, about 1 inch (2.5cms) down and to the side of the u-shaped notch at the junction of the sternum. Tap and repeat the reminder term.

Then **under the arm**—about 3 inches (7.5cms) down from the armpit. Where a bra strap comes for women. Don't tap too hard as there are lymph glands here. Tap and repeat the reminder term.

Finally—tap the **crown of your head** seven or eight times as you repeat the reminder term again.

Then take a deep breath in through your nose, and release through the mouth.

Tune into your issue and rate how you now feel on the zero to ten scale.

If your score has dropped by only one or two points from when you wrote it down on Step 1, repeat the tapping sequence above again, but begin with tapping the karate spot and repeating this revised statement three times:

"Even though ***I still have*** some of this... (emotion—e.g., fear, anger, whatever, as in the reminder term)... I deeply and completely love, trust and accept myself anyway."

As you progress around the spots above, now say: "This ***remaining***... (emotion term)."

Keep repeating the tapping sequence with this statement to start and the "remaining (emotion)" reminder phrase as you go around the spots until the rate of distress you feel falls to zero or one. Then take a deep breath in through your nose and breathe out through your mouth. If you are not able to drop your rating to zero or one, make a note of the issue you are dealing with and consult an EFT practitioner.

You can download a PDF transcript of this basic EFT procedure, with illustrations, at my website. Go to cwejohnson.com/offerings.

Go to eftuniverse.com for a practitioner listing.

Go to emofree.com for more on EFT and its founder Gary Craig.

Appendix III: The Families of Intent—A More Definitive Guide

The articulation of intent through the human psyche loosely conforms to nine distinguishable forms of expression. Essentially, they are differing developmental paths of activity peculiar to humankind, involved with the growth, learning and evolution of each individual and humanity itself. Although your personality encapsulates *all* forms of human intent, it chooses to experience the physical dimension with certain expressions of intent to the fore.

Seth, perhaps deliberately, only gave a brief outline on how each of the families of intent translates to human activity—through traits within our personalities to preferred physical pursuits. I say *perhaps deliberately* as at the time of delivery of this information (1970s) there was, and still is according to Elias (Mary Ennis), an acute possibility that the casual reader can misunderstand the metaphor's premise, overplay the differentiating factors, and under emphasize the subtleties of this insight on the expression of human consciousness.

A deep understanding of this material is required before attempting to use it in the help of others. This is a precaution that will hopefully prevent the information from being co-opted into yet another distorted belief system in respect of personality profiling.

This said, according to our metaphysical guides, our Essence self *belongs to,* and our current personality *aligns with,* certain families of human intent. We rarely *overtly* express the characteristics of our family of belonging during our lifetime; instead, *they bring an underlying subtlety* to the qualities and characteristics expressed by our personality's family of alignment—our *primary,* overtly expressed, family of intent.

The Elias transcripts, and more recently the teachings of Rose

(Joanne Helfrich), give us a clearer picture as to what actions we can expect of individuals *aligning with* a certain family of intent. Remember, though, that the demarcation lines between the families are as undefined as the overlapping colors of a rainbow. You can *align* with more than one family, or form a mix, a subfamily—although one family of alignment is the norm. Furthermore, *your personality continues to encapsulate and express* ***all*** *the differing intentional leanings of the nine families.* You hold the potential to express any of their intentional idiosyncrasies, particularly in relation to the circumstances of the moment.

Essentially, the families of human intent provide a fluid, yet significant guide to the subtleties of intent expressed through human consciousness. As such, and in view of a person's allegiance to the expressions of certain families rather than others, they give indication as to a person's personal motivations, and thereby, a clue as to the general purpose of their current lifetime.

The colors in parentheses are those associated with the family's *tonal frequency*. That is, each family has a vibrational tone that can be roughly matched to the frequency of a color. There is a resonance in vibrational quality. Tone and Color are *relative truths* (see *Chapter 16*)—they are *qualities* of existence that transfer between dimensions of Consciousness other than our physical one.

Innovators/Formers—Gramada—(Orange)

This family of intent is involved with creating, initiating, inventing and innovating. Personalities aligned with this type of human intent are in touch with and attuned to their *conceptual inner senses* (see *Chapter 11*)—ideal for exploiting the *natural principle* of creation. They are truly inspired, able to connect to concepts forming worldviews at the Essence level of our consciousness to offer originality of ideas to the physical realm.

Innovators spread themselves across all occupations, they

tend not to take the spotlight but allow others to take on and develop their originating ideas. They are particularly adept at inventing physical objects as well as efficient *systems* for the benefit of society, business, and politics.

Teachers/Seers—Sumafi—(Black)

This intent involves the act of teaching, the relaying of knowledge to others in its purest form. There is an aim to encourage originality through teaching and promote learning through experience. Along with the action of teaching comes a concern for accuracy when conveying information to maintain the integrity of the information. This may translate to a pedantic trait of the personality, an obsession with detail.

Even though this family of intent includes accuracy of information transfer, there is no adherence to any particular "truth" as there is an appreciation of the futility of imagining there to be one philosophical outlook that can convey or describe the only absolute truth—that of Consciousness.

Personalities aligned with this family of intent are generally playful, flexible, and humorous, although they can also be stern and critical. High amongst their values is an aesthetic sensibility. This aesthetic appreciation is one of many links, overlaps, and involvements with the intent of the family of Artists/Speakers (Sumari).

Healers/Readers—Tumold—(Indigo)

This family of intent is involved with healing and helping others. It is an intent aimed at both individual and cultural healing. Its drive, like that of the Spiritualists/Rememberers (Milumet), recognizes natural principles and natural states of being—not least our natural state of health, which is dependent upon our ability to align with and express the natural power of Divine Love.

Personalities with this alignment express healing from a spiritual perspective. This means that they can channel their energies to assist healing on the many different "layers" of human expression. They are thus adept at societal and planetary healing as well as healing the psychological, emotional and physical states of an individual. This family of intent promotes *self-healing*, in the knowledge that it is only the individual's Self that can facilitate true healing.

Our current belief systems concerning health issues can confuse some personalities aligned with this intent as they imagine that *fixing and preventing* define the requisites of healing. In actuality, "dis-eased" expressions of our consciousness simply require *assistance* in returning to their *natural state of well-being*.

Some personalities, when in full alignment with this intent and engaging their *empathic inner senses* (see *Chapter 11*), can "read" the *vibrational signature* of another individual or life form and effect healing simply by being in their presence.

Reformers/Hearers—Vold—(Yellow)

This family of intent is involved with reform through revolution. The intent originates as a peaceful desire to change the status quo, but core belief systems can distort energies associated with this intentional drive by misinterpreting the *natural aggression* (see Glossary of Terms) that is closely bound to the expression of this intent. In other words, a personality aligned with this intent, but misinterpreting its motivational impulses, may attempt to justify violence as a means to achieving reform—which it can never be.

The intent activates reform at all levels, from personal belief systems to collective belief systems reflected in world institutions—political, religious, financial and educational—to family values and societal mores.

Such aligned personalities like to change themselves, their location, and their environment. They are restless, passionate, *com*passionate, understanding, and very much attuned to their emotions. These personalities have excellent precognitive abilities, indicative of an affinity with the *time-based inner senses* (see *Chapter 11*). They have a *feeling* for probabilities.

Spiritualists/Rememberers—Milumet—(Red)

The title "spiritualists" should not be confused with the term's popular use to describe those people who practice spiritualism—communicating with the dead. The intent of this family is far subtler in meaning; it emphasizes the spiritual nature of everything in existence and is very much concerned with keeping us aware of the natural rhythms of life, such as *natural time* (see Glossary of Terms). Perhaps a better expression to personify the intent would be *spiritual counselors*.

This drive is of particular importance to us at present as we observe the suppression of it reflected in many environmental issues. It is a family of intent involved with true spiritual connection (to Essence), directing our energies inwardly to review and apply the *natural principles* that steer the creativity of Consciousness to our lives.

Personalities aligned with this intent tend to manifest within primal cultures—Native American Indian tribes and the Australian aboriginal people, for example. They tend to keep their *Selves* to themselves! They are deeply involved in the divinity of nature, having an extraordinary connection with all living things—on empathic and telepathic levels. They attune themselves to their *empathic inner senses*, which facilitates an awareness of the energy potentials of inorganic matter such as crystals and mineral compounds.

This family of intent nourishes humanity's collective psyche—reminding us of our own divinity.

Imagers—Zuli—(Violet)

This is an intent that focuses upon the expression of form in the physical domain. It is primarily to do with the human form, but also the design of other living forms and all physical structures. It is an intent dedicated to perfecting the beauty, elegance, and performance of a physical body. Like the Teachers/Seers (Sumafi) and Artists/Speakers (Sumari), it facilitates a deep appreciation of beauty.

Personalities with this alignment of intent tend to manifest as athletes and artistic performers, such as ballet dancers. They have inspired design capabilities, being excellent manipulators of the physical form, so can enjoy being involved in the broad spectrum of artistic design, from graphic design and architecture to choreography.

According to Rose, this family of intent is under-utilized at present in the design of our physical constructions. We often neglect the spiritual *desire* for beauty for the secular *want* of functionality.

Nurturers/Bearers—Borledim—(Pink)

A family of intent concerned with nurturing. This drive to nurture includes all creatures of the Earth, but in relation to humanity, it promotes a complete and spiritually astute nurturing of our young. There is an underpinning concern with manifesting a healthy, balanced, human "Earth stock"—a bank of physically healthy, psychologically well-adjusted, emotionally aware, "quality" individuals.

Personalities aligned with this intent often belong to, or produce, large families, but the intent focuses on nurturing, so it is not incumbent upon such a personality to produce many children, if any at all. They are, though, family oriented, with excellent parenting skills.

Nurturers demonstrate great affection, patience, fairness, and understanding—while guiding without being pushy. The intent brings awareness of the importance of learning through experience, so they don't block or admonish impulsive or spontaneous behaviors in children as there is a subconscious understanding of these important inner energies seeking expression.

The expression of this family of human intent helps to diminish the judgmental attitude within us that we all struggle to control.

Exchangers/Tellers––Ilda––(Green)

This family of intent is to do with communication and the exchange of information and knowledge. We require this intent in order that we spread ideas, attitudes and concepts across differing cultures. It is an intent that brings an individual the ability to see the bigger picture and form connections.

Personalities aligned with this intent enjoy traveling and trading, often satisfying such activity as merchants or seafarers pursuing a nomadic lifestyle. They are colorful characters, extremely vocal, and keen to express humor whenever possible as a device for leveling communication between peoples of contrasting belief systems.

In the medieval period, the Court Jester was an example of a personality with the Exchangers intent to the fore—a necessary psychological go-between, bridging the enormous gap in ideas, imagination, and thinking between the layperson and the aristocracy.

Artists/Speakers––Sumari––(Blue)

Like the intent of the Reformers/Hearers (Vold) family, there is a drive to change the status quo. It is an intent, like the Teachers/Seers (Sumafi), which concerns itself with the aesthetics of physical expression, thus encouraging actions of change through the language of art. This intent emphasizes the natural principle to be creative in our actions. When we observe those who display great creativity (indicative of alignment with this family of intent), we often label them as the *doers* in society.

Personalities aligned with this family of intent are extroverts, naturally playful, and like the Exchangers/Tellers (Ilda), keen to use humor. They are independent and nonconformist, thus championing individuality and shunning group activities. They revel in thought, initiating new thoughts on a subject, and thoroughly enjoy the spotlight. Personalities of this intent find fulfillment across the breadth of the arts and in the "less conventional" sciences.

Seth mentions that this "family of consciousness" came to the fore in our collective psyche to "stir the pot" and initiate our collective *shift in consciousness*.

Appendix IV: Exercise 1

Touching Your Tone

Read through this script a few times before practicing.

Sit as comfortably as you possibly can without crossing your legs. Close your eyes. Take a couple of deep breaths, breathing in through the nose and out through the mouth. Quickly scan through your body, relax any muscles that appear cramped and allow your jaw to open slightly. Set an intention to experience your own deep vibrational tone within you—no matter how briefly.

Begin to quiet your thoughts and tell yourself that you will deal with any invasive thoughts later.

Similarly, if any emotions come to your awareness, put these aside; they are not what you are wishing to sense at the moment.

Imagine your awareness to be drifting in clear, transparent space. There is nothing above you, below you, or around you. Simply feel the tone of your being. Ask your inner self to allow you to experience this deep rhythm of your Essence.

Maintain a mental stance of gratitude and appreciation for your uniqueness.

There is no right or wrong way of doing this. It is not a meditation; it is simply giving yourself the time to allow the tone of your vibrational signature to appear so that you may familiarize yourself with its feeling. Know that it exists; you just want to be able to sense it in some conscious way.

Keep things lighthearted; everyone experiences their unique tone in their own unique way. You are not concerned at all about *how* it should feel. However, you will *know* it's *your* vibrational tone when it appears within your senses.

Now allow yourself to experience the tone of your vibrational signature.

End of script.

You should realize that this exercise is not some sort of test; you get what you get. Initially, that might not be very much. So be persistent and practice the exercise as often as possible. Do know that once you can sense your vibrational tone quite easily, you can put yourself in touch with it at will—allowing yourself to feel confident and secure in moments of distress.

If you are unable to get past any feelings or emotions that come to the fore while practicing, then you might consider using the EFT exercise (Appendix II) to dissipate any emotional energy getting in the way. Make the specific feeling or emotion "the problem" when using the EFT Exercise. Be persistent and run through the protocol at least twice. Remember to keep this exercise and EFT work as lighthearted as possible. Treat it as *first conscious contact* with your Essence––the nonphysical part of your Self that exists before you are born. I promise you, it won't bite.

Appendix V: Exercise 2

Tapping for Self-Worth

Have a pen and your work journal to hand for making notes.

Refer to the Basic EFT shortcut procedure (Appendix II) for where to tap.

A freely downloadable PDF of the Basic EFT procedure and this Exercise (see "A Core EFT Exercise"), both with illustrations, is available at the cwejohnson.com/offerings page.

Begin by relaxing yourself

Preferably seated in a straight-backed chair, keep an upright posture, cross your feet, then cross your hands opposite to the feet. So, if your right foot has crossed on top of the left foot, put your arms out in front of you and put your left hand on top of the right. Slide your left hand around to the back so that your palms are together, and your fingers interlinked. Then draw your arms into the chest keeping the fingers interlinked. Your right wrist should now be facing outwards. Keep your arms and feet in this position, sit up straight, close your eyes and focus your mind on **BALANCE**.

Just focus on whatever or however your mind conjures up BALANCE. It may be a visual image, but just go with what your mind brings you.

- **Remain in this position for about 2 minutes, keep your focus on balance, and breathe in through your nose and out through your mouth.**

After 2 minutes, unravel your arms and uncross your feet. Place both feet on the floor, keep the upright-seated position, put your hands in your lap or on your thighs, take a deep breath in through the nose and release through the mouth. Remain deeply relaxed as you slowly follow the steps below:

Step 1

Firstly, find your left sore-spot, and while rubbing it continuously in a circular motion (not too hard!), repeat the following affirmation—with conviction—three times:

"I deeply and completely love, trust, and accept myself, without judgment, even with all my challenges and problematic beliefs."

Secondly, while continually tapping the side-of-hand (karate) point recite three times—with conviction—the statement:

"Even though I have this issue to do with my self-worth and am not consciously aware of it, I deeply and completely love, trust, and accept myself anyway."

Step 2

While tapping each of the points in the following sequence seven or eight times, say aloud this shortened phrase: "My issue to do with self-worth."

Eyebrow > Outside of Eye > Under Nose > Under Lip > Under Eye > Collarbone > Under Arm > Collarbone > Under Eye > Little Finger > Collarbone > Index Finger > Collarbone > Middle Finger > Thumb > Karate Point.

The fingers and thumb points are located at the base of the nail on the inward facing side (towards the body). Absolute precision is not required when tapping any of the points, so use the ends of a couple of fingers whenever you can.

When you have completed the sequence, locate the "Gamut Point" on the back of either hand (an inch back—2cms—from between the little finger and ring finger knuckle joints) and continuously tap this point for about 20 seconds as you repeatedly say aloud the shortened phrase, "My issue to do with self-worth."

Step 3

Take a deep breath in through your nose and release it through your mouth.

While tapping the karate point, recite the following:

"Even though I may well have this deep-seated issue to do with my self-worth that is affecting my self-esteem, my self-confidence, and my self-image, I deeply and completely love, trust, and accept myself anyway.

Even though my ego-self doubts whether I have this issue and can't believe that I inherited it from my mom while still in her womb, or picked it up in some other subconscious way, I deeply and completely love, trust, and accept myself anyway."

Now continually tap **the eyebrow point** (both if you can, one will do) while reciting this statement:

"I'm eliminating ALL OF THE SADNESS in all of the emotional roots and the deepest causal belief of any issue I have that belittles my self-worth."

Now continually tap **the under-eye point** (again, both if you can, but one will do) while reciting this statement:

"I'm eliminating ALL OF THE FEAR in all of the emotional roots and the deepest causal belief of any issue I have that belittles my self-worth."

Now continually tap **the little finger point** (base of the nail on the side facing the neighboring finger) while reciting this statement:

"I'm eliminating ALL OF THE ANGER in all of the emotional roots and the deepest causal belief of any issue I have that belittles my self-worth."

Then **return to the eyebrow point** and continually tap as you recite this statement:

"I'm eliminating ALL OF THE EMOTIONAL TRAUMA in all

of the emotional roots and the deepest causal belief of any issue I have that belittles my self-worth."

Now take a deep breath in through your nose and release it through your mouth.

Step 4

While continually tapping the LITTLE FINGER point, recite each of the following statements three times:

"I'm eliminating all of the anger that I hold towards my ego-self for having this issue of self-worth."

"I'm eliminating all of the anger that I hold towards my mother for unconsciously passing on this issue from her psyche to mine."

Then, **still tapping the LITTLE FINGER point**, use this statement for anyone else that you may feel anger towards for the adoption of this self-worth issue, using the name you call them by (for example, your father–Dad, brother–Steve, sister–Kay, a teacher–Miss Smith, a grandparent–Ganky, or even God–Lord):

"I'm eliminating all of the anger that I hold towards (Dad/Steve/Kay/Miss Smith/etc.) for reinforcing this issue within me."

When you've exhausted everyone you feel may have contributed to you having this issue, take a deep breath in through your nose and release it through your mouth.

Step 5

It is now important to forgive yourself and the people named in Step 4 for the adoption of this self-worth issue.

While continually tapping the INDEX FINGER point (bottom of the nail on the side facing the thumb), recite the following statement three times in forgiveness of yourself:

"I deeply and completely forgive my ego-self for maintaining this issue, for I know that it's doing the best that it can."

Then, **still tapping the index finger point**, repeat three times for your mother:

"I deeply and completely forgive you (your name for your mother—e.g., Mom) for passing on this issue to me, for I know that you were doing the best you could for me at the time."

Then, **continue tapping the index finger point** and repeat the following statement three times for each further person you may have named.

"I deeply and completely forgive you (Dad/John/Sally/Lord) for I know that you are/were doing the best you can/could for me."

When you've exhausted your list, take a deep breath in through your nose and release through your mouth.

Step 6

To end this tapping marathon, do a "round" of tapping of the basic points:

At each point repeat the statement:

"I deeply and profoundly love, trust, accept, and appreciate the totality of my Self."

Begin with the KARATE point, move to the EYEBROW/s point, then SIDE-OF-THE-EYE/s point, then UNDER THE EYE/s, then UNDER THE NOSE, then the CHIN point, then the COLLARBONE point/s, then UNDER THE ARM, and finish with the CROWN OF THE HEAD.

Repeat this exercise whenever feeling a little low or lacking in confidence.

Appendix VI: Exercise 3

Finding Your Alignment

This exercise is about recording those moments in your life that have brought you a deep sense of fulfillment.

You will call to mind those times when your actions naturally and effortlessly flowed. You are going to identify those times when you felt passionate and energized about doing something—it doesn't matter what it was you were doing, but it made you feel really good about yourself.

You will recall the interests and activities that have consistently drawn your attention to them. They could be actions that others may have commented upon as being something not worthy of your energies—*you* though have a sense that such actions are right for you. You will recall those moments when time just flew by, as you were so absorbed with and enthused by what you were *doing*.

You will recall episodes that made you feel *good* about yourself—doing an activity or fulfilling a role of some description. These are moments in your life that brought you more than just a feeling of satisfaction—as when eating a favorite food or enjoying physical activity.

Set the intention to enjoy recalling those moments in your life when you were enjoying yourself utterly. Allow your inner self to bring you recall of the times when you were in total alignment with your primary intent for this lifetime.

Read through this script a couple of times so that you know what to do after closing your eyes. Have paper and pen to hand for notes/sketches. Don't worry about opening your eyes and reading from this script to remind yourself.

Sit as comfortably as you possibly can with legs uncrossed, feet on the ground.

Close your eyes. Take a couple of deep breaths, breathing in through your nose and out through your mouth.

Mentally scan slowly through your body, starting at your feet, relaxing any muscles that appear cramped, and allow your jaw to open slightly when you get to your head. Quieten your thoughts and instruct yourself that you will deal with any invasive thoughts later. Just relax.

Count from five down to one, and on each count you can relax more and more... and you can allow your relaxation to double through your entire body... becoming twice as relaxed by the time you get to one. For example:

5... relaxation begins to double... 4... feeling wonderfully comfortable and relaxed... 3... relaxation doubling more and more... 2... going deeper and deeper... relaxation almost doubled now in my entire body... 1... the state of relaxation has now doubled in my entire body... every nerve, every muscle... every tissue doubled in its relaxation... more relaxed, letting go... deeper down... further and further.

My body now feels perfectly comfortable... all discomforts are now gone... completely gone from my body. My whole body is functioning properly and is deeply relaxed.

Begin to cast your mind back to your early childhood. Take yourself to a time when you were a small child... you had few beliefs to think about, you just did things; particularly things that brought you pleasure. Settle upon a time when you were very young and enjoying yourself, doing something you loved to do, either on your own or with others. Recall your favorite way of playing—if told to "go and play," what would you do?

What was your favorite color when you were a young child?

Take a moment to focus your attention on that time, and when you have a bit of detail to record, open your eyes and note down what you recall—or make a quick sketch if you like.

Now close your eyes again—still feeling deeply relaxed—bring your awareness now to another time when you were young, perhaps in your teens, when you were absorbed in what you were doing, a time when doing what you were doing made you feel really good about yourself.

Did you love to wear clothes of a certain color?

After you have captured some details of this second moment, open your eyes again and make a note or a little sketch of what you were doing. If others were involved, note this down. Begin to feel *right now* the pleasurable emotions you felt then.

Take a few moments again—don't think too much—just get down what comes to your mind as you recall this time that made you feel so good about yourself.

Now close your eyes once again and let your emotions and thoughts take you to another time, it may be a time as an adult, when you experienced similar emotions in doing what you were doing.

This is another past time when the experience was totally absorbing you because it was an experience that stimulated positive emotions—your actions flowed naturally and with no mental effort, no resistance, even though physically it may have been demanding. Were you fulfilling a particular role?

Take a few moments to recall some details of this experience, and when ready, open your eyes and note down the experience. Remember to make a special note of the *doing* aspects of the pleasurable experience and any colors that may have come to mind. Were you engaged in a specific activity? Were you doing something with others or alone? What was the general theme behind what you were doing?

Don't worry if you only have a few sketchy notes or could only recall one or two moments of great fulfillment. Take your time and go over what you have, and as you focus upon an experience feel free to add anything, however abstract, to your notes. Just add any more details that have now come to mind.

What you can do next, when you're satisfied you have all you can recall for the moment, is focus your thoughts on any predominant theme of activity or consistent role you seem to be playing that appears to link together the different moments of recall.

What, if anything, appears to emerge from your notes that stands out as significant? If you can figure out a theme to your activities, or spot a role you would like to adopt, but have no colors noted down, ask yourself which color would resonate with your predominant theme or role—don't think about it—just note what color first comes to mind.

After the exercise:

Armed with your notes, primary theme, and color if any, go to *Chapter 5* and turn to the brief synopses of the activities and traits relating to the nine families of intent.

- Compare your notes with the family descriptions. Remember that the descriptions of the families are highly generalized, and they overlap and interrelate with each other, so you may find that more than one family appears to connect with your notes.
- Jot down the family (or two) that most closely aligns with your mental and physical notes about your predominant or significant activity.
- When you have done this, go to Appendix III, where you will find each family's characteristics defined more clearly, together with their assigned colors. Compare your notes on your possible family of alignment with the fuller description and see if the color you have noted marries with the one assigned to it.

If you can easily link the activity to a family of intent, and the color you have confirms the family—intend to pat yourself on the back! Don't worry if nothing quite worked out on your first experience of this exercise; and don't assume that if you *seem* to have a result, then you're done with this exercise. Practice it. Do it a few times over the coming weeks and then take an average of your results. Fluctuations in your results from this exercise are to do with the timing of the exercise. A particular family, not necessarily your family of alignment, may be to the fore because of the circumstances affecting your personality at the time of doing the exercise.

You will know when you are done when you *feel* a deep connection to the family of intent that consistently surfaces in this exercise.

Appendix VII: Exercise 4

Accepting Your Inner Self

Begin with some Balanced Breathing

Preferably seated in a straight-backed chair, keep an upright posture, cross your feet, then cross your hands opposite to the feet. So, if your right foot has crossed on top of the left foot, put your arms out in front of you and put your left hand on top of the right. Slide your left hand around to the back so that your palms are together, and your fingers interlinked. Then draw your arms into the chest keeping the fingers interlinked. Your right wrist should now be facing outwards. Keep your arms and feet in this position, sit up straight, close your eyes and **focus your mind on BALANCE**.

Just focus on whatever or however your mind conjures up BALANCE. It may be a visual image, but just go with what your mind brings you.

- **Remain in this position for about 2 minutes, keep your focus on balance, and breathe in through your nose and out through your mouth.**

After 2 minutes, unravel your arms and uncross your feet. Place both feet on the floor, keep the upright-seated position, put your hands in your lap or on your thighs, take a deep breath in through the nose and release through the mouth. Remain deeply relaxed as you slowly read the passage below. Close your eyes when you can to help visualize:

Now picture within your mind an image of your *ideal* companion. It may take the form of an ideal you, someone of the opposite sex, an animal, an imaginary being—whatever image comes to mind is perfectly fine. This image represents the most caring, loving, and trustworthy companion to your ego-self as it goes about dealing with everyday life. Your companion is always listening to and communicating with you and can assist you in reaching your own perfection—easily, safely, and beautifully. Greet your imaginary companion in your mind now. Embrace your companion and thank them for their constant support. Suggest to this nonphysical, but supremely powerful part of your whole Self, that you recognize them as your ***inner self***, and you would like them to facilitate the coming exercise.

The EFT exercise:

Have the Basic EFT procedure to hand for reference, see Appendix II. You can download a PDF transcript of this basic EFT procedure, with illustrations, at my website. Go to www.cwejohnson.com/offerings.

Step 1: Find your ***sore spot*** on the left side of your chest—about 3 inches (7cms) down and the same across from the u-shaped notch at the base of the neck. Using the ends of 2 or 3 fingers, find the spot by pressing around this area until you find a place that is more tender or sensitive than the area around it.

While gently rubbing your sore spot in a circular motion, say aloud (preferably) or in your head:

"Even though I haven't achieved my ideal situation in life yet, I deeply and completely accept, trust, and value myself. Even though I still worry and feel the pain of not having everything that I want yet, I deeply and completely accept, trust, and value myself. Even though I most often battle alone, ignoring the assistance of my inner self, I deeply and completely accept, trust, and value myself." **Hold your fingers on the spot, take a slow deep breath in through the nose, and release it through the mouth.**

Step 2: While tapping the side-of-hand spot (karate point), say aloud or in your head:

"Even though I may be afraid of taking back control of my life and reclaiming my true sense of powerfulness, and even though I may not believe that I am worthy enough to express my power, I deeply and completely love, trust and accept myself anyway." **Hold on the spot and take a slow deep breath.**

Step 3: While tapping both eyebrow spots, say aloud or in your head:

"I am calling forth the extraordinary resources of my inner self, to gently release, completely and permanently, any and all, trauma and sadness from my emotional roots and my deepest beliefs, that are still in my way to experiencing my own joy, freedom and growth." **Hold on the spots and take a slow deep breath.**

Step 4: While tapping both side-of-eye spots, say aloud or in your head:

"I am calling forth the extraordinary resources of my inner self to gently eliminate, completely and permanently, any and all, deep rooted pain and limiting beliefs that are still causing me to feel angry, irritated, anxious, impatient, or out of control." **Hold on the spots and take a slow deep breath.**

Step 5: While tapping both the under-eye spots, say aloud or in your head:

"I am calling forth the extraordinary resources of my inner self to gently release, completely and permanently, any and all fear or self-pity from my emotional roots and my deepest beliefs—and to strengthen my ability to deliberately look for things that make me feel good, safe, and satisfied, no matter where I am, or whether I am with others." **Hold on the spots and take a slow deep breath.**

Step 6: While tapping the under-nose spot say aloud or in your head:

"I am calling forth the extraordinary resources of my inner self to gently release any shyness I may have, and draw to me many new and exciting opportunities, especially designed to purposefully enrich my life." **Hold on the spot and take a slow deep breath.**

Step 7: While tapping the chin spot, say aloud or in your head:

"I am calling forth the extraordinary resources of my inner self to gently release any feeling of shame I may have, and enhance my vitality, creativity, natural talents, intellectual abilities, and overall sense of well-being." **Hold on the spot and take a slow deep breath.**

Step 8: While tapping both collarbone spots, say aloud or in your head:

"I am calling forth the extraordinary resources of my inner self to keep me in a constant state of fun-loving appreciation of my life experience." **Hold on the spots and take a slow deep breath.**

Step 9: While tapping the third eye spot (about 1 inch (2cms) above and between your eyebrows), say aloud or in your head:

"I am calling forth the extraordinary resources of my inner self to always keep me safe, healthy, and prosperous, and to help me stay in perfect alignment with my higher purpose and mission in life." **Hold on the spot and take a slow deep breath.**

Step 10: While tapping or rubbing the occipital protuberance (small bony bump on base of skull at back and center), say aloud or in your head:

"I am discovering daily the wonderful resources of my inner self, leading to much growth and expansion in my life.

I am thrilled to experience the extraordinary changes that are happening in my life, under the care and safe guidance of my inner self. I easily see all the good things that are present in my life and I am grateful and appreciative for all of them. I love my Self and ALL aspects of my Self—including my occasionally misguided ego-self! I live my life knowing that I am where I am meant to be in my self-development and, from my inner self's standpoint, cannot get it wrong!" **Hold on the spot and take a slow deep breath.**

(Adapted from an exercise devised by Sophie Merle: www.sophiemerle.com.)

Appendix VIII: Exercise 5

Reframing an Unwanted Behavior

Have pen, paper, and the Basic EFT guide (Appendix II) to hand for reference.

Begin with some Balanced Breathing

Preferably seated in a straight-backed chair, keep an upright posture, cross your feet, then cross your hands opposite to the feet. So, if your right foot has crossed on top of the left foot, put your arms out in front of you and put your left hand on top of the right. Slide your left hand around to the back so that your palms are together, and your fingers interlinked. Then draw your arms into the chest keeping the fingers interlinked. Your right wrist should now be facing outwards. Keep your arms and feet in this position, sit up straight, close your eyes and focus your mind on **BALANCE**.

Just focus on whatever or however your mind conjures up BALANCE. It may be a visual image, but just go with what your mind brings you.

- **Remain in this position for about 2 minutes, keep your focus on balance, and breathe in through your nose and out through your mouth.**

After two minutes, unravel your arms and uncross your feet. Place both feet on the floor, keep the upright-seated position, put your hands in your lap or on your thighs, take a deep breath in through the nose and release through the mouth. Remain deeply relaxed as you slowly follow the procedure below.

Reframing an unwanted behavior

First identify an unwanted behavior you would like to bring under control and eventually stop doing. This could be a physical behavior like smoking, eating too much of something such as chocolate, or an emotional reaction to something—perhaps anger, anxiety, feeling overwhelmed or overexcited (highly impatient) about a particular issue.

- **Write down the unwanted behavior in the following statement and read it aloud:**

  "I want to communicate with the part of me that is causing me to [unwanted behavior]."

  (E.g., "become overly anxious when I watch young children playing near water.")
- **Write down a setup statement along the following lines:**

  "Even though a part of me is causing me to [unwanted behavior], I deeply and completely love, trust, accept, respect, and appreciate that part of me—as I know that it is doing the best it can for my care and well-being."
- **Next, gently rubbing the chest "sore spot" (see basic shortcut version of EFT, Appendix II) in a circular motion, state aloud, three times:**

  "I deeply and completely love, trust, accept, and appreciate myself, without judgment, even with all my challenges and problematic beliefs."
- **Then tap the side-of-hand (karate) spot continuously as you repeat aloud, three times, your setup statement.**

  When completed, take a deep breath in through the nose and release through the mouth. Then rest either of your hands palm down on your thigh, the arm of your chair, or comfortably on a table.
- **Keeping your palm and other fingers resting,** as you lift your index finger upwards to its fullest height say aloud the following statement as if talking to your index finger:

"I won't be able to return my index finger to the rest position until my subconscious mind has generated and begun to utilize at least three new ways of behaving which my inner self feels are more beneficial than what I've been doing, and which are totally appropriate and acceptable to all of my Self; and I will be delightfully surprised to discover how easily I am able to achieve the change in my behavior that I desire."

- Now wait for the internal processing to complete itself. This will be apparent when the finger returns to rest. This may take seconds or several minutes—exercise the natural principle of patience!

You may or may not have an idea as to the better choices of behavior now programmed into your subconscious. It would be interesting to note what you now tend to do in situations like those which before triggered the unwanted behavior.

This exercise usually requires only one application. If the problem behavior has many "layers" to it or is an addiction of some kind, then repeat the process for as long as you feel is necessary.

Note:

You may decide to bring the index finger down quite consciously, that is, with your own intent rather than being patient. This will not interfere with the internal processing; however, you may find later that if the processing was incomplete your finger may automatically pop back up when relaxed and your attention is elsewhere. This is simply a sign that further processing is taking place. Eventually your finger will come to rest of its own accord.

(Adapted from a procedure devised by Dianne Ruth, PhD: www.dynamicresources.net.)

Appendix IX: Exercise 6

Art Exercise—Depict Your Subconscious Library

Create your own depiction of your subconscious library. It can be a sketch, a painting, a collage—whatever you find easiest to do. Just include as much of the description elements from *Chapter 9* as you can and add as much detail as you like to make the scene an inviting one. Creating a physical picture of your subconscious library is the best way to retain the image in your mind.

Appendix X: Exercise 7

Elias's Clarity Exercise

Elias (channeled by Mary Ennis) maintains that the Clarity Exercise is important if you want to become adept at using your inner senses. The point of the exercise is to focus your attention on your *outer* senses and become familiar with manipulating them, so that you better understand how to notice and manipulate your inner senses.

The exercise gets you practiced in moving your attention—from one outer sense to another. It will eventually allow you to move your attention to where you choose and not have your attention automatically drawn to your thoughts.

With practice, your physical reality, the focus of your waking attention, will become clearer as you begin to appreciate the varied input of information from all your physical senses *in conjunction with information supplied by your inner senses*. Furthermore, as you better appreciate how your outer senses act in union, you will be better able to use your inner senses in union.

If you find difficulty in meditating, perhaps because you are unable to stop your attention moving to certain thoughts, or quieten your thoughts, then use the Clarity Exercise for a few days before meditating again.

The Clarity Exercise:

Begin by getting yourself alone and relaxed and seated comfortably.

- Focus upon any object within your field of vision, but don't concentrate upon the object, just allow it to be at the center of your visual attention so that you are still aware of your peripheral vision. Don't jump from one object to another; decide on an object and keep it at the center of your vision.

- Now tune your consciousness to your outer senses. Begin by letting your vision be as clear as it can possibly be. Then tune into your hearing, noticing all the sounds that are occurring around you. Then tune into your sense of touch, sensing all the clothes and objects touching your physical body—feel the surface beneath your fingertips, feel the air on your skin. Notice the feelings within your body, the pressure of the seat on your buttocks and thighs, the temperature.
- Tune into your sense of smell. There are always smells available to you, it's just that we don't use this physical sense too often.
- Notice what you are tasting. Just because you may not be eating or drinking anything, your sense of taste is still available to you now.
- Without closing your eyes, take a moment now to concentrate upon ***all*** your physical senses.
- (Ninety second pause.)
- Now close your eyes and allow your attention to drift. Stop any focus upon any of your physical senses. Allow yourself to be calm, quiet and comfortably relaxed as your attention simply drifts in clear, transparent space.
- (Thirty second pause.)
- Open your eyes and return to your normal waking state.

You do not need to spend more than thirty seconds with your eyes closed and your attention drifting. You only need to notice what occurs. You may experience flashes of color, mental images, scenic visualizations, or feelings. You may have a series of thoughts flash through your awareness. Just notice whatever occurs and don't concentrate upon the experience. Elias reminds us that it is only an exercise—don't take it too seriously! Remember that it is more important to be, eyes wide open, tuning into your five physical senses in this exercise. As you become more able to manipulate within these senses, you also learn to be more manipulating within alternate realities that your Essence encompasses—not least, the reality of your inner sensing.

This entire exercise should only take you three or four minutes to complete. It may appear deceptively simple, but it is in fact, initially, quite difficult to do. Elias suggests you spend a week, with two to three run-throughs each day, practicing this exercise.

- As your week of practice progresses, begin to manipulate your outer senses. Allow your attention to be on your hearing, and then, intentionally, turn it off. A straightforward way to do this is move your attention elsewhere, to another outer sense. Focus on your sense of touch, for example. Elias clarifies in session:

  Elias: "The only purpose for instructing each of you to intentionally tune out a given sense is to allow you the opportunity to intentionally and purposefully manipulate your clarity [all your senses, outer and inner, form your 'clarity']. It is not to be tuning out."

  Student: "Okay. So, it's sort of like you have your television, and it's fuzzy, and you're just tuning it in, and that's what we're supposed to be doing with this exercise."

  Elias: "Precisely."[1]

As you become better at manipulating your outer senses, you also begin to automatically hone your inner senses, and you will "begin to notice the actions and communications of your inner senses."[2]

A final word on the Clarity Exercise from Elias:

In practicing with the exercise in clarity, you allow yourself to realize objectively that you do incorporate the ability to manipulate your reality in different manners. It allows you to recognize that you actually do incorporate the ability to manipulate your actual senses, and if you can manipulate your actual senses, this reinforces your trust of your ability to be actually creating your reality. In a manner of speaking, it allows you a type of sense of control. It is not actually control, but it moves you out of the role of victim and offers you more of a sense of empowerment that you do incorporate the ability to manipulate whatever is being generated in your reality.

It is a challenging exercise, for your outer senses are quite automatic. It is unfamiliar to allow yourself to actually manipulate them, for you incorporate the perception that they are almost independent of you, that they are things, and that they generate their own experiences being things—but they are not. They are expressions of you. They are avenues of communication, and you can manipulate those avenues of communication.[3]

Notes:

1 Ennis, M. (September 1996) Session 125.
2 Ennis, M. (April 2002) Session 1069.
3 Ennis, M. (September 2004) Session 1629. Available at www.eliasweb.org

Appendix XI: Exercise 8

Utilizing Your Thoughts to Feel Good[1]

This is a truly short exercise you can do once or twice a day—just before going to sleep and/or just before getting up for the day is a good idea. It's not necessary but may prove useful to have your journal at hand for this exercise.

Thinking about a happy event from your life activates positive feelings. With these feelings come memories of other pleasant occasions, along with sensations from both your outer and inner senses—smells, sounds, excitement, feelings of euphoria—all associated with feeling good.

Your body-consciousness is automatically activated whenever you think. It investigates and stimulates cellular memory patterns that relate to what you are thinking about. Very quickly your entire body re-experiences the feeling state achieved at the time of the event.

Your cellular structure changes in recognition of the information contained within your thoughts—it doesn't care about whether the information relates to the "real" world outside the body, it's simply responding to instruction from your body-consciousness.

What you need to realize is that all these psychological associations are "living things"—living energy patterns that frequent a dimension unconcerned with time. Just like cells, thoughts have an identity, a vibrational signature, that reacts to other energies; and they revel in the action of association, drawing to themselves resonant energies while fending off those that threaten their existence.

The exercise:

- For the next 68 seconds[2] focus your attention on a highly pleasant event from your life.

- Only entertain those thoughts, feelings and sensations that are associated with this event.
- If a contrary thought appears, banish it immediately and concentrate on the original event again.

It can take several attempts before you can maintain a purity of thought for 68 seconds. Regular practice will achieve this, and your body's cellular structure will benefit immensely.

Notes:

1 This exercise is adapted from a suggestion made by Seth in: Roberts J., *The Nature of Personal Reality: A Seth Book*. Englewood Cliffs, NJ: Prentice-Hall Inc.; 1974. pp. 153/4; and suggestions on practicing purity of thought found in the works of Abraham (Abraham-Hicks.com).

2 Abraham advises that for a concentrated purity of thought (i.e., uninterrupted by contrary thoughts or feelings) to have an optimum effect on the physical system, it should be maintained for 68 seconds. Don't worry if you run a few seconds over!

Appendix XII: Exercise 9

Art Exercise––Depict Your Own Garden of Beliefs

Creating your own rendition of your personal Garden of Beliefs is both therapeutic and useful to you when working to clear debilitating beliefs or sowing self-empowering ones through meditation and EFT exercises. Producing a visual reference to this psychological "place," and the creative process itself, are an aid to establishing a map to your subconscious area—one that eases any fear of the unfamiliar.

Read through the *Systems of beliefs* subtitle at the start of *Chapter 15* again to spark your imagination. Notice any "issues" that may arise as you create your picture. Use the EFT protocol to work on these if necessary. Choose whatever medium you prefer and allow your inner self to express itself through that medium.

It's a good idea to do this about once a year to see how your garden develops and matures. Try creating it from differing viewpoints and using different media. Enjoy the process.

Endnotes and References

Preface

1 Roberts, J. (1972) *Seth Speaks: The Eternal Validity of the Soul.* Englewood Cliffs, NJ: Prentice-Hall Inc. p. ix.

Introduction

2 Hicks, E. & J. (April 21, 2001) Audio recording of a workshop at San Antonio, TX. Available at www.Abraham-Hicks.com.

3 Melanie (channeled by Tilde Cameron & Tina Fiorda) states, "This is why your Universe is expanding, and contrary to your belief system, the Universe will not shrink." See, Cameron, T. & Fiorda, T. (2008) *A Book of Insight: Wisdom from the Other Side*. British Columbia, Canada: Stone Circle Publishing. p. 27. Available at www.abookofinsight.com.

4 Wilber, K. (2017) *Trump and a Post-Truth World*. Boulder, CO: Shambhala Publications Inc. pp. 91/92.

5 Heisenberg, W. (1958) *Physics and Philosophy: The Revolution in Modern Science*. New York, NY: Harper & Row Publishers. p. 106.

6 Davies, P. (1988) *The Cosmic Blueprint: New Discoveries in Nature's Creative Ability to Order the Universe*. New York, NY: Simon & Schuster. p. 165.

7 Ennis, M. (1998) Elias session 270. Available at www.eliasforum.org/digests.

8 Anka, D. (2015) Extract from the "A Unified Theory" sessions held in Los Angeles, CA. December 2015.

9 Patten, T. (2018) *A New Republic of the Heart: An Ethos for Revolutionaries*. Berkeley, CA: North Atlantic Books. pp. 42/43.

Chapter 1

10 The ancient Greek civilization recognized two ways of

thinking about how the world works: "Logos" is the use of logic and reason, and "mythos" is the use of intuition, feelings, and direct experience. Both can produce a story or an account of a phenomenon, but in a contrasting manner. A part of our evolving new worldview would be to recognize these separate ways of processing information are equally valid and bring them into balanced use.

11 Helfrich, Paul M. (forthcoming) *Seth: The Ultimate Guide*. pp. 14/15. For more on Paul, go to www.paulhelfrich.com.

12 Roberts, J. (July 12, 1979) From a private session in Roberts, J. (1986) *Dreams, "Evolution," and Value Fulfillment: A Seth Book. Volume I*. New York, NY: Prentice-Hall Press. p. 9.

13 According to Seth, all physical matter, from subatomic particles to the elements that make up huge physical objects, has a rudimentary "self-awareness." This is because they are made of "aware-ized" energy that emanates from Consciousness.

14 Goswami, A. (1997) From the article "Scientific Proof of the Existence of God: An interview with Amit Goswami." *What Is Enlightenment?* (Spring-Summer 1997).

15 The God particle is a name given to a theoretical particle in physics, also known as the Higgs boson. In July 2012 the CERN organization in Geneva announced its discovery using the Large Hadron Collider. The Higgs boson particle confirmed the existence of a Higgs field, a uniformly present suffused field that permeates space. The Higgs boson represents a "new form of matter," as unlike any other subatomic particle it has no spin.

16 There is only one absolute truth—Consciousness and its existence. All other truths, such as the laws of physics, are relative to it (refer to *Chapter 16*).

Chapter 2

17 James, W. (1902/1958) *The Varieties of Religious Experience: A*

Study in Human Nature. New York: Mentor Edition. p. 298.

18 Goswami, A.; Reed, R.E. & Goswami, M. (1993) *The Self-Aware Universe: How Consciousness Creates the Material World*. New York: Tarcher/Putnam. p. 215.

19 Tone is a vibrational frequency or signature emitted by an expression of Consciousness. It is representative of the ***identity*** of an individuated expression of Consciousness. For example, your vibrational signature is the primal tone of your overall Self's identity.

20 Divine Love is a primary measure of all existence, "all things exist within this law and are created out of it." (Payne, J.L. (2001) as Omni in *Omni Reveals the Four Principles of Creation*. Forres, Scotland: Findhorn Press. p. 20.) It is a natural principle pertaining to an innate quality of Consciousness that promotes the maximum development of every expression of itself.

21 Seth defines "action" as the process by which the inner vitality of Consciousness (Divine Love) "continually attempts to express itself in endless formations." (Roberts, J. (1998) *The Early Sessions: Book 4 of The Seth Material*. Manhasset, NY: New Awareness Network Inc. p. 92.) Action is a property of existence. It is "basically electrical" in nature and a by-product and part of all realities. We interpret action as movement in the physical plane. Science is yet to explore fully the concept of electrical action beyond its obvious physical manifestations.

22 Abraham (channeled by Esther Hicks) states that, "the *basis* of life is freedom."

23 Your personality is an electrically encoded counterpart to your ego-self. From a linear-time perspective, it begins life along with your ego-self. Its form is electrical in quality, residing within the electrical dimension of *action*. It has a constantly (both in physical time and outside of it) changing and evolving nature.

24 Our "shift in consciousness," and "shift," are the most popular terms used in the mind/body/spirit movement to describe the evolutionary changes occurring in our collective human consciousness during the late 20th Century and first half of the 21st Century. The term "shift" first appears in the Elias transcripts.

Chapter 3

25 This does not mean the impulse to act immediately because our life is in danger (interpreted as a primal fear) goes away. Other than this primal impulse, fear is something we generate from our psychological structures—namely the beliefs we hold and the thoughts we entertain.

26 The totality of your Self (the physical and the spiritual you) has a distinguishing vibrational frequency or *tone* that distinguishes your overall identity within Consciousness. It is what identifies your Self within the Oneness of All That Is (Consciousness). A useful metaphor in understanding your unique cosmic identity is to imagine your Self as a star within the physical universe. In astronomy, spectral analysis of a star reveals that it emits a unique electromagnetic frequency because of the proportions of chemical elements under combustion within it and other variables such as its ionization state and temperature of the photosphere. Thus, each of the countless trillions of stars in the universe has its own individuality. Its spectral specification is the star's vibrational frequency or tone, if you will.

27 An *emotional-signal* is a special kind of feeling that signals the onset of an emotion. A "feeling" is an independent electromagnetic energy form—*distinct from emotions*—that alerts the conscious-mind to information or knowledge about to transfer directly from the *inner self*. The inner self is the conduit through which Divine Love (Consciousness itself) can communicate with the ego-self.

28 For the individual, there comes a point when our inner self, or Essence, will intervene if our ego-self has created or continues to create experiences that are in detriment to the planned overall learning experience of our lifetime. Intervention usually takes the form of physical or mental illness, although the inner self employs a variety of less dramatic methods before this—an epiphany, for example.

At the collective level of human consciousness, there also comes a point when Consciousness will intervene if we continue to learn nothing from our disturbing collective experiences—wars, genocide, ecocide, for example. Our shift in consciousness is such an intervention.

29 Ennis, M. (1998/2002) Elias sessions 275 and 997. Available at www.eliasforum.org/transcripts.

30 Truth is a topic explored in *Chapter 16*.

31 Moorjani, A. (2012) *Dying to Be Me: My Journey from Cancer, to Near Death, to True Healing*. Carlsbad, CA: Hay House, Inc. p. 137.

32 John L. Payne channels Omni. Go to www.family constellations.net.

33 Payne, J.L. (2001) *Omni Reveals the Four Principles of Creation*. Forres, Scotland: Findhorn Press. pp. 23/24.

34 The transitional area within consciousness is where our Self creates certain psychological structures in order that our physical self (ego-self and its psychological structures) can operate within the physical dimension. It is to this area that our ego-self and personality come as they acclimate again to existence after the physical body has died.

35 "Spacious present" is a term used by Seth meant to encapsulate how Consciousness expresses itself outside, as well as inside, the concept of time.

Chapter 4

36 Moorjani, A. (2012) *Dying to Be Me: My Journey from Cancer,*

to Near Death, to True Healing. Carlsbad, CA: Hay House Inc. p. 108.

37 According to Seth, some dimensions of existence are "more physical" than our own, and some less physical. Presumably, he was referring to higher and lower vibrational frequencies of energy outside the electromagnetic frequencies we recognize in physics.

38 The nonphysical realm where emotions exist is what Seth calls Framework 2. Emotions come closest to the physical dimension in the *electric field*, where they exist as independent electric actions. As with all actions, their intent is to find expression, and their dimension for expression is the physical one. Furthermore, humans are not the only physical life forms for their expression. We explore the topic of emotions at length in *Chapters 12 and 13*.

39 I hyphenate *conscious-mind* to distinguish it as a facet of the *Mind*—a *collective* noun, hence the capital M.

40 Feelings of a negative nature drain our biological system of energy, whereas emotions are an energy resource.

41 *Survival instinct* is a complex subject covered extensively in the Seth material. This quote by Seth hints at the subject's complexity:

"The 'drive for survival' is, therefore, a drive that leads ***to*** death and ***beyond*** it, for all consciousness understands that it survives through many forms and conditions." (Roberts, J. (1997) *The Way Toward Health*. San Rafael, CA: Amber-Allen Publishing. p. 160.)

42 I would liken this membrane to that surrounding any cell within the body. Research in the burgeoning field of epigenetics, pioneered by Bruce Lipton, PhD, has revealed that the cell membrane is the "brain" of the structure, not the nucleus. Far from being the point where it separates from the whole, the cell membrane is a surface of transformation—*transference of information*. Receptors and effector proteins

within the cell membrane "decide" on which information to receive and which to release. The "protein complexes are the fundamental units of cellular intelligence. Technically they may be referred to as units of perception." (Lipton, B. (2005) *The Biology of Belief*. Santa Rosa, CA: Mountain of Love/Elite Books. p. 87.) Similarly, your beliefs form the greatest part of your perception, discriminating what you *accept* and affecting what you release.

43 Duplicity is the term coined by Elias to describe the belief system that has grown from our thoughts on the nature of duality and the differences expressed in the physical realm. Difference and contrast occur in the physical realm in order that we can make choices on what we prefer to create. Duplicity involves making a judgment on the choices made—right/wrong, good/bad, etc. This judgmental aspect leads to conflict, both within our minds and in the physical environment. Its strength within our belief systems stems from a lack of trust in our ability to make beneficial choices.

44 Ennis, M. (1997) Elias session 253. Available at www.eliasforum.org/transcripts.

45 Our Essence self is the spiritual "layer" to our Self that knows how our mental and physical behaviors should be to better create the reality of a more joyous, fulfilling life experience—despite the turmoil the Shift can surround us with on occasion! Our inner self (soul if you wish) is an emissary of our Essence self, keeping an eye on our ego-self's creative management on the physical plane. (Refer to *Chapter 6*.)

46 Helfrich, J. (2014) *The Way of Spirit*. Topanga, CA: NewWorldView. p. 180.

47 A more detailed description of the natural principles is available on Amazon Kindle entitled *How To Be In Divine Love: 10½ Principles That Will Make You A Happy, Purposeful Person*.

Chapter 5

48 Described in Roberts, J. (1979) *The "Unknown" Reality, Volume II. A Seth Book*. New York: Prentice-Hall Press. (Pertinent material is primarily in sessions 735–737.)

49 In the notes for session 734 and 737, found in *The "Unknown" Reality, Volume II*, Robert Butts explains how his impending questions into material relating to the families of consciousness were put on hold by an interruption to session 734. In the notes for session 737, Butts states, "Except for the Sumari, which Jane and I choose to be allied with, there's much we don't know about the families of consciousness." There would be no return to the general subject in subsequent sessions.

50 Omni (John L. Payne) supports distinctive groups or families within the human expression of Consciousness, although his interpretation generalizes to seven types rather than nine.

51 Roberts, J. (1979) *The "Unknown" Reality, Volume II. A Seth Book*. New York: Prentice-Hall Press. p. 608.

52 Roberts, J. (1979) *The "Unknown" Reality, Volume II. A Seth Book*. New York: Prentice-Hall Press. p. 609.

53 For more about Rose, go to www.thewayofspirit.com.

54 Your inner self is an aspect of your Essence (elaborated upon in *Chapter 6*). For now, realize that your inner self uses different methods to remind you of your purpose and keep you on its path, including feelings and emotions, impulses, and coincidental or synchronous events.

55 It's interesting to note that the color blue, according to Elias, has a vibrational frequency strongly associated with the tonal frequency of the Artists/Sumari intent family. Perhaps Picasso's *blue period* coincided with an inner impulse to express the Sumari intent within him—*creativity through art to initiate change* in artistic appreciation (Sumari intent). His blue period (1901–1903) coincided

with depressive interludes following the death of his friend Carlos Casagemas.

56 Ennis, M. (1996) Elias session 67. Available at www.eliasforum.org/transcripts.

57 Roberts, J. (1979) *The "Unknown" Reality: Volume II. A Seth Book*. New York: Prentice-Hall Press. p. 562.

58 Ennis, M. (1995) Elias session 59. Available at www.eliasforum.org/transcripts.

59 Ennis, M. (1997) Elias session 185. Available at www.eliasforum.org/transcripts.

60 An absolute truth is something that remains consistent across all dimensions of Consciousness, not just applicable to the physical dimension and human consciousness. (See *Chapter 16*.)

61 For more information on the Enneagram system go to www.enneagraminstitute.com.

Chapter 6

62 Gestalt is a German term with no English equivalent, used to refer to *unified wholes* that we cannot understand fully by simply examining their parts. This concept is foundational to the Gestalt Psychology movement.

63 Roberts, J. (1998) *The Early Sessions: Book 3 of The Seth Material*. Manhasset, NY: New Awareness Network Inc. p. 333.

64 For a compilation of mainstream scientific research that begins to fathom the nature of this domain, see McTaggart, L. (2001) *The Field*. London: HarperCollins Publishers Ltd.

65 Source Energy is a reference to the transformation of the energy of Consciousness into physical expression.

66 Altered states of consciousness are mental experiences related to accessing subconscious information and knowledge from various *areas within Consciousness*, particularly the *Subjective Area* and the *Transitional Area*.

Channeling, hypnosis, astral projection, and dreaming are examples of altered states.

67 Your inner self uses *inner senses* to obtain information from the Subjective Area pertinent to your overall Self's well-being and your expression within the Objective Area. *Chapters 10 and 11* explore the inner senses.

68 Mind, with a capital M, signifies the collective noun used to describe a variety of psychological constructs, not the least of which (according to Seth) is a variety of minds within the Mind, each with their own characteristics and abilities. *Your Mind* is a portion of the *psyche,* situated within your *Essence,* most actively involved with your *inner self* in maintaining your physical existence.

69 Our ego-self and personality are not the same psychological "thing." Our personality is an electrically encoded *counterpart* to our ego-self. It has a constantly (both in physical time and outside of it) changing and evolving nature.

70 Roberts, J. (1997) *The Early Sessions: Book 2 of The Seth Material.* Manhasset, NY: New Awareness Network Inc. p. 71.

71 The announcement (July 2012) from the CERN organization in Geneva of the discovery of the *Higgs boson,* or "God particle," may be our first sighting of Seth's EEs. What we might regard as the definitive God particle, Seth's Consciousness Unit, is not something that would come anywhere within the range of physical electromagnetic frequencies—thus unobservable.

72 In the Subjective Area, time (continuity of existence) translates as an entity's *durability*—one of Seth's "laws of the inner universe." Durability is based upon sustained electrical potential, which has nothing to do with time.

73 Lipton, B. (2005) *The Biology of Belief.* Santa Rosa, CA: Mountain of Love/Elite Books. pp. 26/27.

74 For more information, see Pert, C. (1999) *Molecules of Emotion: The Science Behind Mind-Body Medicine*. London: Simon & Schuster; and Lipton, B.H. & Bhaerman, S. (2011) *Spontaneous Evolution*. London: Hay House UK.

75 Seth first mentions "tissue capsules" in Roberts, J. (1997) *The Early Sessions: Book 1 of The Seth Material*. Manhasset, NY: New Awareness Network Inc. p. 312.

76 Remember, I deliberately hyphenate *conscious-mind* to distinguish it as a facet of the overall structure of the Mind.

77 Seth says that the psyche is impossible to define in conventional terms. It is a nonphysical expression of energy that has form, although the form can manifest in countless ways depending on *how* one attempts to define it and who is attempting it! Seth makes it clear that we should not equate the psyche with the Mind.

Chapter 7

78 We might view the recurrent patterns formed by fractal geometry as a loose reflection of this individuation process. A fractal is a rough geometric shape that contains within itself fragments that are an ever-diminishing replication of its whole. The term *self similarity* describes this diminishing scale of replication. (Perhaps this term would work better with a capital S!) Although generated from a mathematical construct, nature's geometric patterns frequently approximate to that of fractals.

79 Biological science now understands that the egg cell's membrane *chooses* which sperm to accept into itself when several sperm reach the egg's surface. It is not simply a case of first come first served, a premise derived from an assumption that the strongest sperm will arrive first and is therefore better able to penetrate the outer membrane. This assumption is born of the errant pseudo-Darwinian belief in the survival of the fittest.

80 Pinker, S. (2003) *The Blank Slate: The Modern Denial of Human Nature*. Penguin Press Science.

81 Philosophers Friedrich Nietzsche and Ludwig Wittgenstein both make the point that language has one major limitation: it confines our thinking to the language we are familiar with. Any particular language reflects only the ideas and thoughts of the related culture. Therefore, a vocabulary limits itself to describing concepts already explored and *approved* by societal mores. Difficulty in exploring new dimensions of thought ensues because no words exist to describe a new concept. If we don't have the language to explain our thinking, we tend not to further develop those thoughts. Seth often remarked that we simply do not have the language, *yet*, for him to fully convey what he attempted to describe.

82 As the renowned evolution biologist and futurist Elisabet Sahtouris, PhD, remarks in a recounted conversation with the late Willis W. Harman, PhD, in an article entitled "A Scientist's Thoughts about Redefining our Concept of God," available at https://ratical.org/LifeWeb/Articles/whatsgod.html (accessed June 2013): "All nature is thus conscious in my worldview, and all of it has access to non-timespace; all of it is an aspect of God. The acorn knows the oak tree it will become."

83 Roberts, J. (1998) *The Early Sessions: Book 3 of The Seth Material*. Manhasset, NY: New Awareness Network, Inc. p. 329.

Chapter 8

84 Roberts, J. (1998) *The Early Sessions: Book 4 of The Seth Material*. Manhasset, NY: New Awareness Network Inc. p. 227.

85 Cohen, A. (March 2011) *Your Best Friend and Your Worst Enemy*. EnlightenNext presents Andrew Cohen's quote of

the week. (Subscription site no longer in operation.)

86 Roberts, J. (1998) *The Early Sessions: Book 3 of The Seth Material*. Manhasset, NY: New Awareness Network Inc. p. 282.

87 Roberts, J. (1998) *The Early Sessions: Book 3 of The Seth Material*. Manhasset, NY: New Awareness Network Inc. p. 283.

Chapter 9

88 I use a capital *M* for Mind to distinguish it as a collective noun.

89 Our body-consciousness is an electromagnetic "layer" to our physical self working within the subconscious area of the Mind. It maintains all the processing systems of our physical self and not only manages our physical body's functions along with our electrical body's functions but also initiates the transfer of information from the electric field (Subjective Area within Consciousness) to the physical field (Objective Area within Consciousness).

90 Mainstream psychology recognizes a condition named *multiple personality disorder*, a condition where the personality's integrity becomes fragmented, leading to two or more subpersonalities emerging. In exercising the ability to adopt a different mind from the collective Mind in accordance with different social situations and roles, some individuals can lose their sense of appropriateness. In other words, sometimes the ego-self can choose an inappropriate mind to make conscious on certain occasions. A pathology ensues if this mental inefficiency becomes a constant problem.

91 Inspiration for this metaphor comes from Jane Roberts' *Aspect Psychology* works and her vision of a library of the psyche containing tomes of perennial wisdom meant for translation. See Roberts, J. (1976) *Psychic Politics: An Aspect Psychology Book*. Englewood Cliffs, NJ: Prentice-Hall Inc.

pp. 18/19.

92 Roberts, J. (1998) *The Early Sessions: Book 4 of The Seth Material*. Manhasset, NY: New Awareness Network, Inc. pp. 100/101.

93 We can review *Figure 2* for a visual comparison of what Jung is saying here. Jung places the ego within the sphere of the inner self—which isn't too far off the mark from the metaphysical perspective. We can regard our ego-self's small *c* consciousness as still within the consciousness of our Essence, within the inner self if we like, as our inner self is a part of our Essence—although remember that in nonphysical reality divisions and boundaries don't count for much. The other small spheres inside the Essence of *Figure 2* represent other personalities (from other lifetimes) that continue their existence within our eternal Essence—as time doesn't count for much, either, where our Essence is concerned.

94 The term is originally from F.A. Hayek (1899–1992). It stands for a subconscious area within our minds that contains tacit knowledge of extraordinarily complex aspects of the nature of our reality, often in very abstract representative forms—too abstract for the conscious-mind to access and understand. We assume knowledge of the rules of language, for example, to be part of the supraconscious. This concept may be indicative of Hayek's intuitive attempts to understand some complexities of the conceptual inner senses (covered in *Chapter 11*).

Chapter 10

95 Omni points out, "A principle tells of the nature of things, an action or a flowing of energy, more of a state of being." (Payne, J.L. (2001) *Omni Reveals the Four Principles of Creation*. Forres, Scotland: Findhorn Press. p. 23.)

96 Eddington, A. (1928) *The Nature of the Physical World.*

London: Dent. p. 68.

97 Roberts, J. (1998) *The Early Sessions: Book 3 of The Seth Material*. Manhasset, NY: New Awareness Network Inc. p. 42.

98 Roberts, J. (1997) *The Early Sessions: Book 2 of The Seth Material*. Manhasset, NY: New Awareness Network Inc. p. 14.

99 Roberts, J. (1997) *The Early Sessions: Book 2 of The Seth Material*. Manhasset, NY: New Awareness Network Inc. p. 71.

100 Considering Seth's inner universal law of energy transformation, we can surmise that the empirical law of physics pertaining to energy is a scientific *belief*—a *relative truth* (explained in *Chapter 16*)—rather than an absolute law or *absolute truth*. This belief underpins the notion that the universe is of finite energy resources. This notion in turn encourages our collective pseudo-Darwinian belief that all living things are in competition with each other because of finite resources.

101 Our *perception* is the vital instrument through which we create our reality. It incorporates and employs the sum total of all the energies and functions that constitute the Self. These are the nonphysical and physically oriented structures of our consciousness, along with the creational keys of our dreams, thoughts, beliefs, feelings, emotions, and impulses our Mind entertains. Essentially, our perception is how we view and interact with our Self, the physical world, and others that share the physical experience. It forms our worldview.

102 Our conscious-minds are unable to perceive that time is relative as we rely so heavily on our physical senses, which take time (!) to interpret the environment and the expression of an experience. When we awaken our conscious-minds to our inner senses, we will be better able to sense and perceive

what Seth refers to as the spacious present.

Seth makes continual reference to the spacious present throughout his works, particularly to illustrate how the present moment is the only point of action, the "now point," or "point of power." Eckhart Tölle provides an excellent alternative explanation of this notion of the spacious present in his seminal work *The Power of Now: A Guide to Spiritual Enlightenment*.

103 Roberts, J. (1997) *The Early Sessions: Book 2 of The Seth Material*. Manhasset, NY: New Awareness Network Inc. p. 133.

104 Roberts, J. (1974) *The Nature of Personal Reality: A Seth Book*. Englewood Cliffs, NJ: Prentice-Hall Inc. p. 53.

105 Confusion can arise when we compare the LOA (like attracting like) with *magnetism*, as most of us understand it from elementary schooling. We are taught that *opposite* poles of a magnet attract, whereas like poles repel each other. The LOA simply reflects the principle in magnetism that a *permanent magnet* produces an invisible force, pulling to it certain materials and repelling others. We can regard material attracted to the magnet as having electromagnetic properties that *resonate* with those of the magnetic force.

106 *Probable realities* is a subject explored in Book II—*It's About You! Free Your Self.*

107 Anka, D. (Bashar). From an online transcript at www.bashar.org. (No longer available, accessed September 1, 2007.)

Chapter 11

108 Schizophrenia: "It literally means splitting in the mind and was chosen by Bleuler (1911) because the disorder seemed to reflect a cleavage or dissociation between the functions of feeling or emotion on one hand and those of thinking or cognition on the other." (Reber, A. (1985) *Dictionary of*

Psychology. London: Penguin Books. p. 666.)

109 For a fascinating elaboration on the ego-self's protracted split from its inner guidance, see Taylor, S. (2005) *The Fall: The Insanity of the Ego in Human History and the Dawning of a New Era*. Winchester, UK: O-Books.

110 Remember that we are always an individualized part of Consciousness. We can interpret the recent rise in channelers as Consciousness reminding our shortsighted ego-selves that it is time to recognize, as Bashar (Darryl Anka) has said, that we are in fact always channeling—energy that is *in-formation* from Source (Consciousness).

111 See "inner senses" at www.eliasforum.org/digests.html.

112 A vibrational signature is the primal tone of the identity of an individuated expression of Consciousness. *Your* vibrational signature is the primal tone of your overall Self's identity, which transcends and includes the tonal frequency of your current lifetime's personality.

113 Experiments involving spiders fed with flies laced with drugs such as LSD, mescaline, and cannabis show that web production becomes markedly impaired. Evidence perhaps of a disturbance in the spider's ability to access conceptual inner senses. Interestingly, caffeine appears to have the most destructive influence on web design—webmasters take note! See, Witt, P.N. & Rovner, J.S. (Eds.) (1992) *Spider Communication: Mechanisms and Ecological Significance*. Princeton University Press.

114 For more information, go to www.dolphincommunicationproject.org.

115 Dahl, L.M. (1995) *Ten Thousand Whispers: A Guide to Conscious Creation*. Eugene, OR: The Woodbridge Group. p. 24.

Chapter 12

116 Eastern doctrines describe the chakras as nonphysical energy centers that relate to spiritual, mental, emotional,

and physical aspects of our being. Aligned with the spinal column, from the base of the spine to the crown of the head, there are seven in number. Elias states that an eighth bodily "energy center" between the Heart and Throat chakras is forming in association with the human evolutionary shift in consciousness.

117 An *impression* is a communication to our ego-self that may at first appear to be irrational or illogical. It may be confused as coming from our imagination, but imagination is another form of communication from within. Unlike impulses, impressions may translate into thought, an image, or a feeling. Learn more about Elias's mental "impressions" at www.eliasforum.org/digests/impressions.html.

118 Related to Elias's *impressions* is Seth's notion of "mental enzymes," referred to extensively in Roberts, J. (1997) *The Early Sessions: Book 1 of The Seth Material*. Manhasset, NY: New Awareness Network Inc. For example, "[Mental enzymes are] … Something along the line of mental genes. As mental genes are behind the physical genes so to speak, so mental enzymes are behind the physical stuff that you can examine on your plane." (p. 69.) And, "The inner senses are actually the channels through which the entire composition of any particular plane is appreciated and actually maintained. It is through the inner senses that the mental enzymes are enabled to act upon the vitality which is, as I have said, the structure of the universe itself." (p. 98.)

119 In biological terms, this translation process involves a communication platform that we can loosely call telepathy. Seth advises us that telepathy takes many forms, not least one that transfers information between cells in this process. Seth expects the emergence of a new field in biology, "basic organic psychology," that recognizes this necessary intangible communication platform in living structures.

120 Psycho-electric data refer to Seth's "psycho-electric

patterns" that describe the rudimentary configurations of energy that exist in the electric field (see note 122 below) prior to entering the human psychological system, where they transform into thought.

121 Remember that your body-consciousness is an electromagnetic "layer" to your physical self that works within the subconscious area of your Mind. It maintains all the processing systems of your physical self, not only managing your body's functions, but also those of your electrical body. It initiates the transfer of information from the electrical field (subjective area within Consciousness) to the physical field (objective area within Consciousness).

122 The *electric field* is a term used to encompass a variety of electromagnetic energy fields based in the dimension of existence "closest" to the physical dimension.

123 An *emotional-signal* is a special kind of feeling that signals the onset of an emotion. The psychologist Paul Ekman, PhD, recognizes the distinction between an emotional-signal and an emotion through his research on emotions. His studies show there to be an impulse to act prior to the onset of an emotion. Impulses, according to channeled guides, are not feelings or emotional-signals, but a form of direct communication emanating from our Essence self. Even so, Ekman's "impulse" can equate to the "emotional-signal" type of feeling suggested by channeled literature, particularly when Ekman qualifies his use of the term impulse by suggesting it to be "the spark before the flame," a phrase gleaned from Buddhist philosophy.

124 *Feeling-tone* is a term coined by Seth that refers to the unique vibrational frequency of any expression of Consciousness—this of course includes our Essence self.

125 *Impulses* do not go through thought processing as they require an immediate response.

126 An eBook is available on Amazon Kindle, *Feelings Explained,*

Emotions Tamed, that explores the messages contained within certain emotions.

127 *Inspire* derives from the word *spirit* which originally meant *breath.* It's nice to think of inspiration as experiencing the purity of one's spirit, feeling the breath of one's inner self.

Chapter 13

128 Ennis, M. (1998) Elias session 331. Available at www.eliasforum.org/transcripts.

129 Because the messages contained within emotions and feelings are a lengthy subject, a separate eBook that explores their meaning to the individual is available at Amazon entitled *Feelings Explained, Emotions Tamed.*

130 Payne, John L. (2001) *Omni Reveals the Four Principles of Creation.* Forres, Scotland: Findhorn Press. p. 61.

131 We explore the personality's *Garden of Beliefs* in *Chapter 15.*

132 Ekman, P. (Ed.) (2008) *Emotional Awareness: Overcoming the Obstacles to Psychological Balance and Compassion.* New York: Times Books. p. 13.

133 The electric field is a term used to encompass a variety of electromagnetic energy fields existing in a dimension within the Subjective Area within Consciousness "closest" to the physical dimension. More on this in *Chapter 14.*

134 Lakoff, G. & Johnson, M. (1980) *Metaphors We Live By.* Chicago: University of Chicago Press.

135 Fell, L. (2010) *Mind and Love: The Human Experience.* Biosong: Lulu.com. p. 93.

136 See, *New Scientist,* Vol. 130 (1991). p. 149.

137 Sheldrake, R. (2009) *A New Science of Life: The Hypothesis of Formative Causation.* London: Icon Books Ltd.

138 Roberts, J. (1998) *The Early Sessions: Book 3 of The Seth Material.* Manhasset, NY: New Awareness Network Inc. p. 220.

139 Instinct, or "innate impulse," is about tuning directly

into the inner senses. For creatures, the inner sense Seth calls, "Innate Knowledge of Basic Reality," would appear to be the primary inner sense involved in their physical expression. It's a sense that keeps a physical individuation of Consciousness attuned to the basic principles that power the vitality of the universe.

When we imagine an animal to be expressing an emotion, we are witnessing the automatically generated transference of the emotion from the individual associated with the animal.

140 Consciousness itself does not employ emotions, but it does employ feelings. Consciousness with a capital C simply doesn't need to have emotional-signals and emotions as a form of communication within itself. Emotions are peculiar to certain "levels" of consciousness, such as human consciousness, operating within a physical reality.

141 Roberts, J. (1998) *The Early Sessions: Book 3 of The Seth Material*. Manhasset, NY: New Awareness Network Inc. pp. 269/270.

142 Roberts, J. (1974) *The Nature of Personal Reality: A Seth Book*. Englewood Cliffs, NJ: Prentice-Hall Inc. p. 474.

Chapter 14

143 For a description of the various human energy fields proposed by philosophers and scientists alike, see Dale, C. (2009) *The Subtle Body: An Encyclopedia of Your Energetic Anatomy*. Boulder, CO: Sounds True, Inc.

144 For more information on the remarkable properties of our electrical body, see Becker, R.O. & Selden, G. (1998) *The Body Electric: Electromagnetism and the Foundation of Life*. New York: HarperCollins.

145 Dr. Hiroshi Motoyama (scientist and Shinto priest) and Dr. Valerie Hunt, professor of kinesiology at UCLA, are leading pioneers in the study of the electromagnetic systems of

the body. Hunt discovered that radiation emanates from various sites within the body that are typically associated with the chakras. See, Ozaniec, N. (1999) *Chakras for Beginners*. London: Hodder and Stoughton Educational.

146 Electrophysiology studies the electrical properties of cells, tissues, and organs of the body. Advanced Kirlian photography makes viewing our body's electrical discharge (our *aura*) possible.

147 Anastassiou, C.A.; Perin, R.; Markram, H. & Koch, C. (2010) "Ephaptic coupling of cortical neurons." Article in *Nature Neuroscience* advanced online publication. Published online, January 16, 2011; doi:10.1038/nn.2727.

148 For a definitive explanation of thoughts within the electric field, see Roberts, J. (1998) *The Early Sessions: Book 3 of The Seth Material*. Manhasset, NY: New Awareness Network Inc. pp. 219–225.

149 Remember that time does not control the continuity of existence. The universal principle (Seth's "inner law") of *durability* does.

150 Merrick, R. (2009) *Interference: The Grand Scientific Musical Theory*. Fairview, TX: Self-Published. ISBN: 978-0615-20599-1.

151 Walker, E.H. (2000) *The Physics of Consciousness: The Quantum Mind and the Meaning of Life*. New York: Basic Books.

152 Merrick, R. (2010) "Harmonically Guided Evolution: The Universal Pattern of Life." In an article in *Caduceus*, Issue 79, Summer, 2010. p. 15.

153 Hicks, E. & J. (2008) *Manifest Your Desires: 365 Ways to Make Your Dreams a Reality*. Carlsbad, CA: Hay House Inc. #43.

154 Hicks, E. & J. (2001) Audio recording of a workshop in San Antonio, TX. April 21, 2001. Go to www.Abraham-Hicks.com.

Chapter 15

155 Stibal, V. (2010) *ThetaHealing™: Introducing an Extraordinary*

Energy Healing Modality. Carlsbad, CA: Hay House Inc. p. 67.

156 This system of beliefs relates to our individuation from Consciousness. We humans are favored with a *conscious* awareness of Self made possible through the ego-self's capacity for Self-reflection. Because the ego-self believes that it is the totality of the Self, reflection upon how it came into being has produced a belief that it is separate from everything else, even any Source Entity that may be responsible for its creation. This belief generates the *primal fear* of aloneness within the seemingly hostile reality of the physical dimension. This erroneous belief (that the ego-self exists in separation) gives rise to the belief that it is in competition with everyone and everything for the finite energy resources of the physical plane, and it is *this* belief that holds considerable sway over a wide variety of our actions.

157 Burrow, J.W. (Ed.) (1968) *The Origin of Species by Means of Natural Selection: or the Preservation of Favoured Races in the Struggle for Life*. Charles Darwin. London: Penguin Books.

158 Roberts, J. (1978) *The Afterdeath Journal of an American Philosopher: The World View of William James*. Englewood Cliffs, NJ: Prentice-Hall, Inc. p. 90.

159 Allport, G.W. & Odbert, H.S. "Attitudes." In Murchison, C.M. (Ed.) (1935) *Handbook of Social Psychology*. Clark University Press.

160 To remind yourself of exactly what your *perception* is, refer to *Chapter 7, It's all about perception*.

161 *Natural time* refers to natural rhythms and cycles involved in the expression of Consciousness in the physical realm. We can easily discern these rhythms in the natural world—seasonal and human physiological cycles, for example. Natural time accords with the progression of an action in respect of a myriad set of related probable actions occurring in the Subjective Area within Consciousness where linear

time is of little consequence to that progression. In other words, the *timing* of an event in the physical world involves many nonphysical calculations. We squeeze our energies into linear time-confined channels rather than allow them to flow naturally through us in their own natural time.

162 Roberts, J. (1974) *The Nature of Personal Reality: A Seth Book*. Englewood Cliffs, NJ: Prentice-Hall Inc. p. 153.

163 *Mindfulness*: The intentional accepting and non-judgmental focus of one's attention on the emotions, thoughts, and sensations occurring in the present moment.

Chapter 16

164 Ennis, M. (July 2003) Elias session 364. Available at www.eliasforum.org.

165 The natural power of attraction, lately interpreted as the Law of Attraction, has its foot set more on the rung of the natural principles in terms of "truth" than does the natural power of Divine Love. It, like the natural principles, relates more to the *how* of physical creation than Divine Love, which is closer to the *why* of physical creation (Consciousness).

166 Interestingly, or perhaps not, we can consider "time" as our psyche's translation of a facet (Energy Transformation) of the relative truth of *Energy*. Energy is always in motion, constantly transforming itself—always disassembling and assembling itself into *con*-ceivable and *per*-ceivable patterns. For us to *perceive* this "law of the inner universe" (refer to *Chapter 10*), this truth of Energy playing out in our physical dimension, we must don the psychological spectacles of linear-time.

167 Ennis, M. (July 2003) Elias session 1402. Available at www.eliasforum.org.

Chapter 17

168 Roberts, J. (1997) *The Early Sessions: Book 2 of The Seth*

Material. Manhasset, NY: New Awareness Network Inc. p. 276.

Chapter 18

169 Roberts, J. (1979) *The Nature of the Psyche: Its Human Expression*. Englewood Cliffs, NJ: Prentice-Hall Inc. p. 92.
170 Hicks, J. & E. (n.d.) Extract from Abraham-Hicks AB_CD20, #20 *Self Appreciation*. www.Abraham-Hicks.com.
171 Moorjani, A. (2012) *Dying to Be Me: My Journey from Cancer, to Near Death, to True Healing*. Carlsbad, CA: Hay House, Inc. p. 138.
172 Payne, J.L. (2001) *Omni Reveals the Four Principles of Creation*. Forres, Scotland: Findhorn Press. p. 70.
173 Payne, J.L. (2001) *Omni Reveals the Four Principles of Creation*. Forres, Scotland: Findhorn Press. p. 96.
174 Roberts, J. (1979) *The Nature of the Psyche: Its Human Expression*. Englewood Cliffs, NJ: Prentice-Hall Inc. p. 72.

Chapter 19

175 Ennis, M. (1996) Elias session 66. Available at www.eliasforum.org/transcripts.

Epilogue

176 Ennis, M. (1998) Elias session 270. Available at www.eliasforum.org/digests.
177 Tölle, E. (1999) *The Power of Now: A Guide to Spiritual Enlightenment*. Novato, CA: New World Library. pp. 47/48.
178 Bendriss, L. & Loken, C. (2011) *The Shift in Consciousness*. Cambridge, UK: Galileo Forlag. p. 14.
179 Ennis, M. (1997) Elias session 165. Available at www.eliasforum.org/digests.
180 Roberts, J. (1979) *The "Unknown" Reality: Volume 2*. New York, NY: Prentice-Hall Press. p. 646.

Glossary of Terms

Many philosophers are aware that we require a new lexicon for us to understand better the other dimensions and realities of our existence. We must develop a new language with a vocabulary that encompasses terms that describe concepts and phenomenon that as yet only metaphors can give a hint as to their nature.

This Glossary begins this development. It consists of terms we need to come to terms with! Italicized terms within definitions indicate that they are themselves contained within the Glossary.

Action – Action is a property of existence. It is "basically electrical" in nature and a by-product and part of all realities. It arises from the vitality of *Consciousness* and is therefore a property of *Divine Love*. We interpret action as "movement" in the physical plane. Science is yet to explore the concept of electrical action beyond its obvious physical manifestations.

Akashic Records – A term from Hindu philosophy describing the "Mind of God"—a metaphorical library which contains the records of all of God's actions and experiences in all its dimensions of existence. You might conceptualize it as the vastly extending rooms, buildings and grounds of your subconscious library within the *Subconscious Area within Consciousness*. Metaphysical literature suggests that this store of knowledge is accessible through *Astral Projection* or other *altered states of consciousness*.

All That Is – A metaphysical term that often appears in the literature that approximates to the religious concept "God." It means to convey an absolute guiding influence steering all manifestations in all dimensions of existence. See *Consciousness*.

Altered states of consciousness – These are mental experiences that relate to accessing subconscious information and knowledge from various *Areas within Consciousness*, particularly the *Subjective Area* and the *Transitional Area*. *Channeling*, *Hypnosis*, *Astral Projection*, and *Dreaming* are examples of altered states.

Areas within Consciousness – The term used by the author to distinguish between the various dimensions in which *Consciousness* expresses itself. They are comparable with Seth's "*Frameworks of Consciousness*" or Elias's "Regional Areas." See *Chapter 6*.

Artificial guilt – Artificial guilt stems from the transgression of laws and ethical codes constructed as part of a belief *system*. For example, feeling guilty about performing a sexual act because we believe it to be sinful can produce artificial guilt.

Astral Body – Also referred to as the "*Subtle Body*," a nonphysical body form that loosely resembles the physical form to combat disorientation. It allows us to "travel" within other dimensions of Consciousness. Our *Dream Body* is a form of Astral Body.

Astral Projection – Astral Projection is an altered state of consciousness that utilizes our *Astral Body*.

Belief Systems – The various and many beliefs organized by individuals and groups into core topics that dominate our thinking. These systems are organic in nature, constantly overlapping and interacting with each other.

Beliefs – A belief is a *thought* or collection of synonymous thoughts that incorporates an energy potential capable of influencing our actions.

Bisexuality – *Sexuality* and gender are features of our physical expression. Our Essence selves are, from our physical point of view, bisexual, in that they encompass both energy expressions. Expressing the characteristics of the male and female genders in the physical environment is part of the learning process for our *Essence self*.

Body-consciousness – Our body-consciousness is an

electromagnetic "layer" to our physical self that works within the *subconscious area* of our *Mind*. It maintains all the processing systems of our *physical self*. It not only manages both our physical and electrical body's functions, but also initiates the transfer of information from the *electric field* (*Subjective Area within Consciousness*) to the physical field (*Objective Area within Consciousness*).

Chakra – A spinning vortex of energy that processes *Source energy* as it moves from the *Subjective Area within Consciousness* into and through the physical body. Metaphysical literature confirms the mapping by Eastern traditions of **some** of these "Energy Centers"—seven such vortices aligning with the spinal column. There are others linked to the physical form. Elias describes the formation of an eighth chakra, between the Throat and Heart that will augment energy transfer during and after the *Shift*.

Channeled guides – A term used to refer to the numerous Entities, Essences, "probable selves" and personalities that communicate with the physical realm through *channeling*.

Channeling – One of a variety of *altered states of consciousness* used to access knowledge from the *Subjective Area within Consciousness*.

Collective unconscious – A term coined by Carl Gustav Jung to suggest that our *Mind* contains not just mental activity personal to us, but also impersonal mental activity inherited from the collective mind of humanity.

Conscious-mind – The hyphenated term used by the author to differentiate the chosen mind made conscious by the ego-self from the collection of minds within the *Mind* available to it in the *Subconscious Area*. The hyphen allows for the word "Mind" to be used as a collective noun. See *Mind* in this glossary.

Consciousness/consciousness – Consciousness, with a capital "C," modifies the definition of the concept traditionally referred to as God. Consciousness with a small "c" means to convey an individuated expression of Consciousness, as in *"human consciousness."*

Consciousness Units, CUs – Seth's smallest individuated "portions" of *Consciousness*. See *Chapter 6*.

Coordinate Points – These are mentioned in the *Seth Material* as points where *Source energy* from the *Subjective Area within Consciousness* "enters" the physical plane. Theoretically, these coordinate points facilitate the conversion of *Electromagnetic Energy Units* into physical matter via *Quantum Fields*. We can think of *Chakras* as personal coordinate points.

Death – A period of transition between the physical dimension and the nonphysical dimension. This period can begin sometime before death of the physical body and continue for the personality in the *Transitional Area within Consciousness* as it reorientates to existence outside of the physical realm.

Desire – A desire emanates from our inner self's guidance on our expression of *intent*. It originates as a pure feeling uncorrupted by our *belief systems*. See *Want*.

Dis-ease – A term coined by Seth to infer that illness is a condition created by our *inner self* in cooperation with our *body-consciousness* to indicate that the natural (ease of) flow of energy through our physiology has become impeded.

Divine Love – The term given to the all-pervasive force that describes the vitality of Consciousness. *"Value Fulfillment"* is the term preferred by Seth.

Dream-Art Science – This is a term coined by Seth to describe a future practice that integrates both inner and *outer senses* as well as the ego-self's intellectual faculties in our pursuit of knowledge. He suggests three exemplars of this practice:

- **Dream-art scientist** – a scientist with a less specified, broader range of study that includes dream explorations
- **True mental physicist** – a physicist that primarily uses his mind rather than instruments to identify with the "functions" of the universe

- **Complete physician** – a healer specializing in bringing to light a person's *intent* and *purpose* and reinforcing their spiritual strength.

Dream Body – A form of *Astral Body*. According to Seth, there are three forms of Dream Bodies.

Dreaming – An *altered state of consciousness.*

Duplicity – A belief system (see *Chapter 15*) that has grown from our thoughts on the nature of duality or "dualism" and the differences expressed in the physical realm. Its strength within our *belief systems* stems from a lack of trust in our outer selves and our ability to make beneficial choices. Duplicity is a belief system explored in Book II of the *It's About You!* trilogy—*Free Your Self.*

Ego/Ego-self – The ego or ego-self is a psychological structure within the *physical self* for interpreting what we perceive in the physical field. The ego-self incorporates self-reflection in the process of choosing a *reality* from the myriad *probable realities* available to it in the *Subjective Area within Consciousness*. See *Chapter 7.*

Electric field – The electric field is a term used to encompass a variety of electromagnetic energy fields based in the dimension of existence "closest" to the physical dimension. See *Chapter 14.*

Electromagnetic Energy Units, EEs – Units of energy, formed from CUs (see *Consciousness Units*), within the *electric field* that are "slowing" their *vibrational frequency* in preparation for entry into the physical dimension's electromagnetic spectrum. See *Chapter 6.*

Emotional climate – A metaphor to describe the overall state of our personality's *mood*. See *Tonal frequency.*

Emotional-signal – The special kind of feeling that signals the onset of an emotion. See *Chapters 12 and 13*, and *Feelings.*

Emotions – Emotions are independent configurations of *energy* that exist within the *Subjective Area within Consciousness* and express their energy in the physical realm through the actions of certain animals. In humans they also convey a communication to the *conscious-mind* regarding impediments within the psychological structure (invariably *beliefs*) that affect the natural flow of *Source energy* through the body. See *Chapter 13*.

Energy – We can conceive of Energy (with a capital E) as being the substance of *Consciousness*. This Energy (*Source Energy*) needs to "slow" its *vibrational frequency* if it is to enter the physical dimension to be expressed as matter. *Consciousness Units* and *Electromagnetic Energy Units* perform this task. The energy (small "e") of the physical plane, as described by Einstein in his famous equation $E = mc^2$, represents Source Energy slowed to within the electromagnetic spectrum of light.

Energy centers – The term used by Elias to describe points of *Source Energy* transfer in relation to the human body. See *Chakra*.

Entity – Seth's preferred term for *Essence* self.

Entity/Essence names – Several metaphysical guides suggest that we can ascertain the *Identity* (and name) of our Entity or Essence self through meditation or entering an altered state of consciousness. Seth would call Jane and Rob Butts by their Entity names—Rubert and Joseph respectively.

Essence – The most popular term used in metaphysical literature for the overall structure of the Self and its functions. See *Chapter 6*.

Essence self – The term used by the author to refer to the nonphysical aspects of the Self.

Evolution – Evolution refers to the constant state of change that exists in all dimensions of *Consciousness*. The desire of Consciousness to know itself through experience drives this change. To do this, individuated portions of Itself (*CUs*) cooperate in forming more complex structures capable of creating experiences for themselves, thus adding to the overall experiences of Consciousness.

Expectation – An expectation is a compelling combination of various emotional energies. Desires become expectations as they attract to themselves these emotional energies. The exactness by which a desire becomes manifest through expectation depends upon the degree of conscious control exercised over the emotions involved. See *Chapter 17*.

Families of Consciousness – A metaphorical expression used by Seth to aid understanding of the varying expressions of *intent* within *human consciousness*.

Families of Intent – The author's term for *Families of Consciousness* used by Seth and other metaphysical guides. According to a number of *channeled guides*, the expression of *intent* through *human consciousness* conforms to nine basic descriptive groups. These "psychic groupings" translate as specific activities (roles) and character traits adopted by an individual's *personality*. The most suitable generic terms for these families of intent are: Teachers, Spiritualists, Innovators, Reformers, Exchangers, Artists, Healers, Imagers, and Nurturers. See Appendix III.

Fear – Like *Love,* fear expresses itself through all forms of information transfer. It can come as *impulses* to act or express itself through an *emotional-signal* leading to an *emotion*. See *Chapters 18 and 19*.

Feelings – Feelings are independent electromagnetic energy forms—**distinct from emotions**—that alert the *conscious-mind* to information or knowledge about to transfer **directly** from the *inner self*. The transfer may seem instantaneous, or when the feeling is of the *emotional-signal* variety (which precedes emotional energy about to transfer), a momentary delay occurs for purposes of conscious acknowledgement. We are yet to understand the significance of this delay or exploit its purpose. See *Chapter 12*.

Feeling-tone – A term coined by Seth that refers to the *vibrational frequency* of all expressions of Consciousness, including our Self. See *Chapter 3*.

Focus Personality – The expression used by Jane Roberts in her *Aspect Psychology* work to describe the psychological structures of an individual attuned to the physical world. See *Physical self.*

Frameworks of Consciousness – Seth's term for the numerous levels, layers or dimensions of *Consciousness*. See *Areas within Consciousness*.

Future – Probable energy configurations yet to manifest in the physical realm.

Garden of Beliefs – The Garden of Beliefs is a metaphor introduced by the author to describe the subconscious "place" within the *Mind* where *thoughts, beliefs* and *emotions* combine to produce our *emotional climate*.

Gestalt – A German word to describe something we cannot understand completely by examining its parts. The combination of parts produces a unified whole, which has an indefinable quality, a new identity, which is lost if we separate the parts out from one another.

Hate – Hate is not the opposite of *love*. The opposite of love is *fear*. Hate is a state devoid of love, brought about through an intense fear of separation. It is the fear of losing personal identity, of returning to the fold, of being "One again" with Consciousness.

Human consciousness – A complex, evolving expression of *Consciousness*.

Human love – An interpretation of the qualities of *Divine Love*. See *Chapter 18*.

Hypnosis – An altered state of consciousness and method to induce such a state. See *Altered states of consciousness*.

Identity – The unique "aware-ized" quality of any individuated expression of Consciousness. An Identity (note the capital "I") exists for the smallest indivisible unit of Consciousness—a Consciousness Unit (CU)—and for any cooperative creation formed from them. You, for example, are a complex identity *gestalt* formed from *CUs*. Your Self's overall Identity resides within your *Essence self*. This Identity has a *tone of intent*, a *vibrational signature* unique to your overall *Self*. Your *personality* constructs a *tonal frequency* which your *ego-self* imagines to be representative of its own identity (note the small "i"), unaware of the narrowness of this assumption. See *Chapter 6*.

Imagination – Our imagination is the mental playground of our ideas, *thoughts* and visualizations that formulate our *wants* and *desires*.

Impulses – Impulses are direct instructional prompts to the *conscious-mind*, emanating from our *Essence self*, for us to act in a certain way. Their function is to bypass the thought processing mechanism which may prevent us from acting.

Individuation – The process by which *Consciousness* comes to know itself. Not to be confused with the Jungian term describing the process that integrates the varying aspects of the *Mind* into a cohesive whole, thus attaining "self-realization." See *Chapter 2*.

Inner self – Our inner self acts as an emissary to our *Essence*. It is that part of our *Essence self* that focuses upon looking after and assisting our *physical self* as it explores and experiences the physical world. See *Chapter 6*.

Inner senses – A set of senses that our *inner self* uses to obtain information from the *Subjective Area within Consciousness* pertinent to our overall Self and our physical self's expression in the physical domain. See *Chapters 10 and 11*.

Intellect – A mental faculty that our *ego-self* uses to discriminate between information it perceives as important to the Self and that which is unimportant. *Belief systems* often inhibit this faculty.

Intent – Intent is a directional force **within and part** of *Consciousness* powering learning and growth for it and **all** its individuated forms of expression. See *Chapter 5*.

Intention – An intention is not particularly concerned with our *intent*. It is more to do with our ego-self's concerns as to its immediate needs and wants.

Karma – From Hinduism and Buddhism, we can loosely describe karma as negative actions arising from "the *evolution* of all afflictive or disturbing *emotions*." Resolving these actions may involve more than one lifetime, or reincarnation. See *Reincarnation*.

Law of Attraction/LOA – The popular term used in the Mind/Body/Spirit fraternity that relates to the *natural power* of Attraction. A feature in the teachings of Abraham. See *Chapter 10*.

"laws of the inner universe" – Seth's expression, along with "natural laws," for the *natural principles*. See *Chapter 4*.

Love – Love expresses itself in a vast number of ways. This is because it is constantly seeking expression as it is the vitality of *Consciousness*, the lifeblood of existence. It can be an *impulse* to act or express itself through an *emotional-signal* leading to an *emotion*. This spectrum of expression indicates that love is more a "state of being" rather than a translation of its being like *human love*. See *Divine Love* and *Human love*, and *Chapters 3, 4, and 18*.

Mass event – Co-created realities affecting large numbers of individuals. "Negative" mass events, such as natural disasters and epidemics, along with mass killings and war, convey messages from the collective *psyche* to the collective consciousness of humanity on the nature of our collective *belief systems*.

Metaphysics – Metaphysics has meant many different things. Its meaning in relation to the term's use by the author is that it is an attempt to describe the nature of our existence and the realities we perceive.

Mind – The author uses the word with a capital M to signify a collective noun that describes several psychological constructs, not least a variety of minds within the Mind, each with their own characteristics and abilities. Our Mind is the portion of the *psyche,* situated within our *Essence,* most actively involved with our *inner self* in maintaining our physical existence. See *Chapter 9*.

Mood – Our mood is a measure of the collective *tone* of the *emotional-signals* stored within our *Garden of Beliefs*. See *Emotional climate*.

Natural aggression – Natural aggression stems from natural *impulses* to do with the expression of *intent* through creative actions. Nature displays *natural aggression* through acts such as a flower bursting from its bud, a butterfly emerging from its cocoon, and any birth process where new life comes into the physical realm. Blocking the impulses of natural aggression can lead to inappropriate acts of *Violation*.

Natural approach – A term that describes an emerging post-postmodern *worldview,* which integrates traditional spiritual practices for accessing knowledge from the *Subjective Area within Consciousness,* with the scientific rationale of the modern worldview that seeks to map and clarify the *Objective Area within Consciousness* through reason and logic.

Natural Grace – A term used by Seth to describe a state of joyful acquiescence to the natural power of *Divine Love*. All expressions of *Consciousness* come into existence reflecting this grace of being. Our ego-self's *belief systems* cause us to resist its influence, which our inner selves constantly attempt to remedy. Natural Grace cannot be taken from us and we can never fall from Grace.

Natural guilt – Natural guilt results from transgressing the primary *natural principle* of non-violation. The feeling of natural guilt is essentially a direct message from our *inner self* informing our *conscious-mind* that such a transgression has occurred. Heed the message by ceasing to act in this way—**for your own good**, as well as that of any other party that may be involved. See *Artificial guilt*.

Natural hypnosis – A term used by Seth to describe the constantly occurring psychological process by which our conscious-minds acquiesce to suggestion. This is why a concentrated focus attained in a period of formal *hypnosis* suggesting a desired set of thoughts can be of benefit; the benefit's duration being reliant upon the strength of any countermanding beliefs held. (Think of planting the thoughts in your *garden of beliefs* in the hope that they don't become strangled by the growth of established beliefs.) Seth points out that as our beliefs are integral to the ego-self's structure, it is inevitable that natural hypnosis continually underpins our beliefs, as during the day it is our *ego-self* that is the constant source of suggestion. We can thus think of our *reality* as the result of our ego-self's hypnotizing spell.

Natural laws – Another expression used by Seth for his *"laws of the inner universe." "Natural principles"* is the author's preferred expression for these precepts that underpin physical existence. See *Natural principles* and *Chapter 4*.

Natural powers – A term used by the author to describe *Divine Love* and the *Law of Attraction*.

Natural principles – A set of principles by which *Consciousness* operates when expressing itself through the medium of physicality. See *Chapter 4*.

Natural time – Natural time refers to natural rhythms and cycles involved in the expression of *Consciousness* in the physical realm. We are easily able to discern these rhythms displayed in the natural world – seasonal cycles and physiological cycles, for example. Natural time accords with the progression of an *action* in respect of a myriad set of related probable actions occurring in the *Subjective Area within Consciousness* where linear *time* is of little consequence to that progression. In other words, the "timing" of an event in the physical domain involves many nonphysical calculations. We squeeze our energies into linear time-confined channels rather than allow them to flow naturally through us in their own natural time.

Objective Area within Consciousness – The physical dimension of existence. See *Areas within Consciousness*.

Outer senses – The five physical senses of sight, hearing, smell, taste and touch.

Past – Energy configurations that have passed through expression in the physical domain and no longer have our attention. The configurations continue to exist within the *Subjective Area within Consciousness*.

Perception – Our perception is the vital instrument through which we create our *reality*. It incorporates and employs the sum total of all the energies and functions that constitute our *Self*. These are the nonphysical and physically oriented structures of our consciousness, along with the creational keys of our *dreams, thoughts, beliefs, feelings, emotions* and *impulses* our *Mind* entertains. Our perception is how we view and interact with our Self, the physical world, and others that share the physical experience. It forms our awareness of the *Objective Area within Consciousness* and our *worldview*.

Personal intent – Personal intent is the potential we hold to fulfill our own spiritual ambitions within the pool of probabilities chosen for our current lifetime.

Personality – Our personality is an electrically encoded counterpart to our *ego-self*. From a linear-time perspective, it "begins" life along with our ego-self. It has a constantly (both in physical time and outside of it) changing and evolving nature. Its "form" is electrical in quality, residing within the electrical dimension of *action*. Our personality maintains a unique *tonal frequency*. See *Chapter 8*.

Physical realm/plane/dimension or reality – Conventional terms used to describe the *Objective Area within Consciousness*. Seth refers to this area as "Framework 1."

Physical self – A term used by the author to refer to the three central psychological structures that constitute the part of the *Self* that is concerned with its expression in the physical dimension. The *ego/ego-self, conscious-mind* and *personality*.

Practicing idealist – Someone who seeks to make the world a lovelier place through expressing his or her ideals in the physical world. In doing so, they are fully cognizant of the vital ethical code of non-violation and aware that the end never justifies the means. See *Violation*.

Present – The moment point of now.

Principles – A principle is not a law in the way we conventionally understand the term. As Omni (John L. Payne) declares, "A principle tells of the nature of things, an action or a flowing of energy, more of a state of being." Therefore, principles do not govern us, *Consciousness* does not decide that we must adhere to them; they are **universal** principles that describe the nature of the universe and how things work.

Probable realities – This term relates to the pool of probable events that we have not brought into the physical domain for exploration. They do exist, however, in the *Subjective Area within Consciousness*, where our *Essence self* can explore them. Our *inner senses* allow our *physical self* the opportunity to access these probabilities.

Psyche – The psyche is probably **the** standout term that requires a radical rethink in definition. Seth says that it is impossible to define in words we currently use. The psyche is a nonphysical expression of energy that, although it has form, that form can take on countless definitions depending on **how** we attempt to define it and **who** is attempting it! Seth does make it clear that one psychological form we should not equate it with is the *Mind*.

We have a **portion** of the psyche within our *Self*—which

is our *Mind*. This portion of the psyche is our own inviolate personal "subjective area" within ***the** Subjective Area within Consciousness*. It is a "place" where our nonphysical self resides. As it is within the Subjective Area there are no boundaries such as space and *time;* and as it is a part of *Consciousness* itself—the psyche creates us as we create it! It is an ever-changing place of experimentation.

Psycho-electric pattern – Seth used this term to describe the rudimentary configuration of energy that exists in the *electric field* prior to entering the human psychological system, where it transforms into a thought.

Purpose – Our purpose is our own unique goal that we plan to attain in this lifetime while observing the *natural principles* that describe *Divine Love*. It is a set of actions; a directional path of *intent* we desire to pursue for the expansion, growth and evolution of our own *consciousness*.

Quantum Fields – Quantum Theory postulates that Quantum Fields exist to explain the nature of subatomic particles and their actions. Metaphysical literature suggests such fields exist as an interfacing "area" between the *Objective* and *Subjective Area within Consciousness*.

Rational Approach – The approach to acquiring knowledge that relies upon cognitive (thinking) processes. The approach champions the reason and logic of the *conscious-mind* above the inner intuitional abilities of the *Self*, or indeed, the *Natural Approach*.

Reality – There is not just one reality. Our *perception* of the physical world is a reality personal to our *Self*. There are, therefore, at least as many realities as there are people. In fact, there are as many realities as *Consciousness* has expressions of itself. Mind-boggling as this appears, realities group together in dimensions of existence in accordance with their principles of expression. *Dreams*, for example, are very real in dream-reality, appearing to be "not so real" in physical reality because they do not conform to the laws or principles of physics. There are "types" of reality—primary and secondary realities—that conform to certain truths—see *Truth*.

Reincarnation – Reincarnation or "multiple lifetimes" is a topic that runs through most channeled literature. Our *Essence self* manifests an individuated portion of itself (*physical self*) frequently in the physical dimension. Each manifestation builds a new *personality* that returns to our *Essence* on physical death—expanding and evolving its consciousness. Traditional ideas on "*karma*" in relation to reincarnation are a distortion of its relevance to our Selves brought about by beliefs about *time* and "cause and effect."

Self, self – Self with a capital "S" signifies the entirety of the construct of our Self; a small "s" refers to a part of the Self such as the *ego-self*.

Self-reflection – Self-reflection is an ability that marks an evolutionary stage of an expression of *Consciousness* in the physical realm. All physical objects, from subatomic particles to the elements that make up huge physical objects, have a rudimentary self-awareness. This is because they are made of "aware-ized" energy that emanates from Consciousness. The freedom to "self-express" is an evolutionary step enjoyed by life forms; self-reflection is a further evolutionary step for physical matter as the life form now incorporates a psychological element (a *Mind*) that facilitates this *action*. The ability to self-reflect allows for **conscious self-awareness**. See *Chapter 2*.

Seth Material – The collection of material authored by the "energy personality" known as Seth, and Jane Roberts—transcribed and edited by Rob Butts. Yale University's Sterling Memorial Library now houses the Seth Material in its archives.

Sexuality – According to Elias (Mary Ennis), sexuality and *emotions* are **the** two primary drives in the expression of *human consciousness* in the physical realm—see *Chapter 18*.

Shift – The most popular abbreviated term used in the Mind/Body/Spirit movement for the *shift in consciousness*—the evolutionary changes occurring in *human consciousness* during the late 20th Century and first half of the 21st Century. The terms "shift/shift in consciousness" first appeared in the Elias transcripts.

Shift in consciousness – See *Shift*.

Simultaneous time – An alternative metaphor to Seth's *spacious present* to explain the nine basic dimensions (derived from possible combinations of Past, Present and Future) involved in any "moment point" or "now."

Source, Source Energy – Source is the term used in conjunction with *All That Is* by Abraham (Esther Hicks) and several other channeled guides to refer to *Consciousness*. Source Energy is reference to the transformation of the Energy of Consciousness into physical expression.

Spacious present – A term used by Seth meant to encapsulate how Consciousness expresses itself outside, as well as inside, the concept of time.

Spirituality – Spirituality is to do with our concern for our nonphysical self's needs rather than our physical self's needs. Our ego-selves have become unaware of our primacy as spiritual (nonphysical) beings and that the physical realm is simply our spiritual Self's current focus of amusement. See *Chapter 6*.

Subconscious – The subconscious is an *Area within Consciousness*. **Our** subconscious is an area within our *Mind* that can provide us access to this area within Consciousness. It is a way station or bridge between the Subjective and Objective Areas, a "place" where our *inner self* can communicate and interact with our *physical self*. Our *body-consciousness*, a feature within our subconscious area, controls our autonomic nervous system. See *Chapter 9*.

Subconscious Area within Consciousness – See *Subconscious*.

Subjective Area within Consciousness – The nonphysical dimensions—see *Areas within Consciousness*.

Subtle body – A term widely used in metaphysics and Eastern philosophical traditions that equates with *Astral Body*. According to Seth, we have several "subtle bodies" or "dream bodies" for maneuvering our awareness in the *Subjective Area within Consciousness*.

Survival – Our interpretation of the quality or drive of Consciousness that maintains its existence.

Thought – Thought is a mechanism used by our conscious-mind to translate and interpret information gathered by both our inner and outer senses. A thought, in its **purest** form, is a "psycho-electric pattern" that begins its existence in the *electric field*. This energy pattern then transforms into what we recognize as a thought when exposed to the psychological and physical systems that form our *physical self*. See *Chapter 14*.

Time – Time is a psychological construct that enables us to perceive the progression of *action* in the physical dimension.

Tissue Capsule – A term coined by Seth referring to the energy containment "skin" that encapsulates the energies that constitute our *Essence self*. Review *Figure 1*.

Tonal frequency – Tonal frequency is an expression describing the combined frequencies of the thoughts, beliefs and emotional energies maintained by our *personality*. Because, psychologically, our *ego-self* closely mirrors our *personality*, it regards this combination of frequencies as representative of its identity. See *Identity*.

Tone – Tone is a *vibrational frequency* emitted by an expression of Consciousness.

Transition – A term used in channeled literature to refer to the process we call *"death."* Transition is a process by which our personality transfers itself to Essence for continued existence. It is a process that usually begins well in advance of the physical body's chronological death in preparation for entry into the *Transitional Area within Consciousness*.

Transitional Area within Consciousness – An *Area within Consciousness* where our *Self* creates certain psychological structures in order that our *physical self* can operate within the physical realm. It is to this Area that our *ego-self* and *personality* come as they reorientate and acclimatize to existence after the physical body has died. See *Chapter 6*.

Truth – A truth we hold is a *belief* in which we have invested a lot of energy. There is only one absolute Truth—*Consciousness* and its existence. All other truths are relative to it. See *Chapter 16*.

Unconscious – A condition that occurs when the brain has stopped attending to the outer physical senses—as when in a coma.

Value fulfillment – The alternative term used by Seth to describe the primary *natural power* driving physical existence—Divine Love. See *Divine Love*.

Vibrational frequency – A term synonymous with *vibrational signature*.

Vibrational signature – A vibrational signature is the primal *tone* of the *identity* of an individuated expression of *Consciousness*. Our vibrational signature is the primal tone of our overall Self's identity. This tonal quality of our existence transcends and includes the *tonal frequency* of our current lifetime's *personality*.

Violation – A violation is a deliberate act to end, harm or undermine the physical or psychological freedom of another expression of *Consciousness* in the physical realm. See *Chapter 4*, Appendix I, and *Natural guilt*.

Want – A "want" may be the ego-self's interpretation of a desire (see *Desire*) for a particular experience; or, more often than not, is a constructed need for an experience formulated by the *ego-self* in relation to certain beliefs on what is desirable.

Way of Spirit – An expression used by Rose (Joanne Helfrich) to describe an individual's path of *intent* and *purpose*.

Worldview – A worldview is the complete collection of an individual's or a society's beliefs and values held about the world and how we interact with it. Within our global society there are three prevailing worldviews: **Traditional** (authoritarian, religious); **Modern** (rational, egalitarian, achievement-focused); and **Postmodern** (liberal, sensitive to others, pluralistic). Our *shift in consciousness* heralds a new post-postmodern worldview emerging. We can regard worldviews as the frameworks on which we build our realities. Our own worldview is a unique interpretation of *reality*, a dynamic phenomenon that interacts and combines with other worldviews. See *Perception*.

Author's Biography and Note to Reader

Chris W.E. Johnson MSc began his study of channeled metaphysical literature following a personal life crisis in 1988. His studies of the Seth material awakened a passion for psychology, and by 1998, he had earned an Honours Degree in Psychology from the University of London, a Master's from the University of Surrey, and developed an in-depth knowledge of a variety of metaphysical offerings relating to the spiritual and psychological aspects to our Selves.

Since 2000, he's run Counselling for your Self, a complementary therapeutic practice that marries an eclectic mix of academic psychotherapeutic approaches with alternative procedures such as Energy Psychology techniques and guided meditation. Following his training under Dr. Brian Weiss in 2007, he's added Past Life Regression Therapy to his therapeutic arsenal.

Chris has presented internationally on his interpretations of metaphysical knowledge since 2003. He developed a series of experiential workshops, first rolled out in the autumn of 2009, specifically designed to bring others a fuller appreciation of their "Self" and their life's intent and purpose.

Chris became a member of the Scientific and Medical Network in 2011.

From the Author: I am deeply grateful and appreciative of your interest in *It's About You! Know Your Self*. I sincerely hope that its content has been as revelatory, encouraging, and Self-satisfying as I found it to be while creating it. If you have a few moments, I would be grateful if you would add a review to your favorite online site by way of feedback.

I am currently (November 2018) writing Book II, *Free Your Self*, in the *It's About You* trilogy that will hopefully be published in 2020. Please visit my website for news of this, my other works, recent blog posts, and to sign up for my newsletter:

www.cwejohnson.com

In gratitude and appreciation of you, Chris.

BOOKS

O-BOOKS

SPIRITUALITY

O is a symbol of the world, of oneness and unity; this eye represents knowledge and insight. We publish titles on general spirituality and living a spiritual life. We aim to inform and help you on your own journey in this life.

If you have enjoyed this book, why not tell other readers by posting a review on your preferred book site?

Recent bestsellers from O-Books are:

Heart of Tantric Sex

Diana Richardson

Revealing Eastern secrets of deep love and intimacy to Western couples.

Paperback: 978-1-90381-637-0 ebook: 978-1-84694-637-0

Crystal Prescriptions

The A-Z guide to over 1,200 symptoms and their healing crystals

Judy Hall

The first in the popular series of six books, this handy little guide is packed as tight as a pill-bottle with crystal remedies for ailments.

Paperback: 978-1-90504-740-6 ebook: 978-1-84694-629-5

Take Me To Truth

Undoing the Ego

Nouk Sanchez, Tomas Vieira

The best-selling step-by-step book on shedding the Ego, using the teachings of *A Course In Miracles*.

Paperback: 978-1-84694-050-7 ebook: 978-1-84694-654-7

The 7 Myths about Love...Actually!

The journey from your HEAD to the HEART of your SOUL

Mike George

Smashes all the myths about LOVE.

Paperback: 978-1-84694-288-4 ebook: 978-1-84694-682-0

The Holy Spirit's Interpretation of the New Testament
A Course in Understanding and Acceptance
Regina Dawn Akers
Following on from the strength of *A Course In Miracles*, NTI teaches us how to experience the love and oneness of God.
Paperback: 978-1-84694-085-9 ebook: 978-1-78099-083-5

The Message of A Course In Miracles
A translation of the text in plain language
Elizabeth A. Cronkhite
A translation of *A Course in Miracles* into plain, everyday language for anyone seeking inner peace. The companion volume, *Practicing A Course In Miracles*, offers practical lessons and mentoring.
Paperback: 978-1-84694-319-5 ebook: 978-1-84694-642-4

Rising in Love
My Wild and Crazy Ride to Here and Now, with Amma, the Hugging Saint
Ram Das Batchelder
Rising in Love conveys an author's extraordinary journey of spiritual awakening with the Guru, Amma.
Paperback: 978-1-78279-687-9 ebook: 978-1-78279-686-2

Thinker's Guide to God
Peter Vardy
An introduction to key issues in the philosophy of religion.
Paperback: 978-1-90381-622-6

Your Simple Path

Find happiness in every step

Ian Tucker

A guide to helping us reconnect with what is really important in our lives.

Paperback: 978-1-78279-349-6 ebook: 978-1-78279-348-9

365 Days of Wisdom

Daily Messages To Inspire You Through The Year

Dadi Janki

Daily messages which cool the mind, warm the heart and guide you along your journey.

Paperback: 978-1-84694-863-3 ebook: 978-1-84694-864-0

Body of Wisdom

Women's Spiritual Power and How it Serves

Hilary Hart

Bringing together the dreams and experiences of women across the world with today's most visionary spiritual teachers.

Paperback: 978-1-78099-696-7 ebook: 978-1-78099-695-0

Dying to Be Free

From Enforced Secrecy to Near Death to True Transformation

Hannah Robinson

After an unexpected accident and near-death experience, Hannah Robinson found herself radically transforming her life, while a remarkable new insight altered her relationship with her father, a practising Catholic priest.

Paperback: 978-1-78535-254-6 ebook: 978-1-78535-255-3

The Ecology of the Soul
A Manual of Peace, Power and Personal Growth for Real People in the Real World
Aidan Walker
Balance your own inner Ecology of the Soul to regain your natural state of peace, power and wellbeing.
Paperback: 978-1-78279-850-7 ebook: 978-1-78279-849-1

Not I, Not other than I
The Life and Teachings of Russel Williams
Steve Taylor, Russel Williams
The miraculous life and inspiring teachings of one of the World's greatest living Sages.
Paperback: 978-1-78279-729-6 ebook: 978-1-78279-728-9